SOCIALISM AND AMERICAN ART

SOCIALISM
AND
AMERICAN
ART

IN THE LIGHT OF
EUROPEAN UTOPIANISM, MARXISM,
AND ANARCHISM

BY DONALD DREW EGBERT *1902 -*

PRINCETON UNIVERSITY PRESS

PRINCETON, NEW JERSEY

1967

This essay—a chapter from
SOCIALISM AND AMERICAN LIFE
(Princeton Studies in American Civilization, 4),
edited by Donald Drew Egbert and Stow Persons,
and published by Princeton University Press
in 1952—has been revised
and expanded for this paperback edition.

Printed in the United States of America
by Princeton University Press, Princeton, New Jersey

Preface to the Present Edition

Most of this book was originally published as the concluding essay of the first, or symposium, volume of *Socialism and American Life* (Princeton, 1952, 2 vols.), which I edited with Professor Stow Persons for the American Civilization Program of Princeton University. Throughout that work, and now in the present one, "socialism" has been taken to include not only evolutionary democratic socialism but utopian communism and communitarianism, the revolutionary varieties of Marxism and Marxism-Leninism, and also anarchism—a broad definition of socialism long accepted by experts in this field. Thus Oscar Jászi, "Socialism," *Encyclopaedia of the Social Sciences,* XIV (1934), p. 188, has stated that socialism is the inclusive term.

My original essay has been reissued here with the same plates and without resetting the pages of its text, so that only some limited revisions have been possible. As that original text was published in 1952, while Stalin was at the peak of his power, an Epilogue has been added to indicate the important events within political, social, and artistic radicalism which since then have directly or indirectly affected American artists and their works.

Donald Drew Egbert

Princeton, N.J.
August 15, 1967

v

Contents

List of Illustrations

(See pages 150-151 for the sources of the illustrations.)

SOCIALISM AND AMERICAN ART

Introduction

THAT the visual arts are by no means irrelevant to the socialist way of life has been recognized in one way or another by all the chief varieties of socialism: indeed, the arts raise so many problems vital to socialism that they could scarcely be ignored. For example, not only are works of art the products of a given social environment but they are also the peculiarly unique products of exceptional individuals, and raise with particular immediacy the difficult problem of the place of the gifted individual in a collectivized society. Furthermore, all types of socialism look forward hopefully to some kind of change for the better, to some kind of progress, either in this world or—as some forms of religious socialism would have it—in a future world. This belief in progress inevitably gives rise to questions concerning the relation of progress in the arts to progress in other aspects of society and civilization—questions such as whether modern art, like modern technology, has surpassed that of the ancient world or of the Middle Ages. Then, because socialists look forward so eagerly to future change, they seek ways of bringing the change about as rapidly as possible, which, in turn, usually involves propaganda and the problem of the relation of art to propaganda. And there is still another way in which the idea of progress gives the arts a special relevance where socialism is concerned. For the special sensitivity and insight of the artist make art a kind of mirror in which change is not just reflected, but even dynamically foreshadowed: as Leon Trotsky once phrased it, "Art, don't you see, means prophecy. Works of art are the embodiments of presentiments. . . ."[1]

Thus in many ways the history of art can cast direct light on socialist beliefs and actions. It is true that, in order to study socialism through the medium of art, works of art will have to be treated in this book primarily as historical and social documents, with the result that the *quality* of each as *art* will be insufficiently evaluated. Nevertheless, regarded simply as documents in this partial way, works of art do offer a most revealing means for investigating the presuppositions upon which socialist thought is based, as well as the effects of those presuppositions on socialists and nonsocialists alike. The very fact that most forms of socialism have usually considered art as secondary to religious, political, or economic problems makes socialists likely to reveal themselves through their arts less self-consciously, and therefore with unstudied truthfulness. This secondary position accorded to art also makes it all the more useful for investigating the *indirect* effects of socialism which have perhaps most deeply affected American life.

In studying now the relation of art to socialism in more detail, it will

[1] Leon Trotsky, *Literature and Revolution* (tr. by Rose Strunsky; New York, 1925), p. 110; also see p. 137.

first be advisable to point out briefly the characteristics common to the arts of all forms of socialism everywhere. After that, the characteristics of the arts of each of the important types of American socialism—religious utopian socialism, secular utopian socialism, and Marxism—will be discussed, with some reference also to anarchism. And the art of architecture will be emphasized simply because it is the art which by its very nature involves practical social problems to an especially high degree.

All types of socialism share the implication that some collectivistic mode of life, usually based on common ownership, offers the best possibilities for freeing every man from the material worries that cramp his development—a way of life in which, in theory at least, equality, fraternity, and humanity are customarily stressed. As might be expected, therefore, those arts are emphasized which are either especially useful to the group as a whole (such as housing or craft arts), or which particularly encourage group participation on an equal basis (such as the community singing that once led John Humphrey Noyes, head of the Oneida ·Community, to recognize music as another path to communal sharing).[2] Largely because of the emphasis placed on social utility in art the socialist artist is usually expected to be a craftsman-mechanic trained in several useful arts with no distinction drawn between fine and applied art, which is the reason why the Shaker craftsmen-artists were actually called mechanics.[3] Since the socialist artist is required to subordinate individualistic self-expression, "art for art's sake," to social usefulness, he has at times even been required to remain anonymous.[4] Often he is encouraged to collaborate with other artists in joint aesthetic enterprises: for years the leading cartoonist of Soviet Russia was not a single individual but three men, known collectively as the Kukryniksi, who have customarily worked together on a single drawing. And in many socialist societies, including Soviet Russia, the artist is expected to submit at regular intervals to the collective criticism of his fellows.

Because all forms of socialism look forward to a future event or events as part of their belief in progress, they each subscribe to a belief in some particular goal, some specific "millennium," toward which the world or society is held to be moving. This millennium is customarily prophesied by the founder or leader of the particular group, so that the nature of the given millennium necessarily depends to a considerable degree upon

---

[2] R. A. Parker, *A Yankee Saint, John Humphrey Noyes and the Oneida Community* (New York, 1935), p. 244.

[3] E. D. Andrews and Faith Andrews, *Shaker Furniture* (New Haven, Conn., 1937), pp. 21, 29, etc.

[4] One of the Shaker Millennial Laws is: "No one should write or print his name on any article of manufacture, that others may hereafter know the work of his hands." Quoted by Andrews, *op.cit.*, p. 44.

the character and background of the prophet himself. As the goal of the group primarily determines what it considers worthy of expression in art, the preferences and background of the prophet-leader directly influence its arts: Karl Marx's admiration for the art of ancient Greece, for example, has colored most Marxist aesthetics ever since. Then, the belief in a millennium to come means that among the arts to be encouraged are those considered by the prophet and his followers as the most useful for aiding existence until their millennium has been achieved. In other words, the specific way of life selected for a given socialist community will necessarily affect its art and architecture.

In the last analysis, of course, it is the nature of the specific millennium, or goal, and the way in which it is sought that determine the type of ideology to which a given socialist group subscribes. The spiritual goals of all varieties of religious utopianism clearly distinguish them from both secular utopian and scientific socialism, while the romantic idealism of the secular utopians in many respects contrasts sharply with the materialism of the Marxists. It is the effects of these different goals upon the visual arts which will primarily be considered in the pages that follow.

I. Religious Utopian Socialism and Art

In discussing, now, the characteristics of the art of the religious utopian socialist groups, for the sake of simplicity the illustrations will be drawn from only six of the innumerable communities which have existed in this country at one time or another from the seventeenth century to the present. Three of these six groups (that at Ephrata, Pennsylvania, that at Amana, Iowa, and the group known as the Rappites) were all founded by German immigrants. The other three (the Shakers, the Oneida Community, and also the Mormons, who, however, tended toward socialism in some respects only) were more "native" American in origin even though the first Shakers migrated from England. Nevertheless, despite diverse origins and backgrounds, the arts of all six of these groups have had many characteristics in common in addition to those already mentioned as common to all varieties of socialism everywhere.

Since all of these religious utopian communities were founded on a basis of Christian morality they could naturally be expected to show, as they do, a fear of any kind of art or art theory that is in any way pagan or "worldly." All of them sprang from extremely austere forms of Protestantism, and such arts as they permitted have therefore been marked by a conscious simplicity which represents an attack on vanity, on inequality, and on idolatry, particularly "popish" idolatry. The special emphasis given to the commandment, "Thou shalt not make unto thee any graven image," has often resulted in banning all pictures, and especially portraits. Such a ban long prevailed among the Shakers, and was explained by a Shaker elder in the following words: "We prohibit pictures of individual members because, 1st, of their tendency to idolatry; 2d, the liability of causing personal vanity; 3d, the consequent disunity which might result from preferences given to individuals thus noticed."[5]

Their Protestant belief in the direct equality of individuals in the sight of God as well as their Protestant reliance on the Bible encouraged these religious groups to adopt an equalitarian, communistic way of life largely based on the communism of the Apostles, and led them to allow only those arts which could encourage such a way of life. It should be noted, however, that whereas for other varieties of socialism a communistic way of life was a primary tenet from the beginning, most of these religious groups, on the contrary, only gradually adopted communism, and did so only because it made survival in this world easier. In other words, their communism instead of being an end in itself was really incidental to Christian salvation even though once it had been adopted it was justified on the grounds of precedents found in the Bible. Such communism, therefore, could affect the arts only in a secondary way, and both communism and art were considered entirely secondary to religious belief.

Pietistic Communitarians. Before investigating the relation of American religious utopian socialism to art in more detail, two varieties of this kind of socialism must be distinguished, the first pietistic, the second Calvinistic, in origin. Because the pietistic communities, unlike the Calvinistic groups, strongly emphasized the inward devotional and emotional aspects of religion in which direct personal communication with God was the supreme desire, such communities tended to be unworldly, nonrational, and even anti-intellectual—characteristics reflected in their arts. Almost without exception these pietistic utopians originated either out of German pietism (as in the case of Ephrata, Amana, and the Rappites) or else out of a fusion of evangelical revivalism with Quaker pietism (as in the case of the Shakers, a few of whom still survive). Thus the arts of the pietistic communities of German origin show much German influence: for example, the high roof and flat-topped dormers of the Sisters' House at Ephrata (Fig. 1), built in 1743 and framed without spikes or nails, like Solomon's temple, are clearly survivals from late medieval German architecture. Whereas the Shaker meetinghouses (Fig. 2), with their side entrances and lack of a steeple, just as clearly belong to that simplified version of the Anglo-American architectural tradition which the Quakers had developed for their meetinghouses.

Each of the pietistic groups looked upon itself as a body of elect

[5] W. A. Hinds, *American Communities and Cooperative Societies* (second revision, Chicago, 1908), p. 47.

individuals equal in the sight of God and specially chosen by him for salvation, while the rest of the world was considered inevitably destined for damnation. On this account the body of the elect voluntarily sought to withdraw as completely as possible from contact with the wicked world: one of the twenty-one rules of conduct at Amana was ". . . do not waste time in public places and worldly society, that you be not tempted and led away."[6] Because of their efforts to avoid contact with the outside world, such communities—at least in the case of the German pietist groups—were usually not so interested in actively seeking converts, and for this reason, in contrast to practically all other varieties of socialism, made little use of propaganda and hence of art as propaganda.

In withdrawing from the world they tended to shun all worldly strife; usually, also, they shunned sex and family life and abhorred worldly fashions of all sorts. Their pacifism, so marked in the case of the Shakers, helped to discourage the use of art for any aggressive kind of propaganda for fear of conflict with the outer world. And the celibacy common to most of these groups, Amana and the early Rappites being notable exceptions, inevitably affected the design of their buildings because the sexes had to be segregated. In some cases, as at Ephrata, they were segregated in separate buildings (Fig. 1); in others, as in the Shaker communities, the dwellings were customarily divided into two completely separate parts each with its own entrance (Fig. 3). Since these communities frowned upon worldly fashion, their architecture and other arts, unlike those of other varieties of socialism, were both extremely simple and extremely traditional in style. The Millennial Laws of the Shakers emphasized that "Odd or fanciful styles of architecture may not be used among the Believers";[7] and this simplicity and traditionalism have always made it notoriously difficult to date a Shaker building (Figs. 2 and 3) or piece of furniture (Fig. 4) on style alone. For fear of worldliness, moreover, the pietistic socialist communities abjured nearly all arts except those immediately useful and necessary either for simple everyday existence, such as architecture and the household arts, or for communal worship in some very simple Protestant and evangelical way. Characteristic of their religious arts are the illuminated hymnbooks of Ephrata and of the Shakers (Fig. 5), and also the religious dances of the Shakers (Fig. 6), who danced like David before the Lord and thereby came to play an important part in American evangelical revivalism. For their hymnbooks the Shakers developed a simplified musical notation based on letters of the alphabet (Fig. 5), a notation intended to encourage all members of the Shaker community to participate in singing on an equal basis. As a result of such emphasis

[6] B. M. H. Shambaugh, *Amana That Was and Amana That Is* (Iowa City, Iowa, 1932), p. 244.
[7] Quoted by E. D. Andrews and F. Andrews, *op.cit.*, p. 18.

on both simplicity and social usefulness in art, a very direct and functional expression was often quite consciously sought. The Shakers, for example, held that "Anything may . . . be called perfect which perfectly answers the purpose for which it was designed."[8] And they had a proverb, "Every force evolves a form,"[9] a proverb remarkably similar in spirit to the slogan of twentieth-century functionalism, "Form follows function."

Because their withdrawal from the surrounding world compelled the pietistic communities to be self-sufficient, they had to raise all their own necessities of life. They necessarily followed an agricultural way of life, which appealed primarily to a peasant or farmer clientele; actually the communities of German origin were made up almost entirely of peasants who had emigrated from Germany, while the Shakers drew their converts mostly from American farmers. Such manufacturing as was done grew almost entirely out of agriculture—as, for example, the woolen industry of Amana or the handmade brooms for which the Shakers were noted— and was customarily based on handicraft. Indeed, these communities were hardly able to survive under anything other than an agrarian existence. Elder Frederick Evans, most widely known of all the Shaker leaders, once said, "Whenever we have separated from this rule [that Shaker communities must be founded on agriculture] to go into manufacturing we have blundered."[10] Consequently, the arts of these primarily agrarian communities were almost always limited to the handicrafts of peasant and farmer, while their architecture was based on that of the farmhouses and country villages from which their members had come. For this reason their settlements (Fig. 7) were often laid out in the same naively utilitarian and informal way as the farming villages on which they were modeled; and in this reflected the anti-intellectualism of the founders as well as their fundamental conservatism in everything but their peculiar religious doctrines. Occasionally, however, the leader of the group himself imposed a regular plan on the community, as in the case of the Rappite settlement at Harmony, Pennsylvania, which was laid out by John Rapp in regular blocks. But even here, in spite of axial regularity in plan, the final effect of the village was one of relative informality (Fig. 8).

Calvinistic Communitarians. To be sharply distinguished from the pietistic communities are the other religious utopian socialisms that developed not out of pietism, but out of radical Calvinism. Among the most important of them in this country were the Oneida Community, and also the Mormons who in some respects were organized on a collectivistic basis and at times made efforts—such as the Second United Order—to encourage more complete socialization. The Calvinistic heritage of such

[8] *Ibid.*, p. 17. [9] *Ibid.*, p. 22.
[10] Quoted by Shambaugh, *op.cit.*, p. 156.

communities as these led them to emphasize the importance of the "call-ing" of each individual in this world so that, in contrast to the pietistic groups, their members were expected to participate in worldly activities, albeit in an austerely Calvinistic manner. For this reason business, in-dustry, and the arts related to them were encouraged by Oneida and to a lesser degree by the Mormons, rather than just the agricultural arts of the pietistic communities. The Oneida Community eventually achieved world-wide fame for the silverware and animal traps that it manufactured so profitably. And significantly enough, John Humphrey Noyes, founder and leader of the Oneida Community, urged all socialist groups owning a "domain" to "sell two-thirds of that domain and put the proceeds into a machine shop,"[11] a point of view appealing much more to the nonagrarian middle class, from which Oneida drew so many of its members, than did the agrarianism of the pietistic communities.

Although, unlike Oneida, the Mormons in Utah necessarily had a rural rather than an industrial setting, their Calvinistic heritage is doubtless reflected in the fact that they have always been noted for their financial acumen. Yet in spite of their rural setting, the encouragement which they gave to some arts was at least as strong as that given by the Oneida Community; and in the end the Mormon artistic contribution was to surpass that of Oneida because of the greater extent, wealth, and duration of Mormon society.

Certainly, both of these communities had a much more worldly point of view than any of the pietistic groups, and this greater worldliness undoubtedly helped them to participate in more different kinds of art, with greater emphasis on being up-to-date, even though Calvinistic austerity did usually prevent any ornamental elaboration. While, as noted above, the villages of the pietists were rarely designed in any geometrically formal way, Salt Lake City (Fig. 9), founded by the Mormons in 1847, was laid out by Brigham Young in the regular and financially "practical" gridiron plan that any up-to-date real-estate devel-opment of the period was expected to have, but with wider streets and larger lots. The same up-to-dateness can be seen in the buildings of the Mormons and of the Oneida Community, especially after these groups had obtained a certain amount of wealth, and with it more awareness of worldly fashions. Thus the early Mormon temple at Kirtland, Ohio, completed in 1836, was a naive mixture of the late Georgian and the newer Greek Revival and Gothic Revival styles. The slightly later temple at Nauvoo, Illinois (Fig. 10), erected between 1841 and 1846, was designed in a considerably more sophisticated version of the Greek Revival style, though still with a somewhat Georgian cupola. Within a few years, however, the Greek Revival was dying out, a change promptly

---

[11] *Loc.cit.*

9

reflected in the Mormon temple begun at Salt Lake City in 1853 (Fig. 11) and designed in the now dominant Gothic Revival style. By the time the main building of the Oneida Community (Fig. 12) was built in 1860-1871, fashion had changed once more, and now an up-to-date Victorian Mansard style was employed. Yet all of these buildings, diverse as they seem, are characteristically American, as might be expected of communities whose members, unlike so many of the pietistic utopians, were nearly all native-born Americans.

Unlike the pietistic communities, too, these Calvinistic ones made use of architecture—as their large and impressive community buildings show—to demonstrate their leadership and success in worldly affairs, to serve as a kind of propaganda. Nor did their members hesitate to indulge in many forms of art frowned upon by the pietistic groups, provided that these arts either could be made to yield a financial profit for the community or else could encourage a communal spirit. The drama, for example, which the pietists looked upon as a snare of the devil, was for both Brigham Young and John Humphrey Noyes (Fig. 13) a favorite art because it required collective participation. Individualistic expression in art was correspondingly frowned upon as too often failing to deal with the real issues of life, as being, in Noyes's words, "an enemy to earnestness."[12]

It should be remembered that whereas the pietistic utopians were nearly all celibates who had withdrawn *voluntarily* from the world, such groups as the Oneida Community and the Mormons were compelled to withdraw from everyday society by the strong opposition of their neighbors to their unusual and noncelibate sex mores. Needless to say, these sexual customs affected architectural design. The plan of Salt Lake City (Fig. 9) with its many separate houses reflects the Mormon emphasis on the family as the unit of society, while at the same time Brigham Young's own large and complicated house (Fig. 14) gives architectural expression to the complicated organization of the Mormon family under polygamy. In sharp contrast, the single enormous communal dwelling at Oneida (Fig. 12) by its very architecture suggests the denial of ordinary family life implicit in Oneida's "complex marriage," or, as the enemies of the Community called it, "free love."

II. Secular Utopian Socialism and Art

Like the various forms of religious utopian socialism both pietistic and Calvinistic, the many and varied secular utopian socialist communities in this country also have had many fundamental characteristics in common, characteristics reflected in their points of view toward the

[12] Quoted in Parker, *op.cit.*, p. 236. Nevertheless, the works of the highly individualistic William Blake were much admired at Oneida: see *ibid.*, p. 237.

arts. The three most important groups of secular utopians, from whom our illustrations herein will be drawn, were followers respectively of Robert Owen (d. 1858), of Charles Fourier (d. 1837), and of Étienne Cabet (d. 1856), the last of whom was the author of that celebrated utopian novel, *Voyage . . . en Icarie* (1840), from which his followers took the name of Icarians. While our discussion of secular utopianism and its art will be based primarily on the beliefs which these three leaders held in common, it must be remembered that in many respects they differed sharply with one another and that the beliefs of each were by no means completely accepted by all of his followers.

Owen, Fourier, and Cabet were all inspired, directly or indirectly, by the rational-romantic ideals earlier reflected in the Enlightenment and in the French Revolution, so that they all tended to stress equality and fraternity and were absolutely certain that man is indefinitely perfectible. As the word "secular" indicates, these utopians looked forward to a millennium in *this* world achieved through rational processes of education and social reform, so that when the evils of society had at last been overcome by socialism, each person would be free to develop his potentialities to the full.

Like all such utopians, Owen, Fourier, and Cabet subscribed to the romantic belief that "natural" man is good but is made evil by ignorance resulting from unfavorable environmental conditions. Conversely, in believing that man is rational and indefinitely perfectible, they maintained that he can be redeemed by a favorable environment in which the arts could play a part, and to them the most favorable environment was that offered by a communal existence under conditions of relative equality which, in turn, necessarily affected their architecture. Convinced that such an environment can be brought about through proper exercise of human reason without any supernatural aid whatsoever, the secular utopians were frequently not interested in religion and were often atheists, as in the case of Robert Owen, or—still more frequently—were deists who looked upon God as merely the great watchmaker who had created the universe and set it in motion but whose services were no longer needed. Even those who had religious inclinations were likely to be disenchanted Protestants or spiritualists, so that they too had little or no interest in religious art.

Their utter confidence that man is a fully rational being and that human nature is completely malleable led them to the optimistic belief that all men would hasten to adopt socialism once its benefits had been rationally explained and demonstrated, once mankind had been properly educated. Thus educational propaganda (which had been minimized by the pietistic utopians for whom human nature could be modified only by God's grace) became extremely important here, so that those arts which could best be used for such propaganda were heavily stressed. It was because of this confidence in the complete efficacy of precept and example for convincing and changing the human mind that the leading secular utopian socialists wrote in such detail describing their own particular projected communities, often illustrating their descriptions with elaborate drawings of the proposed community buildings (Figs. 15 and 17). And for the same reason, whenever possible these men sought to establish actual communities as examples and models of the socialist way of life, examples which, it was thought, would inevitably convert to socialism every rational human being who saw them.

The belief of these utopians that social equality is fundamental to the good life is reflected in many ways in the specifications set down for their socialist settlements. It appears, for instance, in one of the three basic rules which Étienne Cabet proposed for his ideal community of Icaria, namely, "that we admit only those pleasures which every Icarian can enjoy equally."[13] And it appears also in the insistence of most of the utopian leaders that their settlements should be organized on the basis of great communal dwellings, generally with equal, or nearly equal, apartments like those of the polygonal socialistic "palace" (Fig. 16) illustrated in 1848 in the *Harbinger*, a Fourierist publication. The *Harbinger* stated that this "palace" was inspired by the octagonal type of house invented by Orson Squire Fowler, the celebrated phrenologist who earlier in 1848 had published a book entitled *A Home for All; or, the Gravel Wall, and Octagon Mode of Building*. Although Fowler said that, because he believed in separate family dwellings, he himself was far from advocating Fourierism, he was nevertheless a friend of Horace Greeley and others interested in the doctrines of Fourier. It is thus not surprising that in his book he carefully mentioned that his octagonal type of plan was well suited to Fourierist communities because it could house several families even more efficiently than a single one. And since Fowler particularly stressed social usefulness in architecture, since he was chiefly interested in the problem of economical housing (and for such housing had developed his "gravel wall," an inexpensive kind of concrete construction), in several respects his book strongly appealed to socialists.

But although a communal, multifamily kind of housing was desired by most utopian socialists, housing ordinarily planned with equality in mind, it should be noted that there was considerable variation in the degree and kind of equality recommended. In contrast to Owen and the Fourierists who proposed communities based on a single great communal structure (Figs. 15 and 17), Cabet would allow as many separate homes as there were households. Yet the interiors of the Icarian houses were

---

[13] [Étienne] Cabet, *Voyage en Icarie* (3rd ed., Paris, 1845), p. 272.

all to be laid out in the same way (although varying in size with the size of the particular family), and the exteriors of all dwellings on the same street were to be alike.[14] Indeed, in Icaria a prize was even offered for the best scheme for a model house with standardized parts, a scheme to which all houses were expected to conform. Such relatively complete equality in housing clearly reflects Cabet's insistence on equality in the distribution of all goods.

In most respects both Owen and Fourier were a good deal less equalitarian in spirit than Cabet although, unlike him, they both desired communal housing. While it is true that Owen's views varied considerably at different periods in his life, at the beginning and end of his career he firmly believed that the individual producer should have "a fair and fixed proportion of all the wealth which he creates."[15] Correspondingly, he usually stated that there would be four distinct economic classes within his ideal community, and in one early proposal published in September 1817, he promised the upper classes that "their accommodations of all kinds will be in proportion to the capital they can at first advance or may hereafter acquire." And even though he wanted to house all classes in apartments within large communal buildings, or "parallelograms," he ordinarily separated the quarters of the different classes. Thus in the project of September 1817 Owen actually segregated them in different villages, while in one of his last great projects, issued in 1841, the four classes were to occupy different sides of the same parallelogram.[16]

Fourier, too, was far from being an equalitarian for he was primarily interested in reforming capitalist methods of production rather than doing away with them entirely. He basically sought *justice* in the distribution of wealth rather than absolute equality. In his description of a "phalanx," or ideal Fourierist community, he therefore did not propose to have equally priced apartments for all, although he insisted that the costly and inexpensive apartments were to be intermixed. Nor did he require everyone to eat together even though he, like Owen and most other utopians, did emphasize community dining rooms.

In all these utopian projects the arts were usually considered important insofar as they could help to educate mankind to socialism and thereby help to bring about an environment in which man could develop his personality to the full: in short, the arts were approved primarily on the basis of social utility. Usefulness, the secular utopians believed, must come before beauty, a point of view well exemplified by another

[14] *Ibid.*, pp. 67, 22, and 46.

[15] Robert Owen, "Report to the County of Lanark" (1820), in *A New View of Society and Other Writings* (New York, 1927), p. 262.

[16] For Owen's changing views on equality see A. E. Bestor, Jr., *Backwoods Utopias* (Philadelphia, 1950), pp. 78-93.

of the three fundamental rules which Cabet laid down for Icaria, "that the agreeable be sought only when we have the necessary and the useful."[17] However, both Cabet and Fourier insisted that once the necessities of life had been achieved, their communities must be decorated with paintings and sculpture[18] in order to create the best possible environment for developing well-rounded, and therefore socially minded, human beings.

This ideal environment, in addition to being beautified by the artistic handiwork of man, must also—these utopians felt—be one which permits man to live close to "nature," a Rousseauistic point of view reflecting their romantic heritage. Their problem, however, was to harmonize this rustic impulse with their profound concern for "attractive industry." Because they felt that country life and agricultural pursuits were necessary aspects of a well-rounded existence, they proposed that their individual communities, ideal and actual, should be restricted in size and located either in the country or in a suburban setting (Figs. 15 and 19, also 17 and 20) away from the more sordid aspects of industrial civilization. And it was largely because Owen and Cabet both considered the American frontier to offer a suitable natural setting that both of these men came in person to the United States to establish their own model communities in what is today the Middle West.

Yet in spite of insisting on a "natural" environment, the secular utopians did not reject machinery and industrialization as the pietists had tended to do. On the contrary, like Marxians later, they tended to glorify the machine provided that it was not permitted to dominate mankind; for the machine could free men from drudgery and thereby allow them much more time for achieving a fuller personal development. Because of this, Étienne Cabet extolled the advantages of mass production, or, as he described it, fabrication "in enormous masses mechanically," while Owen said that "mechanism may be made the greatest of blessings to humanity" instead of "its greatest curse."[19]

Such mechanization of industry under suitable human control was regarded by most secular utopians as an important factor in progress toward a universal socialist society. This progress, they believed, could and should be steady and continuous, so that to them the process of socialization was to be a peaceful one, despite the fact that it might well develop rapidly because mankind, being rational, would soon see its advantages. Since there would be no violent break with the past, no bloody

[17] Cabet, *op.cit.*, p. 272.
[18] Cabet, *op.cit.*, p. 47. Fourier had recommended that "aptitude for the fine arts" be one of the qualifications of those admitted to Fourierist communities: see Julia Franklin, *Selections from the Works of Fourier* (London, 1901), p. 141.
[19] Cabet, *op.cit.*, p. 137, where he was referring to the manufacture of hats; and Robert Owen, "Second Address," Aug. 21, 1817, quoted by Bestor, *op.cit.*, p. 75.

revolution, they were ready to make use of any past styles of art which could be considered worthwhile for human culture even though these past styles would presumably be put together in new and original ways to express the progress that was taking place. In other words, these utopians encouraged eclecticism in art. Cabet said that in the capital of Icaria there were to be "all the varieties of architecture. Here, you would believe that you were at Rome, in Greece, Egypt, India. . . ."[20] As might be expected, also, the eclecticism of the secular utopians often reflected their pride in keeping up with the most "progressive" styles of the day. Until the 1820's, the various projects of Robert Owen were designed in the prevailing Georgian style. However, his model for an ideal socialist community at New Harmony, Indiana (Fig. 15), a model designed for him in 1825, was mostly Gothic Revival with some touches of Greek Revival, and thus combined two of the newest fashions in architecture. At the same time, the various elements borrowed from these styles of the past were all freely treated and were assembled in untraditional ways in order to suggest that such a socialist community, while making use of the past, had now progressed beyond it.

Thus the art and architecture of the secular utopians were supposed to symbolize and exemplify the progress which man could achieve by proper exercise of his reason. So completely did the leaders believe in the powers of the intellect that they sought to arrive a priori at rational principles of social organization good everywhere and for all time. Some leaders did not hesitate to impose their own principles on their followers with considerable dogmatism so that subordinates who violated the leader's principles were often subject to rigid censorship in art as in other matters. Cabet, for example, as president of the Icarians at Nauvoo, Illinois, carefully reserved for himself the power to censor all their theatrical performances,[21] in spite of the fact that in his theory, as expressed in *Voyage en Icarie*, decisions were all to be made by a committee of experts.

Complete faith in reason also often led these utopians to urge a "scientific" approach to art. Josiah Warren—once a member of Robert Owen's New Harmony colony and a participant in many other utopian experiments—developed a new system of music notation which he believed would enable music to be played or sung with scientifically exact fidelity to the composer's intention. And he hoped his method would give the art of music a wider social appeal by making scores easy to read.

This utter confidence of the secular utopians in abstract reason often resulted in an extraordinary mixture of practicality with extreme impracticality, a mixture well illustrated by their idealized architectural projects. On the one hand such projects were considered to exemplify

[20] Cabet, *op.cit.*, p. 47.
[21] Jules Prudhommeaux, *Icarie et sa fondateur, Étienne Cabet* (Paris, 1907), p. 336.

the practical economies which could result from cooperative living; and with such economies in view Owen and Fourier both insisted that the community buildings should be centrally grouped, the various parts being connected by enclosed passageways. But while Owen arranged his "parallelograms" on the four sides of a square (Fig. 15), the ideal Fourierist phalanstery was conceived by Fourier's chief follower, Victor Considérant, as a single great palace with symmetrical wings (Fig. 17), with the intent that men should live like kings in the ideal society. Needless to say, the shortlived colony which Considérant (who became an American citizen) founded at Reunion, Texas, in 1855 was not like this.

The fact that these various projects are all characterized by rigidly geometrical and symmetrical planning clearly indicates that their designers were not nearly so practical as they thought. For such symmetry could only be achieved by largely disregarding those specific practical problems which would inevitably arise with different sites and climates. And this, combined with the general fancifulness and the enormous scale of the projects, shows that the designers, despite their vaunted rationalism, were actually romantic—if often inspired—visionaries, which is of course the reason why Marx scornfully called them utopians. Despite their glorification of socialism, their praise of cooperation, they were really romantic individualists too often incapable of subordinating their own temperaments to the good of the community as a whole. For this reason, among others, the settlements founded by them could hardly hope to approximate the ideal ones so glowingly described and illustrated in their writings. The contrast between the community which Robert Owen actually established at New Harmony, Indiana, in a village bought from the Rappites (Fig. 19), and the projected edifice in which he promised to house the community eventually (Fig. 15), clearly shows how very different the actuality was from the ideal.[22] And a similar contrast is evident if a Fourierist ideal phalanx (Fig. 17) is compared with the North American Phalanx, the most successful Fourierist community actually established in this country (Fig. 20). Indeed, most of the secular utopian communities collapsed chiefly as a result of the disappointment which this contrast between the ideal and the reality brought to those who participated in the experiment.

III.   Marxism: The Marxian Philosophy of Art

Because Marxism has affected American art to a much greater degree than has utopian socialism, its influence will be investigated here in much

[22] Owen promised to erect the ideal edifice on the higher land commanding the Wabash River about three miles from the village of New Harmony. Although some work was actually done at the proposed site, the value of the project was primarily propagandistic: see Bestor, op.cit., pp. 128-30.

more detail. However, it should not be forgotten that the influence of the utopians has to a considerable degree been felt through Marxism itself, for although utopian socialism has been scorned by all varieties of Marxism, nevertheless, as Lenin pointed out, secular utopian socialism was one of the main sources of Marx's thought. Like the utopians, Marx believed in a kind of millennium—in his case, a revolution of the proletariat followed by a classless society. Like them, also, Marx emphasized collectivism, humanitarianism, and equalitarianism insofar as he sought to abolish all classes in society. All of these aspects of his thought have greatly affected the Marxist point of view toward the arts; yet the fundamental contributions to socialist theory and practice made by Marx himself were destined to affect the arts even more than those that grew out of utopianism. Chief among these contributions were Marx's economic and historical materialism, his emphasis on historical and social organicism and on the dialectical process, and his doctrine of a class struggle eventuating in a classless society after the triumph of the proletariat in its revolution. Although Marx never found time to develop a detailed philosophy of art based on these doctrines, he was much interested in the arts and in the late 1850's had even made some annotations for a projected work on aesthetics. In the absence of this work, his philosophy of art has to be investigated on the basis of his general philosophy in relation to the occasional and brief statements about art made by himself or by his friend and colleague, Friedrich Engels.

That Marxism is a form of philosophical materialism is clearly indicated by Engels' statement: "The material, sensuously perceptible world to which we ourselves belong is the only reality. . . ."[23] Marxians believe that man, like animals and insects, is a product of nature and is subject to the laws of nature including those of the geographical environment. However, unlike animals and insects, "man produces independently of physical needs"[24] and throughout recorded human history has exchanged the products of his labor with other men. He thus is a social being, so that for Marxians reality for mankind is primarily a *social* reality with, in the last analysis, an *economic* basis. And the economic conditions resulting from the prevailing mode of production ultimately exert a determining influence on the processes of human life—on the intellectual processes, including those of art, as well as on social and political processes.[25] Art, then, being characterized by intellectual processes, is a

[23] Friedrich Engels, "Ludwig Feuerbach and the Outcome of Classical German Philosophy," in Karl Marx, *Selected Works* (New York, 1936?), I, p. 435.

[24] Karl Marx, "Ökonomisch-philosophische Manuskripte aus dem Jahre 1844," *Marx-Engels Gesamtausgabe*, Pt. I, Vol. 3, p. 88; translation from *Literature and Art, by Karl Marx and Friedrich Engels* (New York, 1947), p. 14.

[25] See Karl Marx, Preface to "A Contribution to the Critique of Political Economy," *Selected Works*, I, p. 356.

form of ideology, and consequently works of art differ from purely material goods although equally determined by the prevailing mode of production. Thus, in the Marxian view ancient Greek society, for example, necessarily had a very different kind of art from that of twentieth-century capitalism because, in the last analysis, the mode of production under the slave economy of ancient Greece was so different from that of industrial capitalism. As Friedrich Engels phrased it, "Political, juridical, philosophical, religious, literary, *artistic* [italics mine], etc., development is based on economic development. . . ." He was careful to add, however, "It is not that the economic position is the *cause and alone active*, while everything else only has a passive effect. There is, rather, interaction on the basis of the economic necessity, which *ultimately* always asserts itself."[26] In other words, art, though determined by economic development, can itself affect other aspects of life, and—being a means of communication and a form of ideology—can help motivate men's minds in bringing about social change.

Since for Marxists the processes of human life, including those of art, are in the last analysis determined by the prevailing economic situation, they therefore are not determined by God (as the religious utopians had believed) or by the human reason (as the secular utopians maintained). As a consequence, religion is considered to be merely the opium of the people,[27] so that religious art is to be frowned upon. And human reason, so all-powerful to the utopians, is believed to be free to operate only within the confines of the laws of nature and of human society. In Engels' words, "Men make their history themselves, [but] only in given surroundings which condition it and on the basis of actual relations already existing. . . ."[28] Hence freedom consists, according to Engels, in "the recognition of necessity," because "necessity is blind only in so far as it is not understood."[29] Man is free, then, insofar as he understands how the laws of nature and society operate, and he can plan human goals, including artistic goals, accordingly.

Marx believed that he had himself discovered the law on which all

[26] Friedrich Engels, letter to Heinz Starkenburg, Jan. 25, 1894, in Karl Marx, *Selected Works*, I, p. 392.

[27] This well-known statement is from Marx's "Contribution to a Critique of Hegel's Philosophy of Law," first published in 1844. It is often forgotten that when Marx stated that religion is the opium of the people, he added that it could not be made superfluous without removing the disease of society which encouraged the use of this opiate.

[28] Engels, letter to Starkenburg, *op.cit.*, p. 392.

[29] The translation followed here is from V. I. Lenin, "The Teachings of Karl Marx," in Emile Burns, *A Handbook of Marxism* (New York, 1935), p. 540. Lenin was quoting from Engels' *Herr Eugen Dühring's Revolution in Science* (usually known as *Anti-Dühring*), first published in German (Leipzig, 1878). This Marxist and Leninist concept of freedom derives, of course, directly from Hegel.

social change is based, namely, that social change occurs inevitably and necessarily with changes in the mode of production. All human history, including the history of art, develops, he maintained, in accord with this economic law of the motion of society. Consequently, if man understands this law, he can so act as to accelerate (or hinder) human progress. And for Marxians, progress consists primarily in advancing toward the goal of the classless society.

Because of their belief in progress, Marxians are frequently interested, at least to some degree, in encouraging new artistic media and progressive artistic techniques which may help in achieving this Marxian goal. However, the question at once arises as to whether politics, law, science, philosophy, art, etc. (all of which, be it remembered, are for Marxians primarily determined by the prevailing mode of production), are all progressing simultaneously and uniformly in the march toward the classless society. Here the problem is complicated further by the early education and preferences of Marx himself, because as a university student he had spent considerable time in studying the literature and art of classical antiquity and had come to the conclusion, to which he always subscribed, that Greek art is the greatest art to date, or as he called it, "in certain respects . . . the standard and model beyond attainment."[30] Marx therefore had to relate this belief to his seemingly contrary one that in other respects—such as the organization of society, scientific knowledge, etc.— mankind today has progressed far beyond the Greeks; and this he did in the following way. "It is well known," he said, "that certain periods of [the] highest development of art stand in no direct connection with the general development of society, nor with the material basis . . . of its organization. Witness the example of the Greeks as compared with the modern nations or even Shakespeare."[31] For although, like Engels, Marx insisted that all development is grounded upon economic development, he also said, "In considering . . . transformations [in the economic foundation and hence in its superstructure] the distinction should always be made between the material transformation of the economic conditions of production which can be determined with the precision of natural science, and the legal, political, religious, *aesthetic* [italics mine] or philosophic—in short ideological forms. . . ."[32]

Clearly, then, Marx believed in the nonuniformity of historical development, so that for him artistic progress does not have to parallel economic progress, or social progress, or scientific progress, etc.;[33] and in this he

[30] Karl Marx, *A Contribution to the Critique of Political Economy* (tr. from second German ed. by N. I. Stone; New York, 1904), pp. 311-12.
[31] *Ibid.*, pp. 309-10.
[32] *Ibid.*, Preface, p. 12.
[33] *Ibid.*, pp. 309-12.

differed from the secular utopians, who customarily implied that progress
is uniform in all fields. Marx could therefore regard Greek art as the
finest in history while also maintaining that capitalism, because it is
nearer in time to the classless society, is a far more advanced form of
social organization than the slave economy of ancient Greece. Yet despite
the advanced social organization of capitalism, "capitalist production,"
said Marx, "is hostile to certain branches of spiritual production, such as
art and poetry."[34] In sum, although capitalistic society has gone beyond
previous societies in economic development, and still further beyond
them in the science and technology which have aided its economic
development, Marx believed that it cannot hope to equal certain earlier
forms of art. Capitalist technological supremacy, for example, is of no
use for aiding modern man in a vain attempt to equal the epic poetry
of the Greeks: "Inasmuch as we have so far surpassed the ancients in
mechanics, etc., why [should we] not also create an epic poem?"[35] asked
Marx sarcastically.

Since for Marx artistic progress does not have to parallel economic
progress, it is clear that he did not regard works of art as economic
commodities. Indeed, he accounted for the decline of art under capitalism
on the grounds that "all the so-called higher forms of labor—intellectual,
artistic, etc.—have been transformed into commodities [by bourgeois
capitalism] and have thus lost their former sacredness."[36] Under capitalism, he said, "even the highest forms of spiritual production are recognized
and forgiven by the bourgeoisie only because they [i.e., artists, men of
letters, etc.] are represented and falsely labeled as direct producers of
material wealth,"[37] so that works of art are admired for what they will
fetch rather than for their quality as art. In other words, capitalism is
accused of stressing quantity and exchange value instead of the quality
and use value that ought to be emphasized, that will be emphasized in
the classless society, and that had even been recognized to some degree
in societies previous to capitalism, notably those of classical antiquity and
of the Middle Ages. As Marx phrased it, "In most striking contrast with
this [capitalistic] accentuation of quantity and exchange-value, is the
attitude of the writers of classical antiquity, who hold exclusively by
quality and use-value."[38] Similarly, though to a lesser degree, "Among the

[34] Karl Marx, *Theorien über den Mehrwert* (2nd ed., Stuttgart, 1910), I, p. 382;
translation from Mikhail Lifshitz, *The Philosophy of Art of Karl Marx*, Critics Group
Series No. 7 (tr. by Ralph Winn; New York, 1938), p. 78.
[35] *Loc.cit.*
[36] Karl Marx, "Arbeitslohn," *Marx-Engels Gesamtausgabe*, Pt. I, Vol. 6, p. 472;
translation from Lifshitz, *op.cit.*, p. 80.
[37] Marx, *Theorien über den Mehrwert*, I, p. 385; translation from Lifshitz, *op.cit.*,
p. 78.
[38] Karl Marx, *Capital*, I (Chicago, 1909), p. 401.

20

craftsmen of the Middle Ages there is still to be observed a certain interest in their particular work and in their skill, which was capable of rising to some degree of artistry," in contrast to "the modern worker, who is indifferent to his work."[39]

Thus, according to Marx, the precapitalistic emphasis on quality and use value, which characterized the ancient and medieval societies, produced workmen and artists who as men were better rounded and therefore happier than they could possibly be under capitalism, and who, as a result, were able to produce better works of art. For Marx insisted that in antiquity and under feudalism, despite slavery and serfdom, individuals still retained some real community ties, and had not yet been desocialized and depersonalized as they later became under the inhuman and mechanistic spirit of capitalism.

But although Marx maintained that in early periods of history the workers were able to have a sense of workmanship and artistry impossible in capitalist society, he also felt that Greek art and, to a lesser degree, medieval art represent the social childhood of man, the time when mankind was still in a relatively immature state. So even though he considered ancient art superior to any other, it should be emphasized that he did not seek to turn the clock back by attempting to revive the conditions of precapitalist society. Believing firmly that the laws of history, aided by human action, foreordained progress toward the triumph of the proletariat and the classless society, he insisted that the future should surpass the past, that the social maturity of mankind should surpass its childhood. Said Marx, "A man can not become a child again unless he becomes childish. But does he not enjoy the artless ways of the child and must he not strive to reproduce its truth on a higher plane? . . . Why should the social childhood of mankind, where it had obtained its most beautiful development, not exert an eternal charm as an age that will never return? . . . The Greeks were normal children. The charm their art has for us does not conflict with the primitive character of the social order from which it had sprung. It is rather the product of the latter, and is rather due to the fact that the unripe social conditions under which the art arose and under which alone it could appear can never return."[40]

Nevertheless, paradoxically enough, Marx held that the very decline of art, which he saw in capitalist society, does in a major sense represent progress even from the standpoint of art itself, because the decline of art is one of those many evils of capitalist society which are helping to pave the way for the revolution and for the classless society. And the classless

[39] Karl Marx and Friedrich Engels, "Die deutsche Ideologie," *Marx-Engels Gesamtausgabe*, Pt. I, Vol. 5, pp. 41-42; translation from Lifshitz, *op.cit.*, p. 80.
[40] Marx, *A Contribution to the Critique of Political Economy*, pp. 311-12.

society, by taking advantage of the methods of production developed under capitalism and adapting them to a new social order, will be marked by enormous new productive possibilities in art as in everything else. Only in this classless society, Marxians believe, can the full development of the productive powers of society and the creative powers of the individual human personality be achieved, powers which have been inevitably cramped under capitalism.

As all students of Marxism know, the cornerstone of Marx's economic doctrine is the labor theory of value, the theory that the value of a commodity must depend solely on the amount of socially necessary labor time expended in producing it. Although Marxians do not consider works of art to be commodities, they do say that art and labor are closely related: in fact, following Engels, they hold that art originated out of labor during the early period of history when human society first reached the stage of trade and industry, and that the skilled hand is actually the product of labor. Moreover, as the production of commodities requires the planned labor of workmen, so the production of works of art, they say, requires the planned and therefore conscious labor of artists. For this reason only human beings can produce art, because, as Engels remarked, "The further men become removed from animals . . . the more their effect on nature assumes the character of a premeditated, planned action directed towards definite ends known in advance."[41] Or as Marx himself expressed it, "But what distinguishes the worst architect from the best of bees is this, that the architect raises his structure in imagination before he erects it in reality."[42] Unlike animals or insects "man . . . creates according to the laws of beauty,"[43] laws which nevertheless are in the last analysis relative to the prevailing mode of production.

In recognizing that artists are not direct producers of material wealth, of commodities, Marx recognized also that the worth of works of art, unlike that of other products of human labor, should *not* ordinarily depend on the amount of socially necessary labor time required for producing them. Unlike other workmen, the artist usually does not work for a fixed wage, and unlike other products of human labor, works of art are ordinarily unique, so that there can be no real criterion of comparability between two works of art. In this respect they differ from commodities, for if commodities are to have value there must be some criterion of comparability between them on the basis of which they can be exchanged. To Marx therefore the very uniqueness of a work of art meant

[41] Friedrich Engels, *Dialectics of Nature* (New York, 1940), p. 290.
[42] Marx, *Capital*, I, p. 198.
[43] Marx, "Ökonomisch-philosophische Manuskripte aus dem Jahre 1844," *Marx-Engels Gesamtausgabe*, Pt. I, Vol. 3, p. 88; translation from *Literature and Art*, p. 15.

that it customarily does *not* have a value, but merely a price; and he was convinced that under capitalism this price depends either upon the whims of millionaires or upon artificial scarcity deliberately caused by a dealer or by the artist himself—an unsocial state of affairs of which he thoroughly disapproved. Furthermore, as indicated above, he believed that under capitalism works of art are treated—wrongly—as if they were commodities.

Only in a few rather exceptional cases can a standard of comparability exist between works of art so that, according to Marxian doctrine, only in exceptional cases can art have a value instead of just a price. For example, such a standard does exist with certain kinds of art, such as prints, which, by the very nature of the medium, are more or less mass-produced. Some Marxists point out that it can exist also in those instances, comparatively rare in capitalist society, under which the artist is paid a fixed wage like other workmen, as occurred with the American artists who worked for the W.P.A. during the depression of the 1930's.[44] For here the wages of the artists could be compared and, on that basis, a value could be arrived at for the works of art produced.

Like Marx's economic and historical materialism, his belief in the concept of organicism has also involved special problems for art. Marx held that nature is an organic whole which resembles a living organism insofar as it is more than the sum of its parts, including its human parts. Then, because he regarded human society as a kind of natural phenomenon, he, like Comte, considered that all the parts of society are organically interrelated and that the whole again is more than the sum of its parts. Since Marx thought that the social organism evolves according to definite laws of history, the concept of social organicism is closely connected with the concept of evolution. Consequently, the idea of process and development is fundamental to Marxism: Engels spoke of "the great basic thought that the world is . . . to be comprehended . . . as a complex of *processes*. . . ."[45] And because the social development of the world, fostered by the efforts of all good Marxians, is held to be proceeding toward the Marxian goal of the classless society, the Marxist believes not only in process but in progress as well.

All this has profound implications for Marxian art. As part of the Marxian concept of organicism, the human individual is considered to be subordinate to society, for the social organism is more than the sum of its individual parts. Marxists therefore frown upon individualistic self-expression in art, upon "art for art's sake," or, to put it more accurately, they believe that the artist should achieve self-expression by devoting

---

[44] See W. J. Blake [Blech], *Elements of Marxian Economic Theory and Its Criticism* (New York, 1939), pp. 434-36, 554, and 557 for a summary discussion of Marxian theory of price and value in works of art.

[45] F. Engels, "Ludwig Feuerbach," in Karl Marx, *Selected Works*, I, p. 453.

himself and his art to social action in order to help bring the goal of the classless society ever nearer. Only in the classless society, they say, can the all-sided development of individual personality become complete, and only then, too, can the arts reach new levels of excellence transcending even those of Greek art, so greatly admired by Marx himself.

In contrast to this future classless society, all class societies (that is to say, all societies since primitive man) and especially industrialized capitalist society, are considered to suffer from profound evils caused by the narrow specialization resulting from the division of labor. Wrote Marx and Engels, "The exclusive concentration of artistic talent in certain individuals, and its consequent suppression in the broad masses of the people, is an effect of the division of labor. . . . With a communist organization of society, the artist is not confined by the local and national seclusion which ensues solely from the division of labor, nor is the individual confined to one specific art so that he becomes exclusively a painter, a sculptor, etc. . . . In a communist society, there are no painters, but at most men who, among other things, also paint."[46]

In short, Marxians maintain that the division of labor, especially in its capitalist phase, has produced individually specialized artists who are therefore neither socially minded nor well-rounded men. This has given rise, they hold, to an evil regionalistic and nationalistic chauvinism in art, an evil distinction between the artist and the masses, between production and consumption, between work and enjoyment, between intellectual and manual labor, between aesthetic significance and utility, between high art and folk art, and between fine arts and crafts. Unlike the narrowly specialized artists of capitalism, Marxian artists are expected to participate in the life of the masses as well as to design many different kinds of things—and are expected to deal with both applied and fine art while obliterating any distinction between them. Moreover, their works must have social significance, must be socially organic and functional, and therefore must in the last analysis reflect the social conditions which are produced by the particular economic and natural environment. Like all socialist art, then, Marxian art tends to be functionalistic in spirit (although, it must be reiterated, by no means all functionalistic art is socialist).

The concept of progress which grows out of this Marxian concept of organicism is very different from that held by the secular utopians, who believed that man is progressing continuously and in a relatively straight line. For Marxians insist that progress, in art as in everything else, takes place in accord with the Hegelian dialectic, or law of motion, according to which any given tendency, or "thesis," inevitably gives rise to a

[46] Marx and Engels, "Die deutsche Ideologie," *Marx-Engels Gesamtausgabe*, Pt. I, Vol. 5, p. 373; translation from Lifshitz, *op.cit.*, pp. 92-93.

countertendency, or antithesis, and eventually to an unavoidable conflict between them ending in a synthesis, whereupon the process begins again. In other words, Marxians look upon dialectics as—in Lenin's words—"the study of the contradiction within the very essence of things,"[47] so that "development is the 'struggle' of opposites."[48] Such conflict of opposites is considered inevitable whenever changes in the social structure, in social relations (which basically are relations of production), fail to keep up with changes in the forces governing the mode of production. And conflicts of this sort mean that progress can occur only in an irregular zigzag manner once described by Lenin as "a development . . . in spirals, not in a straight line; a development in leaps and bounds, catastrophes, revolutions. . . ."[49] In spite of its irregularity, however, all parts of the process are regarded as organically interrelated, like all natural phenomena. As Stalin once said, "dialectics does not regard nature as an accidental agglomeration of things, of phenomena, unconnected with, isolated from, and independent of, each other, but as a connected and integral whole, in which things, phenomena are organically connected with, dependent on, and determined by, each other."[50]

Because of their belief in a zigzag kind of progress Marxists are in theory willing to turn sharply away from the past, to have a revolution in art as in everything else; so that Marxist art is often markedly anti-traditional and thereby emphasizes the present rather than the past. This is in harmony with the statement of Marx and Engels in the *Communist Manifesto*: "In bourgeois society . . . the past dominates the present; in communist society the present dominates the past." Yet because all parts of the dialectical process of development are organically connected, the past is organically related to the present. Indeed, the past casts light on the present because, according to the doctrine of historical materialism, the present grows out of the past and is very largely determined by it; therefore the Marxist must understand and make use of his knowledge of past art in creating the art of the present. Thus tradition is regarded as one of the inescapable determinants of art. As Lenin said, ". . . one can become a Communist only when one enriches one's mind with all the wealth of knowledge created by mankind";[51] and again, "Proletarian culture must be the result of a natural development of all the stores of

[47] V. I. Lenin, *Philosophical Notebooks*, Russian ed., p. 263; translation from Joseph Stalin, "Dialectical and Historical Materialism" (1938), *Leninism* (London, 1940), p. 595.

[48] V. I. Lenin, *Selected Works*, XI, pp. 81-82; translation from Stalin, *loc.cit.*

[49] V. I. Lenin, "The Teachings of Karl Marx," in Burns, *op.cit.*, p. 542.

[50] Stalin, "Dialectical and Historical Materialism," *Leninism*, p. 592.

[51] Lenin in his speech to the third congress of the Komsomol on Oct. 2, 1920, *Works* (Russian ed.), XXV; translation from Jack Chen, "The Graphic Arts in the U.S.S.R.," *Studio*, Vol. 127, No. 611 (Feb. 1944), p. 38.

knowledge which mankind has accumulated under the yoke of capitalist society, landlord society and bureaucratic society."[52]

The all-important role which Marx ascribed to the proletariat in bringing about progress toward the revolution and then toward the classless society likewise has major implications for art. The very existence of a proletariat implies the existence of a highly industrialized civilization to produce it, and since to Marxists, art, like everything else, is ultimately an expression of the economic organization of society for production, the question arises as to how art must express and reflect the productive relations of an industrialized society. Needless to say, because Marxism glorifies the proletariat as the class which will bring about the classless society against the opposition of the bourgeoisie, bourgeois subject matter in art is necessarily rejected as inimical to the masses, and only those kinds of art are stressed which best answer the needs of the proletariat itself. One of its most important needs is, of course, adequate housing, but it is interesting to note that on this question there has been a sharp split among the various factions of Marxism. The "orthodox," or theoretically revolutionary, Marxist often takes the position expressed by Engels in *The Housing Question* (1872) that new housing for the proletariat is to be rejected *before* the revolution, for fear that by thus ameliorating the condition of the masses their zeal for bringing about a revolution will be lessened and the revolution thereby postponed. In the meantime, the only kind of additional housing to be countenanced is housing seized from wealthy capitalists by the proletariat. However, aside from some revolutionary Marxists practically all recent kinds of socialists —including the evolutionary or gradualist Marxians (who, as their name implies, oppose a violent revolution), the state socialists, the Christian socialists, etc.—have supported the cause of more adequate living quarters for the masses even before the proletariat has triumphed.

All Marxians believe that economic change is inevitable and inevitably brings changes in all other aspects of life, including the artistic aspects. Consequently, principles of composition in art are held to be ever changing and relative to the period and place even though they ever more closely approximate absolute truth as mankind progresses.[53] And while Marxians do maintain that an absolute standard exists, they hold that in any specific instance it can only be approximated, for it is the sum total of all relative truths. This relativism (which, according to Engels,

[52] Lenin in *ibid.*; translation from Jack Chen, *Soviet Art and Artists* (London, 1944), pp. 77-78.
[53] For the Marxian concept of the nature of absolute truth see especially Engels, *Herr Eugen Dühring's Revolution in Science* (New York, 1939), pp. 94-105; and V. I. Lenin, *Materialism and Empirio-Criticism* (New York, 1927), pp. 103ff. The latter is Volume 13 of *Collected Works of V. I. Lenin.*

is necessarily even more pronounced in the historical sciences, including the history of art, than in the natural sciences)[54] implies that human nature is ever changing. And in this the Marxian point of view contrasts sharply with more absolutistic philosophies of art, notably with those of all the various kinds of academicism which stem from the classic tradition. For the academic artist, believing that human nature never fundamentally changes, holds that good art must be based on general principles of design considered to be valid universally and for all time.

Marxians also maintain that, like the principles of composition prevailing at a given time, the artist's personal style is basically determined by his environment—not merely by the geographical environment, but also, and primarily, by the social environment. And this manifests itself in the class structure which eventually results from such environmental conditions, and basically from the prevailing mode of production, the prevailing division of labor. As Marx and Engels once said with reference to Raphael, an artist is "conditioned by the technical advances made in art before him, by the organization of society and the division of labor in his locality, and finally, by the division of labor in all countries with which his locality maintained relations. Whether an individual like Raphael is able to develop his talent depends entirely upon demand, which in turn depends upon the division of labor and the consequent educational conditions of men."[55]

That a particular great artist such as Raphael happens to arise at a specific time is held to be a matter of chance, although if he had not existed, a substitute would necessarily have been demanded and eventually found. In the words of Engels, already quoted in part: "Men make their history [including their art history] themselves, [though] only in given surroundings which condition it and on the basis of actual relations already existing, among which the economic relations . . . are still ultimately the decisive ones. . . . That such and such a man . . . arises at that particular time in that given country is of course pure accident. But cut him out and there will be a demand for a substitute, and this substitute will be found, good or bad, but in the long run he will be found."[56]

Because Marxians believe that the "good" man and the "happy" man is he who helps to move history forward, they consider that the good

---

[54] See Engels, *Herr Eugen Dühring's Revolution in Science*, pp. 97ff. Engels remarks (p. 98), for example, that the natural sciences are called the exact sciences because "*certain* results obtained by these sciences are eternal truths, final and ultimate truths." But he adds, "As time goes on, final and ultimate truths become remarkably rare in this field."

[55] Marx and Engels, "Die deutsche Ideologie," *Marx-Engels Gesamtausgabe*, Pt. I, Vol. 5, p. 372; translation from Lifshitz, *op.cit.*, p. 92.

[56] Engels, letter to Starkenburg, Jan. 25, 1894, in Karl Marx, *Selected Works*, I, pp. 392-93.

artist is inevitably a propagandist of the deed. It must not be forgotten that, although Engels said, "political, juridical, philosophical, religious, literary, artistic, etc., development is based on economic development," he added, "But all these react upon one another and also upon the economic base."[57] Thus, although the artist is ultimately conditioned by the given economic and social situation, his art in turn reacts upon that situation and inevitably plays a role of social action which can help or hinder progress. In short, all art is propaganda for good or bad and is considered good only if it helps to bring about the Marxian goal of the revolution of the proletariat followed by the classless society. Art must therefore be useful for training the leaders of the revolution (and Marxian communists sometimes restrict the word propaganda to this meaning). But it must also be suited to the needs of the masses and to their understanding, and in addition must spur them to action—must serve, in short, the purpose of "agitation" as well as education. In the process of arousing the masses, morality and truth, like everything else, are to be considered as basically relative to the particular economic and social situation. "We maintain," said Engels, ". . . that all former moral theories are the product, in the last analysis, of the economic stage which society had reached at that particular epoch,"[58] a doctrine implicit also in Lenin's statement that communist morality "is entirely subordinate to the interests of the class war. . . ."[59] Consequently, to non-Marxians the Marxian seems to act as if the end justified the means in art as in other aspects of life; whereas Marxists themselves would prefer to say that the end cannot be separated from the means because the two are dialectically interrelated and interpenetrated.

Since good propaganda is considered to be that which best educates the masses, as well as the leaders of the revolution, in their historic social role, and which therefore spurs the proletariat to action, Marxians give particular emphasis to those artistic media which best lend themselves to propagandizing the masses. It is for this reason that Marxians stress the kinds of art which can most easily be seen and understood by large numbers of people, such as newspaper cartoons, murals, great buildings, monumental sculpture, the drama, motion pictures, mass parades, and pageants. Frequently monuments and buildings are made enormous, both to be seen more easily and to impress the masses by sheer size. And

[57] Engels, *ibid.*, p. 392.
[58] Engels, *Herr Eugen Dühring's Revolution in Science*, p. 105.
[59] Lenin in his speech to the third congress of the Komsomol on Oct. 2, 1920, *op.cit.*; as translated somewhat freely in René Fülöp-Miller, *The Mind and Face of Bolshevism* (New York, 1929), p. 278. What Lenin literally said was ". . . our morality is subjected entirely to the interests of the class struggle of the proletariat. Our morality is derived from the interests of the class struggle of the proletariat." See G. S. Counts and Nucia Lodge, *The Country of the Blind* (Boston, 1949), p. 22.

also, as might be expected, the varieties of art considered as the most important of all are usually those which best lend themselves to mass production and distribution, and which—like the motion picture, or like newspaper and poster art—can therefore reach the largest possible audiences when treated in an easily understandable way.

These, then, are the general characteristics usually found in Marxist art everywhere. And no matter where or by whom a particular Marxist art form was originated, if successful it has usually spread widely and rapidly because of the international spirit of Marxism. This spirit (which Marxians believe had already been foreshadowed and made possible by the growth of great international cartels and monopolies under capitalism) is reflected in such statements of Marx and Engels as: "With a communist organization of society . . . the artist is not confined by . . . local and national seclusion. . . ."[60] By this internationalism the different currents of Marxist art—currents which have varied in character both with the particular variety of Marxism and with the country of their origin— have been encouraged to intermingle and become modified by one another in many different ways. Not only has Marxist internationalism encouraged the spread of Marxist art into countries where Marxism is strong, but even where it is weak. And at times it has also helped to spread the forms of Marxist art where there is no *direct* Marxian influence at all. For frequently the *forms* of Marxist art, quite apart from its *content*, have been admired and imitated by internationally minded nonsocialists, or by other nonsocialists who for one reason or another have ignored or forgotten the original Marxian content of those forms. And at such times, as has often been the case in the United States, the Marxian forms have usually been much modified by the non-Marxian environment.

In order, therefore, to comprehend, first, the different manifestations of Marxian influence—direct or indirect—on American art, and, second, the modifications in them resulting from the American environment, the previous history abroad of those aspects of Marxist art which have affected art in the United States will be indicated briefly. Most of them have originated in countries where Marxism was not so swallowed up in trade-union movements as it was, for example, in France under syndicalism. Most of them, indeed, have originated in England, or Germany, or Soviet Russia; and for the sake of relative brevity, though at the risk of great oversimplification, our survey of developments abroad will be almost entirely restricted to those countries.

This means, of course, that various important questions more or less related to socialism—such as the contributions to modern housing made by the Swedish cooperatives—will have to be omitted. Even when thus

[60] For reference see note 46 herein.

abbreviated, the subject is still so complex that probably no one author can hope to treat it with the completeness that a specialist would desire; yet even a relatively superficial survey, to be of any use at all, must deal with so many facts as to become necessarily hard reading for the layman. However, in spite of such difficulties, an attempt to discuss this European background must be made here because otherwise the relations of Marxian socialism to American art and life simply cannot be understood.

IV. Marxism (continued): Marxian Art and the European Background

England. In considering the origin and development of the varieties of postutopian socialist art and art theory which have exerted the most influence on American art, we shall turn first to England, because the first great socialist leader who gave a primary place to the arts was the celebrated English author, poet, artist, and medievalist, William Morris (d. 1896). Morris was chiefly inspired by the ideas of John Ruskin, who in many respects was a Christian socialist in everything but the name and who taught drawing for a time in the Workingmen's College in London founded by the noted Christian socialist, Frederick Denison Maurice. Like Ruskin, Morris was led toward socialism chiefly by his interest in the Middle Ages. Originally a liberal (he was treasurer of the National Liberal League in 1879), Morris increasingly felt that the medieval social organization, with its spirit of cooperative effort as expressed in the medieval guilds, had integrated art and society and was far superior to the laissez-faire capitalism of his own day. Even though he realized the impossibility of returning to the conditions of the Middle Ages, to him medieval society was—comparatively, at least—an ideal society, a kind of utopia, and one which in many ways he deliberately sought to recall. His utopian spirit is reflected also in his famous romances of reform, including *The Dream of John Ball* (1888), named for a celebrated medieval leader of the lower classes, and *News from Nowhere* (1891).

However, Morris was much more than just a utopian. Among other things, he was greatly interested in the ideas of Henry George, the American exponent of the single tax; and as befitted one who had originally been destined for the church, there were also elements of Christian socialism in his thought. He himself stated that he was "a good deal influenced by the books of Charles Kingsley," the famous Christian socialist, poet, and novelist. Toward the end of his life he fell under the direct influence of Marxism, for in 1883 he became a member of the Marxian [Social] Democratic Federation in England, which had been founded only a little over a year before. He withdrew from this in

1885—together with Karl Marx's daughter, Eleanor Marx Aveling—to found the Socialist League; and when this organization was taken over by anarchists, he founded the Hammersmith Socialist Society. Yet Morris' concept of socialism—though not that of most of his associates in these groups—simply called for the realization of a society of fellowship, of cooperation, in which everyone would be guaranteed complete equality of condition by the community.

Because in Morris there came together so wide a variety of the chief social and artistic movements of his day, his influence, artistic and otherwise, was many-sided and was able to spread to many different places for very different reasons and with diverse results. For one thing, Morris' mediovalism made him a very prominent figure in the Gothic Revival in art. In connection with his attempt to revive the medieval guild system, Morris sought to revive handicraft as a means of restoring the well-being of the individual worker dehumanized by the machine age. Through handicraft and applied arts, he felt, the workman could become once more a self-respecting personality instead of merely a human tool; and at the same time the products of the worker's hands would themselves be much improved in quality. Besides, the separation between fine arts and applied arts, a separation also deplored by Ruskin, would be abolished.

It is obvious that Morris' criticism of the evils of industry under capitalism, as well as the ultimate social goals which he sought, had much in common with those of Karl Marx; however, like Ruskin, Morris called primarily for the *moral* reform of the evils of the industrial revolution and capitalism rather than the *economic* reform which Marx demanded and which Marx thought would bring moral reform in its train. Largely for this reason Morris had great difficulty in bringing himself even to read Marx's works. Moreover, Morris refused to subscribe to the Marxian doctrine of class struggle; and insofar as he sought to revive the medieval guilds and their handicraft, he was, in the Marxian view, both reactionary and utopian. For while Morris was not totally unmindful of the material contributions resulting from the industrial revolution (he once praised the iron steamship as the cathedral of the nineteenth century), it is true that to a considerable degree he and many of his followers did seek to turn the clock back, and in this respect differed sharply from the more completely forward-looking Marx.[61]

[61] For Morris' praise of the iron steamship see Lewis Mumford, *The Condition of Man* (New York, 1944), p. 336. Somewhat similarly Ruskin had praised the old wooden naval vessels: "Take it all and all, a ship of the line is the most honorable thing that man, as a gregarious animal, has produced" (quoted in Mumford, *Technics and Civilization* [New York, 1934] p. 208). Ruskin, too, did not completely reject the machine: he recognized the utilitarian advantages offered by machine power even though he tended to reject the steam engine, which had done so much to make

Morris' influence on the arts of design came chiefly from his revival of handicraft; in fact he was the leading figure in the whole "arts and crafts" movement which was destined to have a tremendous vogue throughout the Western world. Because this represented a reaction not only against the dehumanization of the craftsman by industrialism but also against that Victorian overelaboration in art resulting in part from the misuse of the new machine tools, it tended to foster a straightforward functionalism in art, especially in the applied arts. This functionalism is well illustrated by the simple forms and direct use of materials characteristic of the Morris chair, named after William Morris though not actually invented by him. Although Morris was not an architect himself (despite some training under a Gothic Revivalist, George Edmund Street), he was also to exert enormous influence on architecture through a house—Red House, Bexley Heath in Kent (Fig. 21)—which was built for him in accordance with his ideas by an architect friend, Philip Webb. This clearly reflects Morris' interest not only in a free handling of medieval design according to a native English folk tradition, but also in honest craftsmanship and in the straightforward use of regional materials and methods to give rise to both a better society and a better style.

Many of Morris' ideas were shared by artists associated with the famous Pre-Raphaelite Brotherhood with which Morris himself had close connections. This was partly fostered by the Gothic Revival; and it had considerable influence on art in the United States. One of the founders, in 1861, of Morris' cooperative arts-and-crafts firm—Morris, Marshall, Faulkner and Company—was the painter, Ford Madox Brown, who is sometimes called the source of the Pre-Raphaelite movement. Madox Brown liked to paint realistic pictures of workingmen and acknowledged that, somewhat like Morris, he too had "twinges" of socialism.

As all forms of socialism tend to stress social utility in art, it is not surprising that Morris and the arts and crafts movement have had so much influence on the arts of several varieties of socialism. In England, for example, many of Morris' doctrines were taken over by the two most influential socialist groups, the Fabian Society and the guild socialists. The Fabians (who consider Morris as their ideological ancestor even though he himself regarded them as too materialistic) have been especially noted for their influence on literature—as everyone knows, George Bernard Shaw was one of the leading Fabians. But they have also had considerable effect on the arts of design, a subject to which several of

England ugly, in favor of the more "natural" wind and water power. Similarly, in chapter 15 of *News from Nowhere*, Morris assumed a new kind of power, not unlike electricity, which eliminates smoke. Through this power "all work which would be irksome to do by hand is done by immensely improved machinery," even though "in all work which it is a pleasure to do by hand, machinery is done without."

the most important Fabian tracts have been devoted. One of the best known of these, written by the architect Arthur Clutton-Brock who had recently published a book on the work and influence of Morris, is entitled *Socialism and the Arts of Use* (1915), a title which again reflects the utilitarian and functional spirit typical of so much socialist art. The same spirit is reflected also in many of the writings of Herbert Read, long the most famous English art critic. Read, an anarchist, for a time strongly supported guild socialism, and, as he himself says, has been influenced by the ideas of Morris and John Ruskin as well as by some of the doctrines of Marx, of the syndicalist Sorel, and of Kropotkin, the Russian anarchist, among others.[62]

Fabians and guild socialists alike have played a particularly important part in modern city planning, and especially in connection with the development of the garden city, for some of the best known of all garden-city designers were Fabian followers of William Morris. Among them were Raymond Unwin, Barry Parker, and A. J. Penty, the last of whom became a founder of guild socialism. The garden-city movement, which later was to spread to the United States, was initiated in 1898 when Ebenezer Howard published in England his famous pamphlet, *Tomorrow: a Peaceful Path to Real Reform*, reissued in 1902 under the title of *Garden Cities of Tomorrow*. Howard himself was always as much concerned for free enterprise as for social control. However, the principles of the garden city—its location surrounded by countryside, its informally functional plan, its belt of greenery and many parks, its organization as a cooperative restricted in size and density and possessing a local industry segregated from the residential section (Fig. 22)—offered one answer to that complete isolation of city life from country life under capitalistic industrialism which had been so bitterly deplored by Marx, as well as by Morris, because it produced one-sided human beings. It is therefore not surprising that a Soviet project for rebuilding Moscow, prepared in 1935, called for one, but only one, of the most characteristic features of the garden city, namely, a greenbelt of forest.[63]

Nevertheless, Ebenezer Howard had been led to his conception of the garden city not by Marxism, but by the combined influence of Edward Bellamy's American utopian novel, *Looking Backward* (1888), of the cooperative movement (of which the English utopian socialist, Robert Owen, was the chief founder), and of the English medieval village, recently glorified anew by the Gothic Revival and particularly by William

---

[62] See Herbert Read's autobiography, *The Innocent Eye* (New York, 1947), especially pp. 140-42 and 240.

[63] The proposal was finally rejected, however, as "a rightest counterrevolutionary attempt to weaken the city by separating the proletariat from the technology both physically and morally": see Percival Goodman and Paul Goodman, *Communitas* (Chicago, 1947), p. 35.

Morris. From Morris also came the concept of decentralization so fundamental to the garden city: in *News from Nowhere* Morris—rejecting Bellamy's mechanistic centralization—had visualized the ideal London of the
future as an agglomeration of villages separated by woods, fields, and
gardens.

All of these influences are reflected to some degree in the two famous
English garden cities, Letchworth and Welwyn (Fig. 22). Letchworth,
founded in 1903, was planned by Howard's disciples, Raymond Unwin
and Barry Parker, while Welwyn, begun in 1919, resulted from Howard's
own initiative. Through Unwin, the influence of the garden city was to
be felt everywhere in modern suburban real-estate developments, of
which, however, both Howard and Unwin sharply disapproved. Much
of the best English planning for the period after World War II also stems
from Howard's ideas, notably the Greater London Plan of 1944, the New
Towns Act of 1946, and the Town and Country Planning Act of 1947.[64]

Germany. Like English socialism, German socialism too has made important contributions to modern art and architecture. Some of them have
originated in Germany itself, some have reflected the influence of the
English arts and crafts movement, and others have shown the influence
of Soviet Russian art; for the central position of Germany tended to make
it a kind of clearinghouse for the ideas and artistic developments of all
Europe.

In architecture, many of the chief German contributions have been
made in connection with housing for the poorer classes erected by state
or municipal authorities. Such housing developed in Germany on a large
scale long before it did in England, in Russia, or in the United States,
because Germany and several neighboring countries under German influence possessed a long tradition of housing built by municipal governments, a tradition going back to the Middle Ages. In the nineteenth
century this tradition was given a new impetus by the exaggerated
deification of the state fostered by such German philosophers as Fichte
and Hegel, the first of whom particularly emphasized the planning
function of the state. All of this helps to account for the fact that the
first important program for state socialism was formulated in Germany
by Marx's rival, Ferdinand Lassalle, and also that state capitalism on a
large scale was first developed there by the conservative Bismarck, who
sought to buttress the status quo by adopting a few conciliatory socialist

[64] For the influence of Howard and Unwin see especially the preface by F. J. Osborn
to Osborn's edition of Ebenezer Howard, *Garden Cities of Tomorrow* (London, 1946).
Also see Dugald Macfadyen, *Sir Ebenezer Howard and the Town Planning Movement* (Manchester, Eng., 1933), and James Dahir, *Communities for Better Living*
(New York, 1950).

measures. Although Bismarck's program did not include housing, it did help to foster an atmosphere of social reform in which even many nonsocialists eventually became willing to support public housing as well as other aspects of the socialist program. But it was when German socialism grew particularly strong during the early twentieth century, and especially during the period of the Weimar Republic, that the greatest developments in public housing were made in Germany, developments destined to influence American housing, notably under the New Deal. As might be expected, it was during this general period also that the influence of artists stimulated by William Morris' arts and crafts movement, and later by Soviet Russian art, aroused particular interest in Germany.

No single "socialist style" has ever developed in Germany largely because German socialism has so often been torn by dissension, with major conflicts between the state socialism of Lassalle on the one hand and Marxism on the other, between the revolutionary socialism of the "orthodox" Marxians and the evolutionary socialism of the revisionists, and between social democracy and the Russian forms of communism. Nevertheless, although no one socialist style in art has prevailed in Germany, certain tendencies affecting the arts and common to all or nearly all forms of German socialism can be pointed out.

Thus, for the reasons noted above, nearly all varieties of socialism in Germany long supported housing erected at public expense. The single exception was the strictly revolutionary Marxist group, which took the view of Engels that if the condition of the workers was much improved before the revolution, their eagerness for bringing about a revolution would be abated. Surprisingly enough, the German socialists who favored new housing usually argued for the one-family dwelling until well after the walk-up apartment and row house had developed for hard economic reasons during the Weimar Republic. And this fact suggests that political and economic radicals are often conservatives in those other fields of thought and action which they do not consider so fundamental.

Practically all of the different varieties of German socialism could be affected in various ways—although often for different reasons—by the doctrines of William Morris and the English arts and crafts movement. For instance, Morris' medievalism could appeal to those German Christian socialists who, like the followers of Bishop von Ketteler of Mainz, were also seeking to revive the guild system. And it could appeal to the nationalistic tendencies of those who supported the concept of a specifically German state socialism because the medieval revival could, if desired, be given a specifically Germanic and Wagnerian cast. At the same time, the arts and crafts movement (though not so much the medievalism of

Morris) could attract the various Marxist factions within German socialism because they believed that it offered a remedy for certain evils of the capitalist system including—for art—the separation between fine art and craft art, between the artist and the masses, between intellectual and manual labor, and between work and enjoyment. Many German Marxists, therefore, were much interested in the arts and crafts movement, but often gave it a conscious up-to-dateness in harmony with the Marxian emphasis on the present and the future, on the machine and mass production, rather than with Morris' attempt to revert to the handicrafts of the medieval guilds.

However, Morris' influence in Germany was not restricted to socialists. In many respects, and especially in its protofunctionalism, his point of view was also accepted by many Germans who were not socialists or political radicals, but who were nonetheless considered artistically radical because they subscribed to a native German tradition of functionalism in art, a tradition perhaps best exemplified by the writings of the German architect and aesthetician, Gottfried Semper (d. 1879). Semper—a liberal who was forced to flee from Germany because, with his friend Richard Wagner, he had taken an active part at Dresden in the Revolution of 1848-1849—has been called by the English critic Herbert Read, "the historical materialist in the sphere of art."[65] For Semper explained structure in art as derived from the nature of the use to which the work is to be put, from the nature of the material, and from the nature of the tools and methods employed.[66] In very similar phraseology William Morris avowed a "principle of structure that evolves its forms in the spirit of strict truthfulness, following the conditions of use, material, and construction."[67] It was therefore easy for the ideas of Morris and Ruskin to be assimilated by the followers of Semper and, conversely, for Semper's doctrines to spread among some of Morris' contemporaries in England[68] and elsewhere.

One of the pupils of Semper's son, for example, was the great Dutch

[65] Herbert Read, Art Now (2nd ed., New York, n.d.), p. 41.

[66] Gottfried Semper, Der Stil in den technischen und tektonischen Künsten (Munich, 1878), I, p. 7.

[67] Quoted in W. C. Behrendt, Modern Building (New York, 1937), p. 61.

[68] Nikolaus Pevsner, Academies of Art (Cambridge, Eng., 1940), p. 253, cites the influence of Semper on Owen Jones, the Welsh architect and decorator. Semper, while in exile for participating in the Revolution of 1848, lived for a time in London and played a part in organizing the world's fair of 1851, the Great Exhibition at the Crystal Palace. Henry Cole, the chief organizer of the Exhibition, was the leader of a group which included Owen Jones and which sought to reform design in England by proper use of the machine rather than by reacting against the machine as did William Morris. Cole himself spoke of Semper as the man from whom "our manufacturers would be likely to obtain great help." See Siegfried Giedion, Mechanization Takes Command (New York, 1948), pp. 350-60.

architect, H. P. Berlage, who even though a Marxist regarded Ruskin as "the father of modern art."[69] Nevertheless, Berlage criticized Ruskin as a mere scholar who did not participate in social action through the practice of art, and he maintained that only practicing artists and architects, such as Semper, could really direct modern art upon its right path.[70] Yet like Ruskin (and like Morris, also) Berlage insisted upon the social utility of art while maintaining that, of all previous forms of art, those of the Middle Ages could best serve as the right foundation for the art of modern times.[71] And as a Marxist, he sought to justify in terms of historical materialism his return to a modernized version of the forms of medieval architecture,[72] for he felt that only the Middle Ages had previously possessed that communal spirit of working together which to him was characteristic of the twentieth century as a century of socialism.[73] He therefore insisted that the twentieth century demanded a "pure art of utility,"[74] a functionalistic art comparable to the architecture of the Middle Ages (Fig. 23). Berlage was not only the first great leader of the whole modern movement in Holland, but through his writings, his buildings, his city planning, and housing for workers (especially as exemplified in Amsterdam South, the planning of which in part reflects the influence of the medieval town), he became particularly influential in Germany. And via Germany many of his ideas were spread to other countries.

A still greater influence was exerted in Germany by the theories and works of Henry van de Velde, a famous Belgian architect, designer, and craftsman. Van de Velde, who began his career as a neo-impressionist painter, had suffered a complete physical and nervous collapse in 1889 and, while recuperating, had felt himself strongly drawn to socialism, especially in its more individualistic aspects. At this time, therefore, he spent much time reading the works of the anarchists Kropotkin and Stirner, of the "Christian anarchist" Tolstoy, and of Nietzsche, the highly individualistic glorifier of the superman. He also admired the writings of Edward Carpenter, an English socialist who was stimulated by Thoreau's *Walden*, by the Christian socialism of his friend F. D. Maurice, and especially by the somewhat more Marxian socialism of Hyndman and William Morris. Hence when an artist friend called Henry van de Velde's attention to the writings of William Morris himself, the way had been prepared: they were, Van de Velde felt, exactly what he had been seeking

[69] H. P. Berlage, *Gedanken über Stil in der Baukunst* (Leipzig, 1905), p. 22.

[70] Berlage, *loc.cit.* Together with Semper, Berlage mentioned Viollet-le-Duc, the French Gothic-Revivalist and rationalist architect, who was a radical republican.

[71] Berlage, *op.cit.*, p. 40.

[72] Henri de Man, *Psychology of Socialism* (New York, 1927), p. 246. Marx, however, presumably would not have approved of this return to medieval forms.

[73] Berlage, *op.cit.*, p. 48.

[74] H. P. Berlage in *Tweemaandelijk Tijdschrift*, II (1896), pp. 233-34.

all along. For previously he had been worried by the fact that in socialism there seemed to be no adequate place for the skill of the individual. Now at last in the writings of William Morris he had found a kind of socialism in which the individual, as artist, plays the leading role. And from now on, like Morris and like John Ruskin (the two men who, he later said, had most influenced his art),[75] Van de Velde insisted that the so-called fine arts must be applied to life—must, in short, become applied arts, for in this way the individual artist, while working for beauty, could also work to restore nobility to all mankind. This philosophy of art led Van de Velde, like Morris before him, to turn away from painting to the crafts and, in Van de Velde's case, toward architecture as well. In 1894-1895 he designed, in accordance with the principles of Morris, a house for himself at Uccle in Belgium equipped throughout with furniture, wallpaper, metal work, etc., made from his own designs. More than Morris and Ruskin, however, Van de Velde came to feel that the unintelligent use of the machine, rather than the machine itself, was to blame for the horrors of contemporary industrialized society. And gradually he even came to regard machinery itself as beautiful, recalling his childhood fascination with the engine rooms of steamers at Antwerp—a fact which may serve to remind us not only that Morris had spoken of the iron steamship as the cathedral of the nineteenth century, but that the famous French writer, Edmond de Goncourt, disparagingly referred to Van de Velde's own work as the "Yachting Style."

What De Goncourt called the "Yachting Style" was generally known as *Art Nouveau*, or *Jugendstil*—contemporary terms which clearly indicate that the movement was regarded as artistically radical.[75a] Not only was Van de Velde the chief founder of Art Nouveau but he was mainly responsible for spreading it (and thus the influence of William Morris and the English arts and crafts movement) throughout the Continent. And he became particularly influential in Germany, where from 1902 until 1914 he was director of the Arts and Crafts School at Weimar, a school destined to form part of the celebrated *Bauhaus* after World War I. Years later, with two other architects he designed the Belgian pavilion at the New York World's Fair of 1939-1940.

In addition to Berlage and Van de Velde, a third foreign artist whose influence profoundly affected German design was the French architect Tony Garnier. Garnier was born at Lyons, which ever since 1848 had

[75] Henry van de Velde, *Die Renaissance im modernen Kunstgewerbe* (1901), p. 23. For Van de Velde's life see especially K. E. Osthaus, *Van de Velde* (Hagen, 1920), and Henry R. Hope, *The Sources of Art Nouveau* (unpublished Ph.D. thesis, Harvard University, 1942).

[75a] It is significant that another Belgian founder of the Art Nouveau style, Victor Horta, was the architect of the *Maison du Peuple* (1899), headquarters of the Social Democratic Party in Brussels. Horta, too, was an avowed follower of Morris.

been a chief French socialist center, and was raised in a socialist family. He himself had socialist leanings described by one of his biographers as resembling the mild socialism of a Saint-Simon or a Fourier.[76] Although trained at Paris in the highly traditional and academic École des Beaux-Arts, where he won the highest student honor, the Grand Prix de Rome, Garnier partly rebelled against his academic training. Interested in the social problems raised by the expansion of industry, between 1901 and 1904 he made designs for a whole imaginary *cité industrielle* (Fig. 24) in the new and unacademic material of reinforced concrete, designs published in 1917. In 1905 the Radical Socialist (i.e., liberal) mayor of Lyons, Édouard Herriot, commissioned Garnier to redesign a large part of Lyons along the lines of his project for an industrial city. Both the work at Lyons, which was published in 1919 in a book with a preface by Herriot, and especially the project for the *cité industrielle*, aroused much interest among modern architects in postwar Germany as well as in France, and eventually throughout the world. In this way Garnier became one of the chief founders of modern architecture.

Thus in Germany the native radical movement in the arts, stemming particularly from Semper, could be encouraged in part by the socialism of Morris and Marx and of foreign artists such as Berlage, Van de Velde, and Garnier, though without being by any means completely socialist in either origin or development. Insofar as this movement sought to develop a new or revived respect for the personality of the craftsman-artist, and insofar as it tended to stress the nonseparation of fine and applied art as well as a straightforward "functional" expression in the arts, it appealed to socialists. Likewise its anti-academic "realism" appealed to many more or less radical German artists and architects who, disillusioned by World War I and its immediate aftermath, were turning to the left in art or politics or both. Among them was the artist Käthe Kollwitz, whose work was later to be admired by many Americans, and who, without ever being a member of the German Communist Party, became one of its venerated "People's Artists." Among them also was George Grosz, a painter and cartoonist world-famous for his satirization of the German bourgeoisie, who was then sympathetic to communism (Fig. 25) and is said to have worked for the Spartacist group of left-wing communists. In the 1920's Grosz—who left Germany for the United States in 1933—was the leader of a group of artists to whose work was applied the term, *die neue Sachlichkeit* (i.e., the new objectivity, the new realism), a term which the inventor once said was intended to "apply as a label to the new realism bearing a socialistic flavor."[77]

[76] Giulia Veronesi, *Tony Garnier* (Milan, 1948), p. 10.

[77] Quoted by A. H. Barr, Jr., in Museum of Modern Art, *German Painting and Sculpture* (New York, 1931), p. 13, note. The term, *Neue Sachlichkeit*, was coined

However, it must be emphasized that this radical movement in the arts, stemming in part from Semper and reinforced by *die neue Sachlichkeit*, appealed not only to socialists but also to many nonsocialists who were interested in solving in an "objective" functional way various economic, social, and artistic problems which had been raised by the industrial revolution but which had come to a head in Germany after World War I. In other words, at that time in Germany it was easy for many socialists and many nonsocialists, Marxians and many non-Marxians, to use the same art *media* and *forms*, although often with a very different *content*.

All this is well illustrated by an association of artists called the *Novembergruppe*, founded in Berlin in the autumn of 1918 and named for the month of the republican revolution. On November 9, the Kaiser had fled from Germany and the social democrats had formed Workers and Soldiers Councils which fostered a general strike and brought about the appointment as chancellor of Friedrich Ebert, vice-president of the Social Democratic Party. The members of the Novembergruppe (which soon included most of the leaders of modern art in Germany) called themselves "revolutionaries of the spirit," insisting that a revolution in the arts should accompany the postwar political and social revolution, and urging the closest possible interrelation between art and the people. In 1919 the Novembergruppe founded a Workers Council for Art which issued a questionnaire on the subject of the relation of the artist to society, and investigated among other things the duty of a socialist state to support art, the problem of housing, the relation between fine arts and industrial arts, and the production of works of art collectively. One hundred and fourteen painters, architects, sculptors, critics, and art historians sponsored the questionnaire. Among the sponsors—many of them simply artists with little or no interest in politics—was Walter Gropius, the architect who was the first director of the newly founded Bauhaus. And several other artists who became members of the Bauhaus staff were connected with various activities of the Novembergruppe, including the architect Ludwig Mies van der Rohe and the painters Kandinsky, Klee, and Feininger.

The Bauhaus, destined to be the chief focus of the various currents of modern art in Germany during the 1920's, in some respects and in a nonpolitical way continued the spirit of the Novembergruppe. As we have mentioned, the Bauhaus replaced the Arts and Crafts School at Weimar, directed since 1902 by Henry van de Velde, one of the founders

by Dr. G. F. Hartlaub in 1923: see Fritz Schmalenbach, "The Term *Neue Sachlichkeit*," *Art Bulletin*, Vol. 22, No. 3 (Sept. 1940), pp. 161-65. The art movement known by this name had been started in 1920 by Grosz and another German painter, Otto Dix. That Grosz worked for the Spartacists is stated by Marcel Ray, *George Grosz* (Paris, [1927]), p. 33.

of the continental arts and crafts movement known as Art Nouveau, or Jugendstil, a movement then considered to be highly radical. After Van de Velde withdrew from the Arts and Crafts School at Weimar in 1914, it was at his suggestion that Walter Gropius, a native German architect, was eventually selected to succeed him. In 1919 under Gropius' leadership the Arts and Crafts School was combined with the Grand Ducal Academy of Pictorial Art and the two were reopened as one establishment with the name of the Staatliches Bauhaus. Under Gropius and his successors the Bauhaus became the most widely known progressive art school not only in Germany, but in the whole world, and at a period when the social democratic governments dominant in so many German municipalities during the Weimar Republic were indirectly helping to foster modern architecture by their large building programs.[78] Because of the Bauhaus' artistic radicalism, it met increasing opposition in conservative Weimar, and in 1925 moved to the industrial city of Dessau, where it was soon housed in a new building erected from Gropius' designs, a building (Fig. 28) which immediately acquired a reputation as one of the most famous monuments of modern architecture.

All political activity was officially banned at the Bauhaus by Gropius.[°] Artistically, however, as a focus of modern movements in art, the Bauhaus was far left of center, so that its principles appealed to many socialists and communists as well as to many others who were simply anticonservative. Gropius himself—justly described by pupils as a liberal—was not a political socialist or communist. But as one whose avowed precursors include Ruskin, Morris, and Van de Velde[79] he has always been interested

---

[78] The Social Democrats, in power in many municipalities, held about half the cabinet posts in the Weimar Republic during the early years, and thereafter were in the minority; see the table in Ruth Fischer, *Stalin and German Communism* (Cambridge, Mass., 1948), p. 125.

[°] The author is most grateful to Walter Gropius for his kindness in reading over, while this volume was in press, the pages dealing with the Bauhaus. Every effort has been made to take his comments and corrections into account, but it is only fair to him to say that he disagrees with a number of the author's major conclusions as well as with the presentation of some of the more factual material. He feels, and rightly, that the picture here given of the Bauhaus is not a balanced one. The Bauhaus was a focal point for most of the currents of modern art, of which the majority had nothing whatever to do with socialism. But some had either been developed by socialists or were admired and made use of by socialists. It is only these which are being investigated in this book.

[79] Walter Gropius, *Idee und Aufbau des Staatlichen Bauhauses Weimar* (Munich, 1923), p. 2. Here Gropius acknowledged as his precursors not only Ruskin, Morris, and Van de Velde, but also Peter Behrens and the *Werkbund*. Behrens, in whose office Gropius, and also Mies van der Rohe, worked for a time before World War I, was such an admirer of Van de Velde's ideas that, like Van de Velde, he too had given up painting to become an architect. The Deutscher Werkbund was founded in 1907 as a result of an impassioned public lecture by Hermann Muthesius, then superintendent of the Prussian Board of Trade for Schools of Arts and Crafts. From 1896 to 1903 Muthesius had been attached to the German embassy in London for

in architecture as an essentially social art, so that the prevailing philosophy of art at the Bauhaus during his directorship can be described as more or less collectivistic, though only in a nonpolitical and non-Marxist way. In a letter to me Gropius himself has written: "The Bauhaus was more than an art institute. We were seeking to find a new way of life. The main tendency with which everyone was imbued was to stress the point that in this world of economic expediency the human being should be again the focus. That is to say, that all the economical and industrial issues are to be subordinated to the life requirements of men. In consequence of this many of the members of the Bauhaus were interested in social improvements but the main tendency was very much anti-Marxist."

In 1928 Gropius withdrew from the Bauhaus because of the ever increasing opposition of the Nazis, and was succeeded as director by one of the teachers, an architect named Hannes Meyer who, to Gropius' surprise, eventually proved to be a communist. After but two years Meyer was dismissed, and then went to the Soviet Union where he resided for some time.[80] He was replaced by Mies van der Rohe, whose philosophy of architecture is similar to that of Gropius and who remained in charge until the Bauhaus closed its doors in 1933 after the Nazis came to power.

Thus for only two years, while Hannes Meyer was director, could the Bauhaus be described as at all "communistic" in tendency in any political sense of the word. Actually the staff of the Bauhaus represented a wide diversity of political opinion, yet the difficulties put in the way of Gropius and Mies by all the conservatives and Nazis who wrongly identified the artistic radicalism of the Bauhaus with political radicalism, were enormous: "I hardly believe you can imagine the amount of troubles we had to go through," wrote Mies van der Rohe in a moving letter to the author of this book.

---

the purpose of carrying on research in English housing. He became a strong supporter of the English arts and crafts movement and of English architecture in the tradition of Ruskin and Morris, though Muthesius placed more emphasis on machine production. Demanding a "pure and perfect utility" and a new *Maschinenstil* (which he felt were lacking in Art Nouveau), he called for realism and objectivity in art— "a reasonable *Sachlichkeit*." He thus foreshadowed the somewhat different *Neue Sachlichkeit* which was to develop in German painting after World War I largely under socialist influences. For Muthesius and the Werkbund see Nikolaus Pevsner, *Pioneers of Modern Design* (New York, 1949), pp. 15-17.

[80] On the authority of Mr. Arthur Voyce, who adds that Meyer was an influential figure in Soviet architectural circles during the early years of his stay in the U.S.S.R. There Meyer was for a time on the teaching staff of the Academy of Architecture, contributed a number of articles to Soviet architectural magazines, and as late as 1935 was elected a member of the board of governors of the Moscow "House of Architects." He later went to Mexico. Walter Gropius has told the writer that he himself recommended Meyer for the directorship of the Bauhaus, not being then aware of Meyer's communistic leanings.

As mentioned above, Gropius was admittedly stimulated by some of the ideas of the socialist William Morris without being a socialist himself, a fact which clearly indicates that one artist can be stimulated by another without necessarily adopting the whole political and economic creed of his mentor. Moreover, it must be remembered that artists are frequently given commissions by clients to whose political philosophy they do not subscribe. For example, Gropius—though not a socialist—was commissioned by a social-democratic official of the Ministry of the Weimar Republic to design a monument to those killed in the rightist and nationalistic Kapp *Putsch* of 1920, and this was erected at Weimar in 1921 (Fig. 26). Four years later Mies van der Rohe—not a communist—was commissioned as architect of the monument (Fig. 27) erected near Berlin in 1926 in memory of Rosa Luxemburg and Karl Liebknecht, the two communist leaders shot by German officers following the Spartacist uprising of 1919.

Obviously sheer accident can often play a large part in the commissioning of works of art. Yet the fact that socialist and communist clients commissioned these two works supports the view that—other things being equal—political radicals are more inclined than conservatives to be sympathetic to radicalism in other fields, including the radicalism of artists. And this is frequently the case even if the artistic radicals—like Gropius and Mies—are not really interested in specifically political radicalism at all. In other words, the belief in progress so characteristic of socialism in general and of Marxian socialism in particular, often leads the Marxian to be sympathetic to the most advanced forms of art unless there are special reasons (for example, the anti-Westernism of Russia under Stalin) for attacking such art. And this is true even despite the fact that many political radicals (including Stalin himself) are relatively conservative in their artistic tastes, a conservatism which in these cases usually results from lack of background and training in the arts and which persists simply because Marxism gives such primacy to economic and political, rather than artistic, problems.

All of these points are well illustrated by the story of Mies van der Rohe's Luxemburg-Liebknecht memorial. Mies has written to me concerning that monument destroyed by the Nazis: "Everything was accidental from the beginning to the end. But let me tell you the facts.

"One of the first houses I built was for Hugo Perls in Berlin. Mr. Perls sold his house in the early twenties to a Mr. Edward Fuchs. Mr. Fuchs had a huge collection of Daumiers and other artists. He told friends of mine he would like to build a wing onto his house as a gallery for his collection and for this he would like to talk to me. A few days later a friend of mine told me he was going to Mr. Fuchs' for dinner. I asked him if it would not be an opportune time for me to meet Mr. Fuchs. This meeting was arranged.

"After discussing his house problems Mr. Fuchs then said he wanted to show us something. This developed to be a photograph of a model for a monument to Karl Liebknecht and Rosa Luxemburg. It was a huge stone monument with Doric columns and medallions of Luxemburg and Liebknecht. When I saw it I started to laugh and told him it would be a fine monument for a banker.

"He must have been very much disturbed by this remark because the next morning he called me and said that as I had laughed at the monument he had shown, he would like to know what I would propose. I told him I hadn't the slightest idea what I would do in his place, but as most of these people were shot in front of a wall, a brick wall would be what I would build as a monument. Fuchs could not imagine how a brick wall could be used as a monument but told me that if I had an idea he would be interested in seeing it. A few days later I showed him my sketch of the monument which in the end was built.

"He was still skeptical about it and particularly so when I showed him the bricks I would like to use. In fact, he had the greatest trouble to gain permission from his friends who were to build the monument."

Despite the large element of sheer accident in this story, it is significant that the communist followers of Liebknecht and Luxemburg finally commissioned not a design in the classical tradition based on principles considered good for all time, but one which so completely represents a belief in the idea of progress. As all students of architecture know, Mies van der Rohe and Walter Gropius are among the leading architects who have reacted sharply against the eclecticism, or imitation of past styles, which was dominating architectural design in the early years of the twentieth century. Consequently, in thus seeking to free building from historical reminiscences and achieve a basic and straightforward modern architecture (albeit partly under the stimulation, conscious or unconscious, of that movement in modern art known as cubism), they were among the chief founders of what has since become known as the "International Style." This is a name they strongly dislike, for they insist that they had no intention of establishing a new "style" but were merely seeking to return to architectural fundamentals. Yet because so many of the fundamentals that these men agreed upon can be basic for architecture everywhere, they do transcend national boundaries so that the name, International Style, has become generally accepted for this kind of architecture. And this in spite of the fact that its originators (most of whom prefer the term "the new architecture") firmly believe that good buildings must always be designed to meet specific conditions of climate and site.

Because of the nonnationalistic and consciously "modern" character of the International Style, because of its direct and "realistic" expression of the inherent qualities of new materials and techniques somewhat in the manner of *die neue Sachlichkeit,* this kind of modern architecture could easily be seized upon by many Marxists as a suitable expression of the international spirit of Marxism as well as of its conscious contemporaneity and belief in progress. As already noted, even at the Bauhaus itself the forms of this new architecture could be regarded by Hannes Meyer as to some degree infused with a Marxian content during the two years (1928-1930) of his directorship. And, as will be indicated in more detail later, the International Style was also briefly accepted in Soviet Russia until a more nationalistic point of view became dominant under Stalin.

On account of the ease with which the International Style lent itself to the international spirit of most varieties of socialism, nearly all of its leaders have at one time or another been called socialists or communists whether they actually were or not: indeed, it was primarily for the purpose of avoiding such accusations that political activity was banned at the Bauhaus by Gropius and later by Mies van der Rohe. Yet in spite of the sincere efforts of these men to be nonpolitical, when the Nazis came to power in 1933 the International Style was so antithetic to the exaggerated nationalism fostered by the Nazis that the Bauhaus was accused by them of being "degenerate" or "bolshevistic,"[81] and was eventually compelled to close its doors. For Hitler attributed "degenerate art" to the influence of the Jews, arguing that "the house with the flat roof is oriental—oriental is Jewish—Jewish is bolshevistic."

As early as 1924, when he wrote *Mein Kampf,* Hitler had attacked all modern art as "bolshevistic," probably because in Germany the influence of Russian artists was then strong. Despite the injustice of Hitler's attack (for the Russian artists in question had left Soviet Russia because Lenin disapproved of their art), from that time on those who have fostered modern art have often been subjected to the same accusation of "bolshevism." For example, the architect and belated Fourierist Le Corbusier, another leader of the International Style (who received part of his architectural training in the same architectural office—that of Peter Behrens—as did Gropius and Mies van der Rohe), has frequently been called "communistic," an accusation rightly denied by his chief biog-

[81] A. H. Barr, Jr., in Herbert Bayer, W. Gropius, I. Gropius, eds., Museum of Modern Art, *Bauhaus, 1919-1928* (New York, 1938), pp. 7-8.

rapher.[82] Nevertheless, it is true that some of Le Corbusier's followers, unlike the master himself, really have been communists, including the great Brazilian architect, Oscar Niemeyer, whose work has been much admired in the United States and who—like Le Corbusier—was chosen as one of the architects for the United Nations buildings in New York.[83]

But even though such leaders of the modern movement in architecture as Gropius, Mies van der Rohe, and Le Corbusier themselves are not Marxists, they are socially and internationally minded and in important respects continue the tradition of the socialist William Morris, so that some of their principles of *art* are not dissimilar to some of those held by many Marxists. Like Marx as well as Morris, the Bauhaus constantly emphasized cooperation between craftsmen and urged that distinctions between the fine arts and crafts be abolished. As Gropius said, "Today they [the visual arts] exist in isolation, from which they can be rescued only through the conscious cooperative effort of all craftsmen. . . . Architects, sculptors, painters, we must all turn to the crafts."[84] In emphasizing the crafts Gropius was distinctly in the tradition of Morris, although where Morris sought to revive the crafts for their own sake, Gropius sought rather to use them as laboratories for modern industry. Like Morris, and like Semper and Van de Velde, Gropius insisted upon straightforward expression of materials in a functional way, but, much more than Morris, stressed modern machine-produced materials and industrialized methods of design and construction (Fig. 29). "The Bauhaus," he said, "believes the machine to be our modern medium of design and seeks to come to terms with it."[85]

At this time an independent emphasis on "machinism" in the arts was being made by the postwar art movement known as "dada," a movement which had connections with communism in Germany.[86] While the

[82] Maximilien Gauthier, *Le Corbusier ou l'architecture au service de l'homme* (Paris, 1944), pp. 175-98. Gauthier also points out (p. 223) that, in 1930 at Moscow, Le Corbusier spoke of "the sacred respect for individual liberty," and thereby made enemies who regarded this as a profession of bourgeois faith held to be Trotskyist. Meyer Schapiro in an essay, "Nature of Abstract Art," *Marxist Quarterly*, Vol. 1, No. 1 (Jan.-Mar. 1937), p. 97, points out that one of Le Corbusier's slogans was, "Architecture or Revolution." In other words, according to Schapiro, Le Corbusier urged technological reform in architecture through housing, etc., with the purpose of resolving the conflict of classes and thereby *preventing* the Marxist revolution.

[83] *Life*, Vol. 22, No. 21 (May 26, 1947), p. 35. As a communist, Niemeyer was later refused admission to the United States when invited to lecture at Yale University. He had previously been one of the two Brazilian architects selected to design the Brazilian pavilion at the New York World's Fair of 1939-1940.

[84] Quoted in H. Bayer, W. Gropius, I. Gropius, eds., *op.cit.*, p. 18, from the First Proclamation of the Weimar Bauhaus.

[85] *Ibid.*, p. 27.

[86] A. H. Barr, Jr., ed., Museum of Modern Art, *Fantastic Art, Dada, Surrealism* (3rd ed., New York, 1947), pp. 23, 25-26.

Bauhaus staff did not join the dadaist group, the preoccupation of dada with "the machine" made for a certain sympathy between dadaism and some aspects of the work done at the Bauhaus. It should be noted, however, that although the machine, industrial production, and functional expression were stressed at the Bauhaus, Gropius came to feel that the term "functionalism" (which he equated with *die neue Sachlichkeit*) was too materialistic and one-sided in its connotations[87]—in other words, Gropius, like Morris, stands for a degree of idealism that is non-Marxian.

Like most varieties of socialists, as well as like many nonsocialists, the staff of the Bauhaus was particularly interested in achieving a functional solution to the humanitarian and social problem of adequate housing for the masses. The particular architectural answer to this problem made under the Weimar Republic, and largely developed at the Bauhaus itself, was the row house oriented to the sun which permitted all the inhabitants to have an equal or almost equal amount of sunlight—a scientific arrangement for health that could and eventually did appeal also to socialistic and democratic equalitarianism. Moreover, the Bauhaus was largely responsible for further developing the superblock type of housing. The extra-large city block, but with single-family houses, had early been exalted in a pamphlet entitled *Nothing Gained by Overcrowding*, published in 1912 by Raymond Unwin, the Fabian socialist city-planner. In the 1920's it had to some degree been used in connection with the apartment housing built for the workers of Vienna by the social democratic city government. In the superblock, distances between streets are much greater than in the ordinary city block so that, by reducing the number of streets, much more of the ground area can be devoted to greenery and gardens between buildings. Like the garden city this kind of housing could therefore be accepted with approval by all but the most revolutionary Marxists because it offered an answer to that separation of city and country which Marx blamed on capitalism. Particularly influential for many socialists interested in housing, as well as for many liberals, were the row houses at Siemensstadt (Figs. 30 and 31) designed by the nonsocialist Walter Gropius, and erected as middle-class housing under the auspices of a public-utility agency in 1929, the year after Gropius had left the Bauhaus.

Since the general approach to art for which the founders of the International Style stood was in certain respects (but in certain respects only) similar to that of many Marxians, the influence of the Bauhaus could also affect some Russian communist art. Consequently, Hannes Meyer, the Swiss communist who succeeded Gropius as head of the Bauhaus, was one of several foreign architects attracted to Russia by the hope of

[87] Walter Gropius, *The New Architecture and the Bauhaus* (London, 1935), p. 19.

designing International Style buildings there. However, as already sug-gested, the influences also went the other way: some forms of Russian art had influenced the Bauhaus. In 1922 a great exhibition of the works of artists from the Soviet Union had been held in Berlin and had created a sensation, and at this exhibition the variety of modern Russian art known as constructivism had been particularly prominent. Although con-structivism will be investigated at greater length later in this book in connection with both Russian and American art, it might be noted here that it glorifies modern technology and the machine age—for it had developed in Russia particularly after the Bolshevik Revolution of 1917 and partly as an expression of the desire of revolutionary Russia for immediate industrialization.

By the time of the exhibition at Berlin, however, constructivism had already fallen into some disfavor in Russia primarily because Lenin considered it, with other varieties of modern art, essentially unsocial since it was too abstract and thus too difficult for the masses to under-stand. But as the Bauhaus, like the Russian constructivists, was interested in emphasizing modern materials, modern methods of construction, and machine-age art, it is not surprising that a few months after the exhibi-tion of modern Russian art at Berlin, constructivism—together with the Russian variety of cubism known as suprematism—was introduced into the Bauhaus by a new teacher, László Moholy-Nagy, who had seen the exhibition of Russian constructivist art in Berlin. For Gropius had become dissatisfied with one of the two men giving the course in basic design at the Bauhaus, because this teacher had "mazdaznan" leanings—that is, he subscribed to an individualistic form of mysticism which Gropius felt was bringing a harmful sectarian spirit into the school. Early in 1923, therefore, Gropius called Moholy-Nagy to collaborate with Josef Albers in giving the course.

Moholy-Nagy, a young Hungarian of exceedingly wide-ranging in-terests, had been greatly stimulated by the many new developments in the art of Europe after World War I. Especially interested in Russian suprematism and constructivism, he had been one of those responsible for calling a Constructivist Congress at Weimar in 1922. He was also greatly influenced by the Dutch post-cubist movement called De Stijl, as exemplified by the works of Van Doesburg and Mondrian, and was not unsympathetic to dadaism, although he never became part of the movement. Elements from these currents, and especially from constructiv-ism, now played a part in the pedagogical method which Moholy-Nagy did so much to develop at the Bauhaus. By this method he sought to acquaint students with the revolution in art made possible by modern materials and techniques (Fig. 32). In this way some forms derived from various currents which originally had possessed certain socialist and revolutionary connotations were fostered not only at the Bauhaus itself, but wherever the influence of the Bauhaus spread.

Although Moholy-Nagy thought of himself as something of a revolutionary, he did so in a highly individualistic way. After World War I he had offered himself and his art to the communist regime in his native Hungary at the time when Bela Kun had led a temporarily successful revolution on the Bolshevik model. But Moholy-Nagy had been rejected by the Communist Party in Hungary partly because of the landholding status of his family, and still more because the Hungarian communists, like Lenin, frowned upon the use of nonrepresentational painting and sculpture as revolutionary weapons.

On his part, moreover, Moholy-Nagy was dissatisfied with Marxian communism because he wished to sweep away all historical art forms and therefore felt that the Marxian historical materialism was insufficiently revolutionary. He also felt that Marxism paid insufficient attention to the individual, and accordingly protested that creative individuality had been excluded from the Hungarian Revolution. Nor could he agree with the Marxian emphasis on the glorification of the proletariat. Because of this fact, when he began to admire constructivism—which he praised as the art of our century, a century characterized by technology, the machine, and socialism—he also praised it for being "neither proletarian nor capitalistic . . . without class or ancestor."[88]

Thus the great influence of the Bauhaus has indirectly helped to foster the spread of art forms derived in part, but only in part, from artistic movements which at one time or another have possessed some socialist or communist implications. These forms (though not necessarily their original socialist content) constitute an important element not only in much modern architecture, painting, and sculpture, but in practically all contemporary "industrial design" throughout the world. And they have particularly affected art in the United States, for after Hitler came to power in Germany, Moholy-Nagy, Gropius, Mies van der Rohe, Josef Albers, and other leading members of the staff of the Bauhaus including Herbert Bayer, Marcel Breuer, and the painter Lyonel Feininger were among those artists from Germany who migrated to the United States. Here they have exerted an enormous influence which will be discussed later in this book.

Soviet Russia. As the whole world knows, under the leadership of Lenin and Stalin Russia has made major contributions to Marxian theory

[88] Sibyl Moholy-Nagy, *Moholy-Nagy* (New York, 1950), p. 19, quoting an article published by Moholy-Nagy in 1922. From this biography most of the facts concerning Moholy-Nagy herein have been taken.

and practice. Many of these have to some degree affected the arts not only in the Soviet Union itself but in most other countries as well, including the United States. In order to understand the Marxian elements as they have affected some aspects of American art and art criticism, it will be necessary to devote what may at first glance seem to be an undue amount of space to tracing and illustrating the chief artistic developments within Soviet Russia itself. For the major twists and turns in Marxian art and art theory everywhere since 1917 have been directly or indirectly, positively or negatively, inspired by events in Russia and by the resulting world-wide changes in the Communist Party line. And since American forms of Marxian art and art criticism, including the theories of the various opponents of the party line as well as of its exponents, are thus in nearly all cases but second-hand versions of specific Russian developments, they can only be understood in the light of what has happened in Russia itself. Yet one might add that, because so few Americans, including Communist Party members, understand Russian, the direct influence of Soviet Russian art theory has been felt in the United States primarily through the medium not of the original Russian sources, but of translations into English. Not only the basic writings of Lenin and Stalin but even the day-to-day changes in the economic and political party line, on which the line for art depends, reach the officials of the American Communist Party almost entirely by way of publications printed in the English language.[89]

It goes without saying that any investigation of the Russian contribution to Marxian theory and practice, in art as in everything else, must begin with Lenin himself. Of the contributions specifically made by Lenin to the materialistic philosophy of Karl Marx, and thence to the theory of art, perhaps the most significant has been his insistence on the importance of practical action for bringing about the revolution of the proletariat and carrying it on to a successful conclusion in the classless society. To Lenin more than to Marx, an armchair Marxist was no Marxist at all, because, much more than Marx and Engels, Lenin was himself a practicing professional revolutionary in addition to being a theoretician. Under his leadership and inspiration, therefore—and still more under that of Stalin, also a practicing revolutionary from early youth—Soviet Russia could be expected to give, as it increasingly did, an extra importance to that practical utility and "realism" in art which

[89] According to L. F. Budenz, *Men without Faces* (New York, 1950), p. 83, where he gives a list of the publications on which the line of the American Communist Party is based. Budenz states that the chief source then being followed by the American party-liners was the *New Times*, the English-language supplement of *Trud*, a Moscow newspaper.

appeal both to the materialist and to the "practical" man of action everywhere.

With Lenin's guidance also, and even more with that of Stalin, the doctrine that power and leadership must be concentrated within a Communist Party was highly developed, and thereby added to Marxism the concept of "democratic centralism," which has had profound effects on Soviet art as on all aspects of Soviet culture. Thus in Soviet Russia, and wherever else the artist has been subject to the power of a Communist Party under Russian dominance, he has been expected, of course, to follow the party line. Anything that smacks of individualistic self-expression, of "art for art's sake," is in theory anathema. Works of art that can serve as propaganda to help carry out the decisions of the party and its leaders have been demanded of artists. Like everything else in Russia, art too became increasingly subjected to the careful centralized planning considered imperative in order to keep the party in complete control and to enable communism to develop in a single country "encircled" by capitalist enemies. And such planning necessarily resulted in curtailing the artist's opportunities for expressing himself in any individualistic way.

The present Soviet Russian point of view toward art, the point of view so long required of communists throughout the world who follow the Communist Party line, has had a slow and stormy development largely because neither Marx nor Lenin ever developed a complete aesthetic. Both Marx and Lenin applied themselves primarily to problems of economics and to the political and social problems arising out of the economic situation simply because, in the Marxian view, these are basic for understanding all other human problems. But although neither of them was ever able to devote much time to art and art history, both were greatly interested in these subjects. Marx's early study of ancient art has already been mentioned. And Lenin once bemoaned his lack of artistic knowledge in the following words: "What an attractive field the history of art is. How much work there for a communist. . . . I regretted very much that I have never had and never shall have the time to occupy myself with art."[90]

As neither Marx nor Lenin had formulated an organized and detailed philosophy of art, for a few years after the Bolshevik Revolution of 1917 there existed in the arts no clear party line which could be followed by communists, whether in Russia or in other countries, including the United States. Since Marx and Lenin had both so clearly approved the study of art, although as a subject second to economics and politics, it

[90] A statement made by Lenin in 1905, quoted by A. Lunacharsky, "Lenin and Art," *International Literature*, No. 5 (May 1935), p. 68.

was to be expected that eventually—on the basis of the relatively few statements about art made by Marx, Engels, Lenin, and a few recognized materialist philosophers such as Chernyshevsky—a Marxist aesthetic would be developed in Soviet Russia. Yet even after a party line had developed in art, the official aesthetic was to remain relatively unsystematized for some time. Hence, as late as 1946 the president of the U.S.S.R. Academy of Architecture could state, "So far we have [in Russia] no systematized work on the theory of architecture, throwing light on the principal phenomena of current architecture and the history of architecture as treated from the viewpoint of scientific thinking, from the viewpoint of Marxism-Leninism."[91] Only later, primarily as a result of a cold war speech made in 1947 by Zhdanov, secretary of the Central Committee of the Communist Party—a speech in which he urged Soviet thinkers in many fields to promote ethics and aesthetics more vigorously— were the strongest official efforts made to formulate a thoroughgoing Stalinist aesthetic. Thus, the aesthetic still prevailing in Russia assumed its present form only gradually, and only after bitter political and ideological struggles had been fought within the Marxist ranks not merely in Russia itself, but throughout the world.

These ideological conflicts revolved especially about three major groups of problems. One of these had to do with the relation of the new communist culture, especially in Soviet Russia, to the cultures of the past. Because the Bolshevik Revolution represented so sharp a break with the past, many artists insisted that only new and revolutionary art movements could express its revolutionary spirit, movements representing a reaction against all earlier historical styles, and especially against the eclecticism which had characterized "bourgeois" art since the middle of the eighteenth century. Of these more revolutionary artists, some maintained that new art *forms* should be emphasized at all costs, even as ends in themselves, with the result that this point of view became known to its opponents as formalism. Others insisted that new *techniques* should be emphasized as ends, and for this reason the machine was glorified both as the product of new technical developments and as making possible additional new techniques. Because machines are designed for sheer functional utility, these artists held that a work of art must be just as functionally useful as a machine. Insofar as these functionalists maintained that form mechanically grows out of function, they tended to neglect specifically Marxian content in art, so that eventually they were accused by more "orthodox" Marxians of a kind of formalism. And formalists and mechanistic functionalists alike could be attacked not only for neglecting Marxian content, but for cutting themselves off too

[91] *Architectural Chronicle*, No. 11 (Nov. 1946; published by the U.S.S.R. Society for Cultural Relations with Foreign Countries, Moscow), p. 2.

completely from the culture of the past, out of which, according to Marxian theory, the present has dialectically developed. Furthermore, both were to be accused of stressing novelty in art to such a degree that their works of art could not be understood by the masses of the proletariat.

This leads to a second series of problems about which the doctrinal struggle raged involving the interrelations between communist culture, and the masses, the party, and the state before it has withered away. Included among these have been questions as to what the role of the party should be in fostering and controlling art, or as to the kind of art which should prevail during the dictatorship of the proletariat until a classless society can be achieved. Related to this has been the dispute as to whether the proletariat must be limited to the industrial working classes, or whether the collectivized and mechanized peasantry can be considered as a kind of agricultural proletariat, and therefore whether peasant art can become a form of socialist art.

A third major ideological conflict has concerned the relation of the culture of Soviet Russia both to contemporary culture elsewhere and to the regional cultures within the Soviet Union. This has proved to be of particular importance for it has raised the whole problem of the relation of Soviet Russian nationalism to Marxist internationalism, and of the expression of such nationalism and internationalism in the arts.

These various ideological problems crystallized only gradually with the result that for a few years after the "October" (Bolshevik) Revolution of 1917, there was a period of relatively free experiment in art and art theory. During this period the various prerevolutionary art movements, both conservative and antitraditional, continued side by side, with each of them now loudly claiming to possess the one true Marxist and Soviet Russian content. However, once the immediate threat of White Russian armies and of foreign intervention had been met, the Russian communist leaders finally began to have more time to devote to art and its problems; and soon clashes within the Communist Party arose over the question as to just what kind of art was best suited to the Russian Marxist ideology.

The more traditional artistic currents which had continued in Russia from the art of the prerevolutionary period included, among others, the general European classic tradition of the Renaissance and post-Renaissance, a tradition first introduced on a large scale into Russia by Peter the Great as part of his program of westernization. After the October Revolution, however, this cosmopolitan academic tradition was for some time frowned upon by many because of its associations with imperial Russia. Similarly, the still older and more national traditions of

Byzantine art and also of primitive Russian art, both of which had been revived in the nineteenth century as part of the nationalistic spirit of the time, were considered unsuitable by the communists largely because both had frequently been used for religious as well as national architecture under the tsars. Also more or less traditional, though more recent in origin, was the "realistic" current which had become strong in Western art in the mid-nineteenth century as an expression of the naturalism and materialism so characteristic of the period. This literalistic kind of realism had grown so powerful that to a considerable degree it had been adopted by the academic tradition in Russia, as elsewhere, and in Russia especially by the Academy at Petrograd. Because it fitted in very well with Marx's materialistic philosophy, realism was the one prerevolutionary movement in art which could most easily be approved by the Russian communists. And they could approve it all the more easily because one of the chief founders of realism in art, the French painter Courbet, had been a leading figure in the Paris Commune of 1871, while that great early realist in literature, the French novelist Balzac, had been Karl Marx's favorite novelist.

In conflict with such older traditions, and also with one another, were various more "modern" trends which at first in Soviet Russia were often lumped together under the generic name of futurism, or cubo-futurism. Within this category fell all the various versions and mixtures of the more abstract varieties of modern art, mostly imported but modified to suit Russian needs. Thus cubism (stressing geometrically abstract simplification and dislocation of nature's forms), expressionism (which often greatly distorts the forms of nature for purposes of expression), Italian futurism (glorifying mechanism and dynamism in art), and functionalism (with its literal expression of materials and use) all contributed in varying degrees to the various art movements within Russian futurism. Because Russian futurism took its name from Italian futurism, it might be noted here that the latter was founded before World War I as a revolutionary, antibourgeois, and anarchist movement in art based on the Marxian-Nietzschean theories of the French syndicalist Sorel. Marinetti, its artist-founder, became a close friend of Mussolini, then a left-wing socialist; and Mussolini himself once said, "What I am I owe . . . to Georges Sorel."[92] Eventually, of course, Italian futurism was to become the semi-official Fascist theory of art in Italy, with Marinetti still its theoretician, but this was mainly after futurism had declined in Russia.

The most important art movements within Russian cubo-futurism during the period of the revolution or shortly thereafter were those Russian varieties of late cubism known as suprematism and—still more important—

[92] Quoted in E. H. Carr, *Studies in Revolution* (London, 1950), p. 163.

constructivism. Constructivism had been developed by Russian artists on the basis of "constructions" made by the Spanish-French painter Picasso as early as 1913 toward the end of his cubist period (Fig 33). However, the constructivists did not regard themselves as cubists even though they admitted that their art derived from cubism. They looked upon cubism as destructive, as a kind of revolutionary art which had disintegrated the old unified world of art. Living as they did in a Russia faced with the need for rebuilding after being almost disintegrated by revolution and civil war, the constructivists proposed to be constructive, to establish a new and unified art the very unity of which would aid in fostering a new and unified world-wide society by strengthening the emotions which make men disposed to work together and build anew. Moreover, the constructivists saw many analogies between science and art, and some Russian constructivists claimed to express by their dynamically mechanistic art the special need of revolutionary Russia for rapid progress in science and technology through industrialization. Many of them also maintained that their emphasis on dynamic movement in art was an expression of the Marxist, and particularly the Leninist, belief in revolutionary action. Interestingly enough, the importance which they gave to expressing the need for industrialization led them to admire American capitalistic technology and industrial efficiency. Similarly Mayakovsky, one of the most famous Russian futurist poets, glorified Chicago in the following words: "Chicago: City, Built upon a screw! Electro-dynamo-mechanical city!"[93]

The most widely known example of constructivism in architecture is the project for a monument to the Third International (Fig. 34) designed in 1919 by the Russian artist Tatlin. Tatlin, who recommended "the monument of the machine" as the best architectural expression of revolutionary Russia, of industrialization, and hence of the proletariat, said that his monument to the Third International was an attempt to found "a dynamic-monumental architecture."[94] In the lower part of the steel framework of this structure, 1,300 feet high, there was to be a cubiform legislative chamber for the congresses of the Third International which would rotate once a year, and above this a pyramidal administrative chamber rotating once a month. A spherical section at the

[93] Quoted in Fülöp-Miller, op.cit., p. 23. Stalin once called Mayakovsky "the best, the most talented poet of our Soviet era," in Pravda (Dec. 7, 1935); cited by Jean Fréville, ed., Sur la littérature et l'art: V. I. Lénine, J. Staline (Paris, 1937), p. 100. For the theory of constructivism see especially the essay by Naum Gabo, one of the founders of constructivism, entitled "The Constructive Idea in Art," in J. L. Martin, Ben Nicholson, and N. Gabo, eds., Circle; International Survey of Constructive Art (London, 1937), pp. 1-10.
[94] Fülöp-Miller, op.cit., pp. 99-100.

top, rotating once a day, was to be devoted to instruments of propaganda including a radio station, cinema, etc.

In architecture, the International Style (as it was later named), which was becoming predominant in western Europe after World War I, was soon imported into Soviet Russia, where it has ordinarily been looked upon as a kind of constructivism. As already suggested, the International Style could appeal to Marxists in many ways. For one thing, its nonnational character could appeal to many who believed in the international spirit of Marxism, a spirit particularly strong in Russia in the period following the revolution, as the founding of the Communist International (or Comintern) in 1919 so clearly indicates. And not only were the practitioners of the International Style usually more practical than most constructivists, but their emphasis on new techniques could appeal to the mechanistic functionalists in Russia at the same time that their emphasis on the new abstract forms growing out of cubism was appealing to the formalists. Among the several leading foreign architects of the International Style who eventually were commissioned to design Soviet buildings were the communist, Hannes Meyer, and the noncommunist Le Corbusier (Fig. 35),[95] while many native Russians also worked in much the same style. The Transport Workers' Club at Moscow (Fig. 36), designed by the Russian architect Melnikov in 1929, represents a continuation of Russian constructivism but combined with some influence from the International Style; and here the glorification of the machine has led the architect to compose his whole building in the form of part of a gear wheel, even though a gear wheel has no direct connection whatsoever with the function of the building.[96] An apartment house in Moscow (Fig. 37), designed in 1928 by the Russian architects Ginzburg and Milinis, still more clearly reflects the influence of the mechanistic aspects of the International Style and specifically of Le Corbusier. It well exemplifies Le Corbusier's famous dogma that "A house is a machine for living in," a dogma in entire harmony with the Russian revolutionary emphasis on mechanization and industrialization.

At a relatively early date, however, considerable opposition to such emphatically "modern" tendencies as these was already in existence in Soviet Russia. Indeed, not long after the Bolshevik Revolution, some of the leading Bolsheviki had already come to consider the modern movement in art as too individualistic in temper, too separated from the masses,

[95] Among other leading architects of the International Style who worked in Russia at this period were Erich Mendelsohn, Bruno Taut, and Lurçat. However, most of these architects, including Hannes Meyer, arrived in Russia when the International Style was falling into disfavor, with the result that they designed relatively few buildings in that style.

[96] See Talbot Hamlin, "The Development of Russian Architecture—II," *Magazine of Art*, Vol. 38, No. 5 (May 1945), p. 182.

and hence fundamentally bourgeois rather than proletarian. A new movement toward a consciously proletarian culture was started by a group calling itself Proletcult, but this soon was relegated to a secondary role (though the name was revived in Stalin's regime) partly because the Bolshevik leaders then felt that culture and art cannot be created to order and independent of the past. Thus Lenin himself insisted that modern socialism originated out of the heads of members of the bourgeois intelligentsia; that the seeds not only of socialism but of modern techniques—including artistic techniques—had therefore been sowed not by the proletariat, but by the bourgeoisie under capitalism, or even in still earlier periods of human history.

In 1920 Lenin said, "It is impossible for us to solve the question of proletarian culture without a clear understanding . . . of [all] that culture which was created in the course of humanity's development; it is only by remaking this that proletarian culture is possible. . . ."[97] His disapproval of those modern movements in art which were seeking to cut themselves off from the past is reflected in his statement: "I cannot value the works of expressionism, futurism, cubism, and other isms as the highest expressions of artistic genius. I don't understand them. They give me no pleasure."[98] For although, like all Marxists, Lenin prided himself on looking forward rather than back, in subscribing to the Marxian laws of historical development he maintained that art, like all aspects of culture, is dialectically and organically rooted in the past. He therefore felt that the modern trends in art were seeking to break too completely with history. "We must retain the beautiful . . . even though it is 'old.' . . . Why worship the new as the god to be obeyed, just because it is 'the new'?"[99] And because "it would be a great mistake to believe that you can be a communist without assimilating all human knowledge, of which communism itself is the result,"[100] he considered museums to be highly important and strongly urged their preservation during the revolution.[101] However, it should be emphasized that Lenin did not worship the past for its own sake but for its contributions to the present: as he once remarked, "It is not enough to assimilate all the knowledge that has come down to us, we must also examine it critically from the point of view of its usefulness to us. . . ."[102]

As a materialist Lenin inclined not only toward utility but also toward

[97] Quoted in Arthur Voyce, *Russian Architecture* (New York, 1948), p. 125, from *Collected Works of Nikolai Lenin*, xxv, p. 387.

[98] Klara Zetkin, *Reminiscences of Lenin* (New York, 1934), pp. 12-13.

[99] *Ibid.*, p. 12.

[100] Lenin in his speech to the third congress of the Komsomol on Oct. 2, 1920; as translated (freely) in Fülöp-Miller, *op.cit.*, p. 234.

[101] Fréville, *op.cit.*, p. 149, quoting Lunacharsky in *Iskusstvo* (Jan. 1929).

[102] Lenin, speech to the third congress of the Komsomol on Oct. 2, 1920; translation from Fülöp-Miller, *op.cit.*, p. 234.

realism in art, and this suited his personal preferences which were relatively conservative. According to his colleague Lunacharsky, Lenin "loved the Russian classics, liked realism in literature, in painting and so on."[103] Furthermore, not only did Lenin himself not understand "expressionism, futurism, cubism, and other isms," including constructivism, but he was convinced that the masses could not understand them either, a fact which made him consider such movements entirely unsuited to Marxist art. To him works of art were valuable insofar as they belong to the masses and are understood by the average man. "Art belongs to the people," he said. "It must have its deepest roots in the broad mass of workers. It must be understood and loved by them. It must be rooted in and grow with their feelings, thoughts and desires."[104] And Lenin considered artists unwilling to produce this kind of art, artists who insisted on producing more abstract kinds of art, to be altogether too individualistic and socially undisciplined. To him they were "specialists" cut off from the masses, who arrogantly assumed the right of speaking in the name of the working class and took advantage of the turmoil of the revolution to present as novelties their petty-bourgeois ideas.[105] Their abstract art seemed to him to deny the significance of the material world of nature and of human society which he believed to be the sole reality. Yet in also holding that art must play an active part in fostering the development of the classless society, Lenin further seemed to imply that works of art should be more than mere passive, mechanical, or photographic reproductions of the existing world. And since art must thus be socially significant, the still further implication seemed to be that artists who fail to produce such art should be led to do so by the Communist Party itself.

For these reasons, even though in 1920 Lenin had stated that "Every artist, and everybody who wishes to, can claim the right to create freely according to his ideal, whether it turn out good or not," he added, "But of course we are Communists. . . . We must consciously try to guide this development. . . ."[106] And in the same year he had issued a manifesto condemning all left-wing communism as "an infantile disorder."[107] Although this manifesto was an essay on Marxist strategy and tactics written primarily to uphold a new party line in problems concerning German communism, parliamentarianism, and trade unions, it was taken seriously for all other aspects of Russian life. A split therefore occurred among the more modern artists including the constructivists, some of whom, such

---

[103] Lunacharsky, "Lenin and Art," *op.cit.*, p. 68.   [104] Zetkin, *op.cit.*, p. 13.

[105] See Fréville, *op.cit.*, p. 111. In 1920 Lenin sharply reproved the Proletcult (founded in 1918, and the center of these "petty-bourgeois" tendencies) for neglecting the class struggle.

[106] Zetkin, *op.cit.*, p. 12.

[107] V. I. Lenin, *"Left-Wing" Communism: an Infantile Disorder* (first published June 1920; 1st English ed., London, 1934).

as Tatlin, decided to devote their art solely to the revolution, while others held that art should be carried on independently of the revolution and for art's own sake. Those artists who believed in the independence of art left Russia, and their number was swelled by the fact that state subsidies to artists were reduced with the introduction of the New Economic Policy in 1921. A few of these émigrés, such as David Burliuk, came to the United States, but by far the largest number—including Kandinsky, Gabo, Pevsner, and Lissitsky (who later returned to Russia) —went to Germany where several of them joined the Novembergruppe in Berlin. As has already been mentioned, in 1922 a great exhibition of the works of modern Russian artists, including these men, was held in Berlin, and its influence greatly affected the whole modern movement in Germany, particularly at the Bauhaus. In that very year, the painter Kandinsky (who as a pioneer expressionist is often said to have been the first to paint a purely abstract composition)[108] accepted Gropius' invitation to join the faculty at the Bauhaus, and there he remained for a decade. It was in the next year that Moholy-Nagy, a teacher at the Bauhaus, developed a pedagogical method based in part on Russian constructivism. Moreover, in 1923 Lissitsky (Fig. 58) collaborated for a time with Mies van der Rohe, later head of the Bauhaus. In 1920 Lissitsky had also collaborated in forming a western European constructivist group with Théo van Doesburg, the Dutch artist whose De Stijl brand of postcubism is sometimes said to have influenced the whole Bauhaus group, although this has been vigorously denied by no less an authority than Walter Gropius. Certainly during a visit to Weimar, where the Bauhaus was then located, Van Doesburg—who had strong socialist leanings and who had joined the dadaist movement for a time—highly praised the work of the Russian modernists.[109] And he once described the evolution of modern art as ". . . towards the abstract and the universal . . . which has made possible the realisation, by a common effort and a common conception, of a collective style."[110]

[108] A. H. Barr, Jr., Museum of Modern Art, *Cubism and Abstract Art* (New York, 1936), p. 64. According to T. H. Robsjohn-Gibbings, *Mona Lisa's Mustache* (New York, 1947), pp. 84-86, Kandinsky was influenced by earlier abstractions painted by other Theosophists. It should be added that, though a Russian by birth, Kandinsky had lived in Germany from 1896 until the outbreak of war in 1914 when he returned to Russia. After the Revolution, in 1918 he taught at the Academy of Fine Arts in Moscow and worked with the art section of the People's Commissariat of Public Education. In 1918 he was appointed director of the Museum of Pictorial Culture, and in 1920 professor of scientific aesthetics at the University of Moscow. When abstract art was officially discouraged in 1921, he returned to Germany.

[109] On the authority of Professor Helmut von Erffa, then a student at the Bauhaus.

[110] Théo van Doesburg, "Vers un style collectif," *Bulletin de l'effort modern*, Vol. 1, No. 4 (1924), p. 16; quoted by R. J. Goldwater, *Primitivism in Modern Painting* (New York, 1938), p. 132.

Largely through modern German art and especially through the influence of the Bauhaus, the *forms* of Russian constructivism (though usually not its original Russian revolutionary *content*) were to have considerable effect on modern art in the Western world, including that of the United States. In Russia itself, however, following the departure of so many leading futurists and constructivists because of Lenin's disapproval, art soon became less abstract. Although in 1923 most of the remaining futurists formed a Left Front ("L.E.F."), maintaining that there could be no coalition between them and the art of the past, the Russian Communist Party sharply attacked this point of view in a resolution on literature issued July 1, 1924, which stated that the party "must fight against all frivolous and contemptuous estimates of the cultural heritage of the past." And a year later, in June 1925, another resolution of the Central Committee of the party spoke of the "infinitely more varied forms" in which the class nature of art (as contrasted with politics and economics) is manifested. As a result of this resolution a certain freedom was to be permitted in Soviet art for the next four years or so.

Of all the varieties of modern art, the International Style in architecture was for a time the most successful in surviving the party's disapproval, despite its abstractly cubistic elements. For architecture, much more than painting or sculpture, is necessarily a social art; moreover, the leaders of the International Style have always been particularly interested in social aspects of architecture. In addition, the emphasis which the International Style, in theory at least, has always placed on practical function could help make its architecture more understandable to the masses than most kinds of modern art. On this account it was then acceptable to Russian Marxism, which in the mid-1920's tended to subscribe to a mechanistic philosophy. Only when, under Stalin, the Russian revolutionary internationalism began to be accompanied by a philosophy of art that was more nationalistic, as well as both less mechanistic and less abstract, did the International Style die out in Russia.

Because Lenin believed so firmly that art should arouse the masses, he insisted that art must serve a social and party purpose as propaganda—or, as Leninists sometimes phrase it, must be devoted to moral education. As early as 1905 he had stressed the importance of literature in party propaganda when he wrote, "The socialist proletariat must establish the principle of party literature. . . . Down with non-partisan writers!"[111] And he later included the visual arts when he said, "What I have in mind

---

[111] Lenin in "Party Organization and Party Literature" (1905), *Works* (Russian ed.), ɪɪɪɪ; translation from Joseph Freeman, "Past and Present," in J. Freeman, J. Kunitz, L. Lozowick *Voices of October* (New York, 1930), p. 24.

is something I should call propaganda by monuments."[112] According to Lenin himself, he got the idea of using art and poetry for propaganda from Campanella's *City of the Sun*, a seventeenth-century description of a utopia in which the author mentioned the use of frescoes to serve, said Lenin, "as vivid lessons to the young in natural sciences and history" and "to awaken their civic consciousness"—to play, in short, "a vital part in the education and upbringing of the new generation." "But," added Lenin, "our [Russian] climate is hardly suitable for the fresco[e]s dreamed about by Campanella. That is why I speak primarily of sculptors and poets."[113] Thus Lenin advocated using for propaganda not only literature, but sculpture, and—in warm countries—frescoes, that is to say, murals painted on wet plaster. He also stressed the importance for propaganda purposes of great inscriptions, of newspapers, and especially of the motion picture. "Of all the arts," he said, "the most important for Russia in my opinion is the film";[114] and, ". . . among the instruments of art and education, the cinema can and must have the greatest significance. It is a powerful weapon of scientific knowledge and propaganda."[115] The theater was praised by Lenin not only for its propaganda value, but especially for its ability "to rest hard workers after their daily work."[116]

As everyone knows, with Lenin's long illness ending in his death in 1924, a bitter struggle broke out in Russia between several factions within the Communist Party, a struggle destined to have a profound effect on art and art theory not only in the Soviet Union itself but everywhere the influence of Russian communism has been felt, including the United States. From the point of view of Stalin and his followers, the various factions tended to fall into four main political groups: the Stalinists themselves as the center, the Left opposition or "deviation," the Right deviation, and the nationalist deviation.[117] Because the doctrines of each of the four groups have had some important implications for Marxist art and art theory everywhere, it will be found necessary to summarize them here. Those of the opposition groups will be summarized first in the light of their conflict with Stalinism, a conflict resulting in Stalin's victory over his chief opponents before 1930, followed by the wiping

[112] Lunacharsky, "Lenin and Art," *op.cit.*, p. 66.

[113] *Loc.cit.* In this connection it is worth recalling that some Fourierists, too, had desired to make use of large murals which were to depict modern industry and to be placed in railroad stations and public buildings: see Meyer Schapiro, "Courbet and Popular Imagery," *Journal of the Warburg and Courtauld Institutes*, IV (1941), p. 183.

[114] Lunacharsky, *Lenin and the Cinema* (Russian ed.); see Fréville, *op.cit.*, p. 149; translation from Kurt London, *The Seven Soviet Arts* (New Haven, 1938), p. 270.

[115] Joseph Freeman, "The Soviet Cinema," in *Voices of October*, p. 220; quoting Lunacharsky on Lenin.

[116] Quoted by Max Eastman, *Artists in Uniform* (New York, 1934), p. 127.

[117] See Stalin, "Report . . . to the Seventeenth Congress of the C.P.S.U.(B.)," *Leninism*, p. 515.

out of all opposition in Russia in the great purges of the thirties. In the course of relating the history of this violent political warfare the reasons for many of the characteristics of the Stalinist ideology, in art as in everything else, will become manifest. For many of those characteristics originated in some immediate need for somehow countering the ideologies and actions of the opposing groups. An account of the doctrines of those groups in relation to their struggle with Stalin will therefore help pave the way for a systematic discussion of Stalinist doctrines in art.

In considering now the art theories of the various "deviations," and especially those of the Left and Right opposition, the discussion neces-sarily becomes highly confusing because, in jockeying for power, the Left, the Right, and the Stalinists at times were all opposed to one another in a three-way conflict, but at other times were joined together, two against one, in a series of dubious and changing alliances. The result has been that their respective ideologies, usually in sharp opposition to one another, have nevertheless sometimes overlapped so that they have not always been entirely distinguishable. Moreover, as the party line of the Stalinists has changed, they have called their various opponents by the particular names which seemed most useful at the moment: thus at times opponents regarded as political Leftists have simultaneously held certain views on art considered to be Rightist. As Stalin himself once remarked, "We have always said that the 'Lefts' are also Rights, only they mask their Right-ness behind Left phrases."[118] In short, the Stalinists have never hesitated to change or even to reverse their definition of what con-stitutes Left and Right whenever the historical situation has made it seem advisable to do so—with, from the viewpoint of non-Stalinists, unfortunate or even stultifying effects for art, art theory, and artists alike. In this connection, however, it must be remembered that the frequent changes in the party line, which to a non-Marxian so often indicate a lack of consistency, have seemed justified to Stalinists on the Marxian grounds that truth is almost entirely relative to the particular economic-political situation prevailing at a given time.

In spite of all this confusion, the specific ideologies of the Left and Right opposition can usually be identified with the respective philosophies of Leon Trotsky and Nikolai Bukharin (both of whom, incidentally, had visited the United States, where in 1917 they worked together in New York for a Russian radical paper, *Novy-Mir*). Both became celebrated theoreticians as well as politicians, and by their writings, in which they both frequently referred to the arts, they greatly influenced artists and art critics wherever the various types of Russian communism spread.

[118] *Ibid.*, p. 526.

However, although Trotsky and Bukharin were usually identified respectively with the Left and Right opposition, such was by no means always the case. In 1924, for example, Trotsky was accused by Stalin, Zinoviev, and Kamenev of bourgeois, and therefore Rightist, tendencies. But late in that same year Stalin found it necessary to formulate, with Bukharin's help, the doctrine of "socialism in one country." This encountered the opposition of Trotsky's principle of "permanent revolution" according to which socialism, even to keep alive, must not merely be reinforced by far-reaching economic measures in Russia but must spread as an international movement, a movement based on the idea that a revolution in one country must at once be extended to the next. In attacking this principle Stalin accused Trotsky of Leftism. Early in 1925 he compelled Trotsky to resign as Commissar of War; in 1926 he had Trotsky expelled from the Politburo, in 1927 from the Communist Party, and two years later from the Soviet Union. Correspondingly, in 1925 Ludwig Lore was expelled from the American Communist Party for Trotskyism; then, in 1928 another purge of the American party took place when James Cannon, Max Shachtman, and about fifty others were likewise expelled as Trotskyists. For six years the Trotskyist Cannon group regarded itself as a faction within the Communist Party, then established its own party, which later split and gave rise to several communist parties with slightly different party lines in art as in everything else.

Following Trotsky's decline in power, Bukharin began to fall out with Stalin and to become the leader of the Right opposition within the party—that is to say, he began to insist that the Soviet Union must proceed much more slowly toward complete socialization than Stalin believed advisable. Yet in the years immediately following the October Revolution, Bukharin had been leader of a group called Left Communists; later, as editor of *Pravda*, he had for a time been the chief theoretician of Stalin against Trotsky. Obviously, therefore, he was not regarded by Stalin as a Rightist at all times or in all respects any more than Trotsky was always looked upon as Leftist.

Turning now to Trotsky's theory of art: his belief that communism could not possibly succeed in a single, industrially backward country surrounded by capitalistic nations, as Russia then was, had led him to hold an internationalistic, and thus Leftist, point of view in art as well as in economics and politics. For this reason, Trotsky approved of Tatlin's constructivist project for a monument to the Third International (Fig. 34), remarking that "Tatlin is undoubtedly right in discarding from his project national styles. . . ."[119] For this reason also, Trotsky approved of the International Style in architecture (then not yet known by that

[119] Trotsky, *Literature and Revolution*, p. 246.

name) and the corresponding modern styles in the other arts. To him
the dynamic forms of futurist art, Leftist in seeking to break completely
with traditional techniques and modes of expression, offered an excellent
expression of the dynamism and chaos of the Russian Revolution; and he
implied also that the architecture of the revolutionary period should be
built in the modern materials of metal, concrete, and glass.[120] Trotsky
felt, however, that the relatively peaceful period of the New Economic
Policy (1921-ca. 1928)—which he regarded as a temporary retreat back
to capitalism, and therefore as a regrettable lull in the revolution—
could be better expressed by the calmer, more conservative forms of a
modernized classicism. In Trotsky's own words: "If Futurism was attracted towards the chaotic dynamics of the Revolution . . . then neo-
Classicism expressed the need of peace, of stable forms. . . ,"[121] a point
of view not unlike that adopted by Stalin only a few years after he had
driven Trotsky from Russia.

Unlike Lenin and Stalin, Trotsky had devoted much time to the study
and criticism of literature and art; besides his well-known book of
criticism, *Literature and Revolution,* originally published in 1923,[122] he
had written, among other things, a monograph on Constantin Meunier,[123]
the Belgian sculptor whose favorite subject was the laboring man.
While Trotsky, like other Marxists, believed that art should in the last
analysis serve social ends, he also firmly maintained that it should be
judged not by its social usefulness, as Lenin had implied, but by its
own law, the law of art. For that reason he held that art should be
censored only with the greatest care, and that it should not be directly
controlled by the Communist Party. Wrote Trotsky, "Artistic creation
has its [own] laws—even when it consciously serves a social movement";[124]
and again, "Art must make its own way and by its own means. The
Marxian methods are not the same as the artistic. . . . The domain of art
is not one in which the Party is called upon to command. It can and must
protect and help it, but it can only lead it indirectly."[125]

Because of such statements and because of his interest in the more
radical kinds of modern art and architecture, Trotsky was accused by the
Stalinists of the deadly sin of "formalism." He was accused, in short, of

[120] Trotsky implied this in praising Tatlin's attempt "to subordinate the entire design
to a correct constructive use of material," which is "the way that machines, bridges
and covered markets have been built, for a long time": Trotsky, *op.cit.,* p. 246.

[121] Trotsky, *op.cit.,* p. 113.

[122] This important work is often said to have been published in 1924; however, in "Art and Politics," *Partisan Review,* Vol. 5, No. 3 (Aug.-Sept. 1938),
p. 3, Trotsky himself gives the date of his book as 1923.

[123] According to Louis Lozowick, "Soviet Painting and Architecture," in *Voices of
October,* p. 265.

[124] Trotsky, "Art and Politics," *op.cit.,* p. 10.

[125] Trotsky, *Literature and Revolution,* p. 218.

encouraging art that is abstract, or that is mechanical or experimental for its own sake, art in which the form or the technique is itself the end rather than a vehicle by which suitable socialist subject matter is given a socialist content. The Stalinists therefore increasingly maintained that Trotsky and his followers, in separating form in art from social content, were divorcing theory from practice and thus had become "idealists" who, in believing that mind, ideas, can exist without matter, were *ipso facto* not true Marxian realists. To put it another way, the Trotskyists were accused of holding that there are abstract ideal principles of formal design which are good for all time and independent of the Marxian laws of economic and social change. Insofar as Trotsky fostered art that was thus "idealistic" as well as radical, he was regarded as a Leftist. However, confusingly enough, art in which form is separated from social content in this way was also considered by the Stalinists to be characteristic of decadent bourgeois culture, and therefore as Rightist in tendency. Consequently, although usually regarded as a leader of the Left, on several counts Trotsky was eventually accused of *both* Leftism and Rightism.[126]

Somewhat similarly, buildings like the Transport Workers' Club at Moscow (Fig. 36), at times considered Leftist because of their abstract forms and radical structure, were also attacked as representing experiment for its own sake. They were thus considered expressions of formalism[127] whose designers were to be frowned upon as specialists tainted with bourgeois (and therefore Rightist) individualism and experimentalism, as well as with Leftist radicalism and idealism.

Actually, Trotsky himself had attacked formalism in his book *Literature and Revolution*. At the same time, however, he had denied the possibility of a specifically proletarian culture, had spoken of futurism as a necessary link in the history of art, and had praised aspects of constructivism. He had said, "The wall between art and industry will come down,"[128] and for this reason was also held guilty by the Stalinites of succumbing

[126] For the attack on Trotsky as both an "idealist" of the Left and a "mechanist" of the Right, see G. A. Wetter, S.J., *Il materialismo dialettico sovietico* (Turin, 1948), pp. 198-208.

[127] The architect of the Workers' Club at Moscow was a member of a group of architects called ASNOVA (i.e., Association of New Architects) which was founded in 1923. This constructivist group subscribed to "idealistic"—and therefore Rightist—formalism. It was attacked by a later group called VOPRA (i.e., All-Russian Society of Proletarian Architects). VOPRA was founded in 1929 to champion a proletarian class architecture, and its members claimed to be more orthodox in their allegiance to the Communist Party. This group was dominant during the first Five Year Plan when the emphasis on proletarian culture was particularly strong. See B. Lubetkin, "The Builders," *Architectural Review*, Vol. 71, No. 426 (May 1932), pp. 203-7; and Voyce, *op.cit.*, pp. 134ff.

[128] Trotsky, *Literature and Revolution*, p. 249.

to the claim, early made by constructivist members of the far Left, that art must be a science, an industry. Some of the more extreme Leftists had even gone so far as to hold that a painting is actually nothing but a "machine" for generating certain predetermined human reactions, and that artists should be engineers of form and color.[129] This, the Stalinists maintained, was an attempt to replace the artist with the engineer by making technique and sheer function an end in itself. Indeed, it amounted, the Stalinists said, to a denial that there is any such thing as art; whereas they insisted that art as such not only exists but can and should be an effective weapon in the hands of the proletariat, a weapon of which the Left was seeking to deprive the workers.

The mechanistic aspects of the Leftist point of view in some respects had even more in common with the philosophy of Bukharin, as expressed in his *Historical Materialism* (1922), than with that of Trotsky; yet as long as Bukharin supported Stalin they were widely accepted by many Stalinists as part of the official Communist Party line. They were, moreover, particularly important for art not only because Bukharin himself was a painter,[130] but because Lenin, in his dying statement, had called him "the greatest and most valuable theoretician." However, when Bukharin began to oppose Stalin about 1927, he was increasingly attacked for having interpreted Marx's materialism as a kind of mechanistic determinism. Such statements as "society . . . has much in common with a mechanism,"[131] and, "social phenomena determine at any given moment the will of the various individuals,"[132] clearly indicated, the Stalinists said, that Bukharin believed man to be completely determined by the laws of nature and of social development, and therefore by the environment. This implied, his accusers maintained, that the laws of history, of social development, act automatically so that progress toward the classless society is automatic and inevitable, proceeding in accord with a mechanical process which man can neither accelerate nor retard. In other words, the mechanists were making man merely the *agent* of history instead of a *creator* of history within the framework of society and

[129] Chen, *Soviet Art and Artists*, p. 58.

[130] Lenin's wife, Nadezhda Krupskaya, describes in *Memories of Lenin* (New York, [1930?]), II, p. 112, how she and Lenin first met Bukharin in 1912. The Lenins were at Cracow when they heard about a social democrat "named Orlov [Bukharin], who was making beautiful paintings of the Zakopane Mountains" not far from Cracow. Hè came to call on the Lenins, and Krupskaya says that when they asked about his paintings, he "took a number of splendid paintings by German artists from his bag and we examined them with great interest. Vladimir Ilyich [Lenin] liked pictures very much." Bukharin's theories of art as social expression were partly inspired by the writings of the German Marxist critic, Wilhelm Hausenstein, author of *Die Kunst und die Gesellschaft* (Munich, 1917).

[131] Nikolai Bukharin, *Historical Materialism* (New York, 1925), p. 88.

[132] *Ibid.*, pp. 40 and 42.

of nature—and thereby were denying Engels' statement that "Men make their history themselves. . . ."[133] Thus the works of man, including works of art, were being reduced by the mechanists to nothing but sheer mirror reflections of the natural and social environment unmodified by human mind or will. This mechanistic point of view (which implicitly denied the value of the Communist Party as the leading agent in bringing about the international triumph of communism) could and did encourage both a photographic kind of literal representation in painting and sculpture, and a literalistic and mechanistic functionalism in architecture.

But while such literal and mechanistic functionalism in architecture was particularly characteristic of radical artists of the Left, such literal naturalism in the representational arts was more characteristic of conservative artists of the old academic tradition in Russia which, like the academic tradition everywhere, had already assimilated the nineteenth-century naturalistic current in Western art. Hence Bukharin's philosophy, which in its mechanistic aspects was approved by many Leftists, could in other respects be considered as suited to conservatives of the Right. And in a sense this same split is reflected in his political career because, as already mentioned, although originally a leader of the Left Communists, he eventually became a leader of the Right opposition to Stalin.

In 1927 Bukharin began to oppose Stalin's proposal for the Five Year Plan, primarily because it called for the collectivization and eventual communization of the peasantry, while he had always maintained that the peasants were really inert survivals from older forms of society and thus "lack several elements necessary to make them a communist class,"[134] a view similar to that held by Trotsky. The peasants, Bukharin believed, would automatically have to pass through the stage of capitalism before they could become communists. He therefore maintained that meanwhile it was necessary to consolidate an individualistic and private (and thus capitalistic and Rightist) peasant economy—a point of view which could have important implications for folk art. He also insisted that capitalism outside of Russia was as yet unripe for revolution, arguing that by means of monopolistic organizations capitalists had become stronger everywhere, and that within nations these monopolies were fusing with the state apparatus. The result was that the Stalinists, who identified state industry with socialism, attacked him as believing that capitalism could evolve peacefully into socialism and therefore as abandoning the Leninist concept of revolution. Furthermore, like Trotsky although for different reasons, Bukharin was accused by Stalin of believing that complete socialism is impossible in a single country. And

---

[133] Engels, letter to Starkenburg, *Karl Marx, Selected Works*, i, p. 392.
[134] Bukharin, *op.cit.*, pp. 289-91.

when in 1928 Bukharin sought the aid of Kamenev and Zinoviev (who, after supporting Stalin against Trotsky, had attacked Stalin as an upholder of state capitalism, and then combined with Trotsky), Bukharin himself was accused of joining forces with the arch-foe Trotsky.

Stalin, who had ever increased in power since his election as general secretary of the Communist Party in 1922, showed by his close control of the Sixth World Congress of the Comintern in 1928 that he was now able to dominate Russian policy. He completely gained the upper hand over his last great enemy, Bukharin, early in 1929. In the same year Jay Lovestone and Benjamin Gitlow were removed from the leadership of the American Communist Party and expelled with their friends as Bukharinists and Right deviationists. Whereupon they founded their own small party with its own line, a party which also was to undergo splits, with each faction having its own ideology supposed to cover all aspects of life, including the arts.

Following the political defeat of Bukharin and his friends, the ideas for which they had stood were soon defeated also, a defeat which had direct and international repercussions in Marxian art. The failure of their efforts to uphold a Rightist peasant economy, a failure marked by the destruction of the richer peasants and by the collectivization of agriculture, was accompanied by a reaction leading to a renewed glorification of the industrial proletariat and the class struggle. And the newly collectivized peasants, because of their new farm machinery, were now considered by the Stalinists to be in the process of industrialization, and therefore in the process of developing a point of view like that of the proletarian class—a fact which now made them worthy subjects for Stalinist art. Moreover, the renewed emphasis on the proletariat now brought about a revival of the proletarian culture movement, although in a quite different form. Its revival was formally signalized by a Congress of Proletarian Culture held at Kharkov late in 1930, an international congress attended by delegates from the United States under the leadership of Michael Gold, writer and editor of the *New Masses*. The slogan of the Congress, based on a statement of Lenin, was that "art is a weapon" in the class war, a weapon to be used only under "the careful yet firm guidance of the Communist Party."

About this time, also, the mechanistic philosophy of which Bukharin had been the chief supporter was likewise finally defeated in Russia when, in 1929, a group of philosophers and scientists who subscribed to a form of mechanistic determinism not unlike that of Bukharin himself were worsted in a philosophical controversy. Almost simultaneously, a sharp attack was directed against all forms of art which could be considered mechanistic.

For this reason some Stalinists now began to disapprove of the works of certain conservative academic artists (already long under attack by the more abstract artists of the Left) for their "photo-naturalism," that is to say, for their mechanically literal reproductions of nature. Even Isaac Brodsky (Fig. 38), although he had been one of Lenin's favorite artists, was nevertheless accused by some Stalinists and Leftists alike of being a "photo-naturalist."[135] And practitioners of this photographically realistic kind of painting were now often criticized as "passive observers of life"[136] who therefore denied the Marxist-Leninist doctrine that within the fixed framework of the Marxian laws of historical development man is not only free to create history, including art history, but bears a responsibility to do so. Nevertheless, the fact that Brodsky, in spite of considerable Stalinist criticism, was appointed director of the Academy at Leningrad in 1932 clearly indicates that Stalinist art was itself beginning to reemphasize the academically literalistic kind of realism which Lenin had preferred and which has remained characteristic of official Soviet art.

Just as in theory (though not nearly so much in practice) the followers of Stalin attacked "photo-naturalism" as deterministic, so also they attacked the mechanistic determinism of those "vulgar sociologists" who—exaggerating Bukharin's thesis that "the social sciences have a *class* character"[137]—sought to adhere to the view that every man, and therefore every artist, is completely and mechanically determined by his economic class.[138] This point of view (which, as we have noted, had for a time been the dominant one in Russia) had tended to limit Soviet art to proletarian subjects. Consequently, after its supporters were defeated about 1931 by the exponents of the revised Stalinist line in a series of philosophical and artistic debates, a somewhat wider range of subject matter in the arts was made possible. And on April 23, 1932, a government decree abolished all proletarian art groups, so that once more the Proletcult movement declined in Russia.

The attack on mechanism which marked the defeat of Bukharin particularly affected architecture, and it was at this time that the mechanistic functionalists, who had been very influential in Russian architecture during the late twenties, were reproved for their mechanism with particular sharpness. As a result, the kind of architecture represented by the apartment house in Moscow (Fig. 37), designed in 1928 by two leaders of the functionalistic school, Ginzburg and Milinis, now fell into disfavor.[139]

---

[135] Chen, *Soviet Art and Artists*, p. 54.   [136] *Ibid.*, p. 53.   [137] Bukharin, *op.cit.*, p. xi.
[138] For the "vulgar sociology" controversy see John Somerville, *Soviet Philosophy* (New York, 1946), pp. 118ff.
[139] The architects of this apartment house were members of a group called SASS (i.e., Section of Architects of Socialist Construction), founded as OSA in 1925. The

As this type of architecture had been especially inspired by the works of Le Corbusier, it is not surprising that the whole International Style, in which he was so important a figure, was now also attacked as mechanistic. This attack first became manifest on a large scale in connection with the great architectural competition for the design of the Palace of the Soviets at Moscow. Now the many projects submitted by leading architects of the International Style were all rejected by the committee in charge, which stated in 1931: "Buildings are not machines, and naked functionalism is an insult to humanity. Buildings today, and the Palace of the Soviets above all, must express the fact that man is master of machines and not their slave or servant."[140]

The International Style was vulnerable on several other grounds. For one thing, it had originated not as a national style in proletarian Russia, but under the leadership of "bourgeois" architects in such "bourgeois" countries as Germany, Holland, and France, and therefore could be regarded as a Rightist style. Also it could be assailed by the Stalinists (along with all other kinds of art in which cubistically abstract forms appeared) for its formalism, that is, for glorifying abstraction in art at the expense of "practical" realities, for divorcing theory from practice, and thus for being "idealistic." Largely because of this supposed idealism the International Style now suffered a final defeat. For at this time, 1930-1931, the Stalinists were engaged in rooting out the last major traces of philosophical "idealism," an end achieved when Stalinist philosophers overwhelmed in debate a group of "idealist" philosophers.[141] The final triumph of Stalinism was reflected in a resolution of the Central Committee of the Communist Party, passed on June 25, 1931, which called for unremitting warfare on two fronts in the field of philosophy, warfare against mechanism and idealism simultaneously. This change in the party line meant, of course, that the architects of the International Style, such

---

members of the group had seceded from ASNOVA (see note 127) and, at a conference of OSA in 1928, had adopted a platform of constructivism-functionalism because they believed in a baldly functionalistic and mechanistic kind of building in which architecture tended to become identified with engineering. This they considered to be the best architectural expression of dialectical materialism. When—in connection with the triumph of Stalin over Bukharin and Trotsky—the group called VOPRA was founded in 1929, it attacked SASS as too mechanistic, just as it attacked ASNOVA as too idealistic and formalistic. Twenty years later, Moisei Ginzburg (who, while a member of SASS, was one of the architects for the apartment house mentioned above) was to be attacked by the magazine *Soviet Art* for being the father of "cosmopolitanism" in architecture and of the enthusiasm for "capitalistic architecture": see the *New York Herald Tribune*, May 1, 1949, p. 10.

[140] Quoted by Robsjohn-Gibbings, *op.cit.*, p. 213.

[141] For these controversies see Somerville, *op.cit.*, pp. 213-28. Also see the more detailed account of the triumph of Stalinist dialectical materialism over both idealism and mechanism in Wetter, *op.cit.*, pp. 149ff.

as Hannes Meyer, former head of the Bauhaus, were now unable to design International Style buildings in Russia. Meyer himself eventually
gave up and went to Mexico where Trotsky also had received asylum.

Thus, following the defeat of both the Left and the Right—of
idealistic formalism and of mechanism, now also considered formalistic—
a revised Stalinist party line was in process of crystallization. And this
was already becoming manifest in changes in the leadership of Communist parties throughout the world: in 1930, for example, the year after
the defeat of Bukharin, Earl Browder was made head of the American
Communist Party for the purpose of putting the new line into effect.
For several years it was to be a line which in a sense revived the revolutionary and proletarian spirit of the years immediately following the
revolution, but with a new centralization of power which allowed even
less freedom than before in the arts as in all other aspects of life.

Yet although both the Left and the Right had been defeated ideo-
logically and artistically as well as politically, the question of nationalism
and of nationalistic "deviations" had not been entirely settled, partly
because of ever changing conditions in foreign relations. It is true that
as early as 1924, in opposition to Trotsky, Stalin had developed and
thereafter maintained the doctrine that socialism could be successfully
achieved in one country alone. For his authority he had again and again
cited certain statements by Lenin (which his opponents countered with
other statements of Lenin), and especially Lenin's remark made in
1915 that "the victory of Socialism is possible, first in several or even in
one capitalist country, taken singly."[142] However, despite Stalin's continued insistence that it was possible to bring about the victory of socialism in a single country—Russia—he did not begin to place much
emphasis on a specifically Russian nationalistic spirit until well after
his victory over his chief opponents, Trotsky and Bukharin. But then, in
1931 a final official signal for the beginning of a new nationalism within
revolutionary Marxian internationalism was given by Stalin himself. For
in that year a letter from Stalin was published in *Proletarskaya Revolyutsiya*
under the title "Some Questions Concerning the History of Bolshevism."
In this he attacked "Trotskyism" (now considered as including *all* opposition, whether of the Left, the Right, or of evolutionary Social Democracy) as "the vanguard of the counter-revolutionary bourgeoisie which
is fighting Communism, fighting the Soviet government, fighting the
building of Socialism in the U.S.S.R."[143] The emphasis here on Bolshevik
history, on "the Soviet government" and on "the building of Socialism
in the U.S.S.R.," now clearly reflected the nationalistic spirit which has

[142] See, for example, Stalin, "On the Problems of Leninism" (1926), *Leninism*,
p. 158.
[143] Stalin, "Concerning the History of Bolshevism," *ibid.*, p. 398.

since pervaded Soviet doctrine and has had so profound an effect upon art and art theory in the U.S.S.R.

After the advent of Hitler to power in Germany in 1933, however, it became necessary to modify this Soviet nationalism somewhat by a willingness to join with other nations, including "bourgeois" nations, in opposing fascism. In January 1934 at the Seventeenth Congress of the Communist Party, Stalin first spoke out publicly against the Nazi doctrine as representing "a triumph for the idea of revenge in Europe." At the same congress he attacked as "a departure from Leninist internationalism" all deviations toward nationalism, whether "the deviation towards Great-Russian nationalism" or "the deviation towards local nationalism."[144] He insisted that nationalism is reactionary in spirit and represents bourgeois attempts to undermine the Soviet system by turning to capitalism: he specifically accused the Ukrainian nationalists of having stirred up the peasants to resist collectivization. This antinationalism in the speech meant, of course, that local nationalism and regionalism in art, including folk art, was still restricted within Russia.

Nevertheless, in the very same speech Stalin—while reporting that "deviations" of all kinds had finally been defeated and scattered—stressed the necessity for Soviet patriotic unity, and thereby foreshadowed the encouragement of a still greater all-Russian spirit of patriotism. As a consequence, a great patriotic campaign began a few months later in the Soviet press, signalized especially by an editorial in *Pravda* for June 9, 1934, which fervidly urged love of country and even used the long dis-used word "fatherland." Yet in September 1934 Russia entered the League of Nations; in May 1935 a mutual defense pact was signed with France, and the period of the Popular Front had begun, a period in which an increasing Soviet nationalism was combined with readiness for joint international action against fascism.[145] One result of the Popular Front was that the last traces of the Proletcult movement (which had retained considerable importance outside of Russia, especially in the United States), now had to be abandoned, for its glorification of proletarian culture implied an emphasis on international class warfare hardly reassuring to those "bourgeois" nations with which Soviet Russia wished to collaborate in opposing nazism.

In order to help guarantee Soviet unity in the face of the Nazi threat and at the same time to consolidate his personal position still further,

[144] Stalin, "Report . . . to the Seventeenth Congress of the C.P.S.U.(B.)," *ibid.*, p. 525. For a good brief discussion of nationalism and Soviet patriotism in art and literature, see Rudolf Schlesinger, *The Spirit of Post-War Russia; Soviet Ideology 1917-1946* (London, 1947), pp. 149-59.

[145] A summary of these events is contained in Eugene Lyons, *The Red Decade* (Indianapolis, c. 1941).

Stalin now wiped out all of his chief political opponents in the great purges of 1936-1938. Zinoviev and Kamenev, with several former Trotskyists, were tried and executed as traitors in 1936; several more leading ex-Trotskyists, among others, in 1937; and Bukharin and others in 1938. Two years later Trotsky was assassinated in Mexico by what most people believe was a Stalinist agent. These political purges were accompanied by a new campaign against formalism and leftism in art, a campaign that began in January 1936 when *Pravda* made a violent attack on the music of Shostakovich, which was called "un-Soviet, unwholesome, cheap, eccentric, tuneless and Leftist."[146] And *Pravda* soon followed this with an attack on the modern movement in architecture, which it described as "monstrous trick architecture."[147] In December 1937 *Pravda* accused the great theater director, Meyerhold, of formalism, largely on the grounds that seventeen years before he had dedicated one of his productions to Leon Trotsky.

Thus, in the fifteen years or so between Lenin's death early in 1924 and the completion of the purges, Stalin and his followers destroyed all opposing ideologies within the Soviet Union itself, even though the influence of his opponents has in some respects persisted outside of Russia. In the process of killing off opposing ideologies, Stalin and his followers had to begin to formulate, on what they held to be a Leninist basis, their own interpretation of Marxism, their own systematic ideology which included an ideology for art. By 1939, not long after the purges were over, Stalin's victory was at last so utterly complete that he finally felt free to say in public that Marx and Lenin, like ordinary mortals, sometimes made mistakes, with the implication that Stalin had become at least their equal.

Now that the effects of the various deviations have been indicated and the rise of Stalin to complete power traced, we are in a better position to discuss more systematically the positive effects on art of Stalinism itself, and this with particular reference to the period of Stalin's dominance. For however much one may disapprove of Stalinism, it cannot be denied that the Stalinists have made many important contributions and additions to the Marxian theory of art, and these have affected not only the arts of

[146] *New York Times*, Feb. 15, 1936, p. 17. This editorial in *Pravda* attacking Shostakovich was one of two, both written by Zhdanov according to Juri Jelagin, *Taming of the Arts* (New York, 1951), pp. 151-52. After this attack upon him, Shostakovich remained in official disfavor until after the highly successful première of his Fifth Symphony in December 1937. According to Jelagin (p. 162), this was the first time that official disfavor (rather than dismissal or arrest) was used by the Soviet government as a means for bringing pressure on creative artists to compel them to adjust their work to the party line.

[147] Dwight Macdonald, "The Soviet Cinema: 1930-1938, Pt. 2," *Partisan Review*, Vol. 5, No. 3 (Aug.-Sept. 1938), p. 46.

the U.S.S.R. but the official party line for art in every country in which a Communist Party exists.

As has already been mentioned, perhaps the most basic Stalinist doctrine, and the first to develop, is the doctrine that socialism can be successfully achieved in one country alone. Nevertheless, it must not be forgotten that Stalin, unlike the national "deviationists," customarily maintained that the Soviet point of view must in the end be international if it is to be successful: as he said in 1927, the October Revolution "is not merely a revolution 'within national limits.' It is, primarily, a revolution of an international, world order. . . ."[148]

Remember also that Stalin made an important distinction in terminology between socialism and communism, a distinction in which he followed Lenin. In the *Communist Manifesto* Marx and Engels had used the word communism rather than socialism simply because the latter then meant to most people the "utopian" socialism which Marx was attacking rather than his own "scientific" socialism. But Lenin and Stalin came to mean by socialism what Marx once called the first stage of communism,[149] that is, a transitional period in which each individual receives according to work performed, and in which the state still exists. And by communism they meant only Marx's second stage of communism, namely the classless society in which the state will, as Engels said, have "withered away," and in which each person will receive according to his needs. Therefore Stalinists regarded the Soviet Union as being a socialist society rather than a communist one. And they believed that it became a fully socialist society only following the industrial and agricultural revolution produced by the first Five Year Plan (1928-1932). Not until 1935, however, did Molotov make the official announcement that Russia had become a socialist country.

But though Russia was now considered to have achieved socialism, the official view was that communism, as contrasted to socialism, would not be possible until the Soviet Union had the support of the workers in all countries and until the workers had triumphed in at least a majority of countries. For only then would the capitalist countries be "encircled" and the Soviet Union guaranteed against all possibility of capitalist intervention. As to just when this communism, with its international and classless society, will be achieved is still a matter of discussion. To many non-Stalinists some of Stalin's later statements apparently indicated that he believed that the state would never wither away completely.[150]

---

[148] Stalin, "The International Character of the October Revolution" (1927), *Leninism*, p. 197.

[149] Karl Marx, *Critique of the Gotha Programme* (New York, 1938), p. 10.

[150] For example, L. F. Budenz, ex-member of the American Communist Party, in *This Is My Story* (New York, 1947), p. 162, says that Stalin, "in *The History of*

However, the Five Year Plan which was announced in March 1946 still apparently regarded communism as its ultimate ideological objective, and one which, it was calculated, would be reached in some fifteen or twenty years *if* the industrial revolution proceeded at an accelerated pace.[151]

All of these developments in the party line had most important meaning for art. Thus, Stalin's combination of nationalism with an international "socialism" gave rise to his insistence that all of Soviet culture must be "national in form and socialist in content."[152] To the kind of art which results from this he himself gave the name "socialistic realism," a name he is said to have first used late in 1932 when a group of writers promised him that they would not make formalistic experiments but would hold high the flag of realism. "Say rather of socialistic realism," replied Stalin.[153]

By this kind of realism (which so largely reflected Stalin's own tastes) is meant art suited to the period of socialism, to the period which Marx called the first stage of communism. Such art is expected to have both national and international connotations and to be realistic enough for the masses to understand it without being just a transcript of nature. Furthermore, by definition it must be socially useful, socially dynamic, and educational; so that—as Stalinists insisted—it can be produced only by socially-minded artists, each of whom is participating in the daily activities and emotions of the community as a whole.

A good example of socialistic realism is the sculptured group of two figures entitled *Worker and Woman Collective Farmer* (Fig. 39) which surmounted the Russian pavilion at the World's Fair held in Paris during 1937. This, executed in the highly modern material of stainless steel, was

---

the Communist Party of the U.S.S.R." discarded "the 'withering away' theory as outworn." At the party congress in 1939, Stalin said, "We go forward [from Socialism] to Communism. Will the state be retained by us also in the period of Communism? Yes, it will, if the capitalist encirclement is not liquidated." And after Tito made a speech late in June 1950 reporting that in Yugoslavia (in contrast to Russia) the state had already begun to wither away, Stalin replied with a statement in *Bolshevik* on August 1, 1950 in which he repeated that there could be no withering away of the Russian state so long as it is encircled by noncommunist enemies: see the *New York Herald Tribune* for Aug. 2, 1950, p. 12, and Aug. 4, p. 14.

[151] In 1949, at the celebration of the twenty-fifth anniversary of the death of Lenin, the editor of *Pravda* stated in a speech that the achievement of [complete] communism in the Soviet Union no longer is a remote possibility, although three more Five Year Plans may be necessary to "provide complete safety and ability to meet any emergency." See the *New York Herald Tribune*, Jan. 22, 1949, p. 5.

[152] Stalin, *Problems of Leninism* (10th Russian ed.); quoted in Fréville, *op.cit.*, p. 133.

[153] London, *op.cit.*, p. 139. According to Jelagin, *op.cit.*, p. 75, the new Soviet theory of socialist realism in art and literature was first formally introduced by Maxim Gorky in a speech before the First Convention of Soviet Writers in the fall of 1934.

intended to reflect the new class structure of the Soviet Union, a class structure achieved when, with the completion of the first Five Year Plan, all the "exploiting" classes are considered to have been eliminated, leaving the two working classes of industrial workers and peasants triumphant. Here an industrial worker and a peasant are depicted advancing dynamically side by side, respectively bearing aloft the hammer of industry and the sickle of agriculture to form the Soviet Russian symbol. In this way the artist has sought to symbolize the Stalinist belief that, with the successful mechanization of agriculture, the interests of industrial worker and peasant are now merging as the two march forward together—though with the worker as leader—toward the classless society of complete communism. Only a few months earlier Stalin had stated in promulgating the new constitution for the U.S.S.R. that the first phase of communism had now been achieved, that the working class was no longer a proletariat, and that the peasantry had been integrated into the socialist economy.

All this is symbolized in a style that is a somewhat "realistic"—though "modernized"—version of the Western and international classic tradition which had dominated official art in imperial Russia from the time of Peter the Great. The return to this Russian version of the "classical" tradition was encouraged by the fact that in literature the Russian "classics" were mostly realistic and mostly written by authors who, from Pushkin to Gorky, had been notably progressive in their social views. Actually, Vera Mukhina, the able sculptress of the *Worker and Woman Collective Farmer*, had been trained in the Western classic tradition at Paris before World War I under the celebrated French sculptor, Bourdelle. It can be said with truth that socialistic realism has often implied a return to the more or less classic forms of the prerevolutionary official tradition in Russian sculpture and architecture, forms now, however, made slightly more abstract and hence "modern" to suggest the forward-looking spirit of Marxism. Thus by means of largely traditional and international elements Stalinist Russia attempted to achieve an art which could express a Marxian content, but infused with Soviet Russian nationalism as well as internationalism.

The kind of socialist realism represented by Mukhina's sculpture has sometimes actually been called classical realism. One of the first and best known architectural examples of this classical realism (as it was later named) had been the accepted design for the Palace of the Soviets in Moscow (Fig. 41), which in its original form was prepared in 1931. Although the building was under construction when Hitler attacked Russia, its materials were largely used for defense and it was never erected. The model shows the somewhat simplified and freely-handled classic forms characteristic of so many public buildings (Fig. 40) and other works, including the famous subway in Moscow, which were built in the years shortly before or immediately after World War II. In the design for the Palace of the Soviets, these classical forms are applied to an exceedingly tall structure obviously intended to outdo all American skyscrapers in order to symbolize the great advances in modern technology made by the Soviet Union. And the whole is topped by a statue of Lenin in action, pointing dynamically forward and upward to express dynamic Marxian progress through human action. Stalin, in his role as the direct heir of Lenin, once stated, "Leninism . . . creates a special Leninist style in work. . . . It has two specific features: (a) the Russian revolutionary sweep and (b) American efficiency."[154] The model of the Palace of the Soviets clearly seems to be intended as an expression of such Leninism in architecture during the first Five Year Plan when one of the popular slogans was, "Let us catch up and overtake America." It is significant that a similar style was used for the Russian pavilion at the New York World's Fair of 1939-1940, a building designed by Yofan, chief architect of the Palace of the Soviets and also the architect, in 1933, of Stalin's personal country house on the Black Sea.

The Stalinists justified this return to a somewhat classic style partly on the grounds that it could be considered as continuing the national all-Russian tradition for public buildings and public art found in Russia ever since the time of Peter the Great. They also believed it justified because Marx regarded Greek art as in some respects "the standard and model beyond attainment," and because the art of the Greek city states was a democratic form of public art even though Greek society rested on a regrettable basis of slavery. Moreover, they upheld the use of Roman classic forms on the ground that the Romans had in some respects developed the ideals of Greece by building enormous public-utility works. Thus the spirit of ancient Greece and Rome was sometimes invoked in Stalinist Russia as the inspiration for a kind of proletarian renaissance.[155]

On September 25, 1948, however, a modification in the party line for architecture, and in this classical style, was foreshadowed by an article in *Pravda* attacking "pseudo-Parthenons" and "the excessive use of columns." The same article also contained a sharp reproof for those Soviet architects who were imitating American architecture. The author of the article—Vlassov, chief architect of the city of Kiev—stated that all such "formalism" had crept into Soviet architecture because certain architects "forgot that in the field of architecture there is going on a

---

[154] Stalin, "Foundations of Leninism" (1924), *Leninism*, p. 84. In the same lectures (p. 2), he had previously defined Leninism as "Marxism of the era of imperialism and of the proletarian revolution."
[155] Voyce, *op.cit.*, p. 149.

battle of Socialist realism against bourgeois formalism."[156] This new architectural line was but part of a great postwar cultural purge which paralleled the increasing split between the Soviet Union and its satellites on the one hand, and the Western world on the other, while also reflecting a movement away from the wartime patriotic glorification of Russian history under the tsars. For during World War II not only had anti-Westernism in Russia been less pronounced in deference to Russia's "bourgeois" and "capitalistic" allies in the struggle (with the result that the Communist International and the American Communist Party had been "dissolved" in 1943 and 1944 respectively); but within the Soviet Union nationalist traditions, even including tsarist traditions derived from western Europe, had been fostered to encourage patriotic unity against the German invader. Now, however, the reaction setting in against bourgeois traditionalism and against the capitalism of the Western world was resulting in a new emphasis on Communist Party spirit, on the class struggle, and on the glorification of Mother Russia. It was this shift in the line which brought about the changes in the American Communist Party after the French communist Duclos returned from a trip to Moscow and attacked Earl Browder in April 1945 for having supported the wartime alliances by forecasting "long-term class peace in the United States" and for having dissolved the American Communist Party in 1944. Duclos' attack was published in the *Daily Worker* on May 24, 1945, with the result that Browder was not only replaced by William Z. Foster as titular head of the Communist Party when it was reconstituted in the summer of 1945, but in February 1946 was expelled from the party as a "right opportunist." And corresponding changes took place in the art theory and practice of the American Communist Party, as of Communist parties everywhere, particularly after the Cominform (Communist Information Bureau) was founded in October 1947 as a kind of revival of the ostensibly dissolved Comintern and as an answer to the Marshall Plan, which had been first proposed the previous June.

Even though the change in the party line had been foreshadowed before the end of World War II by such events as the attack on Browder, it was given final and public approval in a speech made by Stalin on February 9, 1946. In this speech Stalin not only publicly attacked his wartime allies by assailing contemporary "monopoly capitalism," but he upheld the unquestioned superiority of all things Soviet. Yet though he said nothing whatsoever about the arts, this had been the clear signal

[156] See the *New York Herald Tribune*, Sept. 26, 1948, p. 1. Specifically, Vlassov was attacking a project for the reconstruction of Yalta. In the following spring the reconstruction of Stalingrad was also criticized before the All-Union Congress of the Young Communist League as reflecting "survivals of formalism": see *ibid.*, Apr. 3, 1949, p. 9.

for a purging of the entire cultural apparatus within the Soviet Union in order to bring cultural affairs into line with the new nationalistic spirit and the new antibourgeois foreign policy.[157] And with this came renewed insistence on the principle of "partisanship," a principle based on the Marxian doctrine that there can be no such thing as complete objectivity and impartiality because the viewpoint of each individual is necessarily affected by his class allegiance. Within this class loyalty Lenin had developed the principle of party loyalty; and now Stalin gave still more emphasis to the importance, for all good Marxists everywhere, of allegiance to Soviet Russia.

The cultural purge formally began on August 14, 1946, with a resolution of the Central Committee of the Communist Party sharply reproving two literary journals of Leningrad for forgetting that literature must be devoted to the interests of the people and of the state. A week later, Andrei Zhdanov, the secretary of the Central Committee, interpreted this resolution in long speeches before the Leningrad branch of the Union of Soviet Writers, and before the leading members of the Communist Party in Leningrad, in which he attacked "bourgeois culture" and "art for art's sake" while calling for a reemphasis on Lenin's doctrine that "literature must become Party." An abridged version of these speeches was published the following December in *Political Affairs*, the theoretical organ of the American Communist Party, as a sign to party members that the cultural line had changed.

On August 26 and September 4, 1946, the Russian Central Committee promulgated two similar "resolutions on ideology," dealing now with the drama and with the motion picture. These were eventually followed by others treating still other major aspects of cultural activity, including music, genetics, and humor. And on the basis of these resolutions of the Central Committee wide-ranging changes were also made in areas of culture not specifically covered by the resolutions and not restricted to the Soviet Union itself.

For example, the new line for art could be seen in an article in *Pravda* published on August 10, 1947, attacking the art of Picasso despite the fact that Picasso had joined the French Communist Party three years before. In this article the celebrated cofounder of cubism and the father of so many other varieties of abstract art, was assailed—together with Matisse—in the following words: "It cannot be tolerated that side by side with socialist realism we still have existing a co-current represented

[157] For a detailed account of these cultural purges see Counts and Lodge, *op.cit.*, on which the account herein is chiefly based. And for an unfavorable review of that book by an American sympathetic to the Stalinist point of view, see Sidney Finkelstein, "Soviet Culture: a Reply to Slander," *Masses & Mainstream*, Vol. 3, No. 1 (Jan. 1950), pp. 51-62.

by worshipers of bourgeois decaying art who regard as their spiritual teachers Picasso and Matisse, cubists and artists of the formalist group."[158]

Two weeks later, on August 25, 1947, a reform of the party line in philosophy and aesthetics began with a speech by Zhdanov at a conference of philosophers and theoreticians called together by the Central Committee of the Communist Party at the instigation of Stalin himself. In this speech (soon translated in *Political Affairs* for the guidance of American party-liners) Zhdanov blamed the chief of propaganda of the party for succumbing to bourgeois philosophical thought, and at the same time urged Soviet "scientific and creative cadres" to seek "to promote more vigorously . . . ethics and esthetics."[159]

A few months after this, the purge of Soviet music began when, on February 10, 1948, the Central Committee issued a resolution accusing the composers Shostakovich, Prokofyev, Khachaturyan, and Myaskovsky, among others, of subscribing to a "formalistic anti-popular tendency," and of writing music reeking "strongly of the odor of the contemporary, modernistic, bourgeois music of Europe and America which reflects the decay of bourgeois culture. . . ."[160]

On the basis of the Central Committee's resolution concerning music a corresponding purge of painting and sculpture took place late in May 1948; and on February 10, 1949, the new line was also established in art criticism when nine Soviet writers were assailed in *Pravda* as "homeless cosmopolitans" who "lack a healthy love of country." Meanwhile, the purge of architecture had begun on September 25, 1948, with the publication in *Pravda* of the article by Vlassov already referred to. The kind of architecture thereafter approved can be seen in Vlassov's own design for the rebuilding of part of Kiev destroyed in the war (Fig. 42), even though this design was submitted by Vlassov early in 1947 before he had promulgated the new architectural line in *Pravda*. For he was no doubt chosen as the exponent of the new line because his recent work, such as

[158] *New York Herald Tribune*, Aug. 12, 1947, p. 15, some editions only.

[159] *New York Herald Tribune*, Aug. 26, 1947, p. 1, reporting Zhdanov's action of the day before. The speech was translated in full in the April 1948 issue of *Political Affairs*, pp. 344-66, under the title "On the History of Philosophy." See also p. 672 herein. Likewise see B. Meilakh, "It Is High Time to Take Up Questions of Esthetics," *Literaturnaya Gazeta*, May 22, 1948; translation in *Soviet Press Translations*, issued by the Far Eastern Institute, University of Washington, Vol. 3, No. 20 (Nov. 15, 1948), pp. 633-35. Meilakh's article was a final signal for the purge in aesthetics.

[160] Counts and Lodge, *op.cit.*, p. 162. For an excellent account of the purge in music see Alexander Werth, *Musical Uproar in Moscow* (London, 1949). In view of the frequent and particularly heavy attacks on instrumental music it is worth noting that Stalin disliked it, according to Jelagin, *op.cit.*, p. 298. The music purge had been preceded by a conference of musicians called by the Central Committee of the Communist Party in 1947 and, as usual, addressed by Zhdanov. For his speech see Andrei A. Zhdanov, *Essays on Literature, Philosophy, and Music* (New York, 1950), pp. 76-96.

this for Kiev, was thought well suited to exemplify the shift in doctrine.

Certainly, in this design the earlier official classicism inherited from tsarist architecture, and ultimately derived from a purely west European tradition, has already been modified so as to be both more Eastern and more "modern" in character. Strictly classic elements have now been partly replaced by elements (such as towers not unlike some in the Kremlin itself) which recall the Muscovite baroque of the seventeenth century, and thus a Russian style that is Eastern rather than completely Western. But these features have been combined with some elements not unlike the expelled International Style of modern architecture in an effort to suggest once more that Marxism looks forward rather than back and that it possesses international connotations even though these are now largely subordinated to specifically Russian characteristics. And although, as part of this "progressiveness," American skyscrapers were still imitated in Russia, the Soviet authorities now claimed that the Russian examples were more advanced than the American prototypes, which, they said, sway in the wind, squeak, and crack.[161]

In addition to this official Stalinist style whose changing character in architecture has just been traced, it must be remembered that there is still another form in which socialistic realism has been expressed—namely, folk art. Communists hold that folk art—which is often created collectively rather than by an individual—has both international and national implications, either of which can be emphasized with changing conditions and hence changes in the party line. On the one hand, folk art can be regarded as having international implications because it is considered to possess the germinating power out of which all great art everywhere arises. It is likewise international insofar as all folk art, all art of the masses and of the common man, does tend to have some characteristics that are much the same everywhere: its content, like that of homely proverbs, is much the same regardless of national boundaries. Yet folk art in Russia can also be considered national in spirit in that it expresses the traditions of some specific nationality or region within the Soviet Union. And perhaps as important as all of these other reasons for the justification of folk art in Russia was the simple fact that Stalin was known to be very fond of Russian, Georgian, and Ukrainian folk songs.

Certainly Lenin and Stalin themselves were significantly responsible for encouraging folk art in Soviet Russia. Lenin—who even before the Bolshevik Revolution had considered the problem of national minorities to be of major importance—admired "folk literature as a veritable creation of the people."[162] Because Stalin, as a native of Georgia, was a member

---

[161] See the *New Yorker*, Sept. 16, 1950, p. 19, quoting *Vechernyaya Moskva*.

[162] See Bontch-Brouévitch's discussion of Lenin's views on poetry in *Na literatournom Postou* (1931), No. 4; quoted in Fréville, *op.cit.*, pp. 148-49.

of one of the national minorities, in 1913 Lenin had selected him as the Marxist-Leninist spokesman on the right of oppressed peoples to self-determination; and with the revolution, Lenin saw to it that Stalin was made Commissar of Nationalities. Nevertheless, by 1918 Stalin came to feel that Lenin, in opposing "imperialistic chauvinism" on the part of dominant nations, was giving too much importance to minor nationalities and to their right of self-determination. Stalin now insisted that the principle of self-determination be used merely as a means in the struggle for socialism, and subordinated to the principles of socialism itself. Stalin therefore attacked "local chauvinism" and tended to reject the idea of maintaining the integrity of a multinational state by means of cultural autonomy. By 1920, however, he had modified his views somewhat and now advocated regional autonomy, when effective both economically and culturally.[163] As a consequence he helped to pave the way for giving regional and folk art a recognized place as approved forms of socialist realism.

During the late 1920's some of the more self-consciously proletarian musicians and artists began to introduce into their work elements of Russian folklore as well as of the folklore of the Asiatic peoples of the Soviet Union. But it was only after the abolition of the proletarian art groups in 1932 that folk art could really begin to achieve a position of primary importance. When in February 1944 a somewhat greater measure of nominal autonomy was granted to the various republics within the Soviet Union, each being authorized to have its own foreign ministry and army, an even greater importance could be placed upon local forms of art. However, as a result of the increased emphasis placed by Stalin on "Mother Russia" in his speech of February 9, 1946, which so clearly marked the postwar change in the party line, the folk art of minorities within the Soviet Union was for a time much less stressed, and artists of the various minor nationalities had to be warned again and again not to succumb to local "bourgeois nationalism." Instead they were now expected to follow the leadership of the specifically Russian people who alone of all the peoples within the Soviet Union were unequivocally assigned a new role of superiority, especially after a purge—aimed at "distortions of ideology" in folk art—began in 1951.

A characteristic example of socialist realism expressed in terms of the regional folk traditions so popular in the Russian art of the late 1930's and early 1940's is the pavilion of the Republic of Uzbekistan (Fig. 43) built in 1937 at the All-Union Agricultural Exposition in Moscow. Designed

[163] See B. D. Wolfe, *Three Who Made a Revolution* (New York, 1948), pp. 397-400, I. Deutscher, *Stalin, a Political Biography* (New York, 1949), pp. 181-85, and E. H. Carr, *The Bolshevik Revolution, 1917-1923* (London, 1950), p. 384.

in the regional, more or less Persian, style characteristic of central Asia in general and Uzbekistan in particular, the plan of the central motif is nevertheless in the form of a star to suggest the Soviet symbol and thereby achieve an all-Russian content which transcends the purely local tradition.

It is this content which differentiates the folk art of socialist realism from that of the nationalist deviation so sharply attacked by Stalin. For while Stalin believed that local historical traditions were to be fostered, he insisted that they must not assume exclusive and anti-Soviet forms. The Stalinists also urged that folk and national art must not hesitate to employ new technical developments—even technical developments originating in capitalist countries—and thereby become somewhat international in spirit. However, according to the official doctrine as stated by Stalin himself all primarily nationalistic forms of expression, including folk art, will eventually be abandoned "when the proletariat has conquered throughout the entire world, and socialism has entered into customs [everywhere],"[164] thus at last making possible the perfect internationalism of the classless society.

Meanwhile, as long as nationalism and the state exist, Soviet artists are to be carefully controlled by the Soviet State under the leadership of the Communist Party to make sure that works of art meet the specifications of socialistic realism. For ever since the Stalinists gained complete control in Russia, the artist, like the literary man, has been expected to do all his work under the "careful and yet firm guidance of the Communist Party."[165] This ever increasing demand for conformity by artists probably became inevitable when—particularly after the ending of the New Economic Policy—the state became the sole middleman between artist and client.

As early as 1918 an Artists' Union had been established in Russia,[166] but, significantly, it was in 1929—the year after Trotsky's expulsion and the year of Bukharin's defeat—that an Artists' Cooperative was established under the control of the state and hence of the party.[167] Through this artists sell their work at prices determined by a committee of the artists themselves, and not, as the Russians delight in proclaiming, by capitalistic dealers or by the whims of capitalistic millionaires. In the spring of 1930 a plan was announced for the development of the theater, the cinema, sculpture, and painting whereby five years of normal development were to be officially telescoped into the remaining three and a half years of the Five Year Plan,[168] and an International Bureau of Revolu-

[164] Stalin, *Problems of Leninism* (10th Russian ed.); quoted in Fréville, *op.cit.*, p. 133.
[165] Eastman, *op.cit.*, pp. 15-16, quoting the circular sent out in 1932 by the organization bureau of the International Association of Proletarian Writers.
[166] London, *op.cit.*, p. 48.　　　　　[167] *Loc.cit.*
[168] Macdonald, *op.cit.*, Pt. I, in *Partisan Review*, Vol. 5, No. 2 (July 1938), p. 44.

tionary Artists was founded in the same year to guide and control communist artists in other countries. When in 1932 the completion of the Five Year Plan made it perfectly clear that Stalin had triumphed over all opposition in Soviet Russia, an official decree directed the reorganization of the entire structure of the artistic and literary societies under still closer government control. As a result, all the existing societies—whether conservative, centrist, or radical—were liquidated, and each professional group was reorganized into a central federation: thus were soon founded the Federation of Soviet Architects and the great Artists' Creative Union.[169] In 1936, which was the first year of the great purges, a Central Committee on Arts was also established[170] in order that the organization of artists and their ideology might be even more carefully supervised by a kind of totalitarian ministry of the arts. All of this has meant that not only the content of art, but to a very considerable degree the methods of achieving that content, are laid down for the artist. The architect Alabyan, then president of the U.S.S.R. Academy of Architecture, said in 1946, "The architect who is not guided in his entire activity by the policy of the Communist Party and the Soviet Government and who stands to one side of it, can hope for no creative progress."[171]

While the attention paid to art by the government and party has meant that Russian artists are favored in many ways, woe to the artist who fails to follow modifications in the party line! In the spring of 1949, when a reorganization of the Academy of Architecture took place as part of the general postwar attack on what was called "bourgeois cosmopolitanism" (that is, the allegedly pro-Western, pro-American, and general cosmopolitan outlook of many artists, scientists, and critics), Alabyan, then acting vice-president of the Academy, was removed from his post. He was accused of having supported the harmful activities of "cosmopolitans" for many years and of failing to safeguard the official line in regard to the "development of the study of architecture."[172]

Thus, while the Soviet artist is, financially speaking, well taken care of by the state, this holds true only if he joins the approved organizations and carefully follows the line laid down by the Central Committee of the Communist Party and hence by the Soviet government. Even some American artists and art critics sympathetic to Stalinism felt that the artistic results under this policy of rigid centralization had not been

[169] Voyce, op.cit., p. 136; and Jack Chen, "Soviet Painting," Studio, Vol. 127, No. 611 (Feb. 1944), pp. 61ff.

[170] Jelagin, op.cit., p. 76.

[171] Architectural Chronicle, No. 11 (Moscow, Nov. 1946), p. 19.

[172] New York Herald Tribune, May 1, 1949, p. 10, quoting Soviet Art. Alabyan—together with several other architects, including Yofan, one of the designers of the Palace of the Soviets, Moscow—had already been attacked in Pravda for displaying bourgeois cosmopolitanism: see the New York Times, Mar. 22, 1949, p. 16.

satisfactory to date, although they, unlike practically all non-Stalinists, insisted that great improvement would become almost inevitable. Regardless of merit, however, it is a fact that the artists' organizations of Soviet Russia, mostly founded in connection with the increasing centralization of power under Stalin, served in significant degree as models for groups of artists in many other countries, even including (as will be seen) the United States.

V. Marxism (continued): Its Effects on Art in the United States

Like most earlier forms of socialism, all the major varieties of post-utopian socialism in the United States have in large part been imported from abroad and can only be understood in the light of their foreign origins. Nevertheless, in the process of importation these forms of socialism, and the arts to which they have given rise, have almost always been modified to some degree by American conditions. It is these American manifestations, and the reasons for them, that will now finally be considered.

For a long time—indeed, from the first appearance of Marxism in this country until just before World War I—Marxism and other socialisms influenced by Marxism had relatively little effect on the arts. The average American socialist of that period still more than most other Americans tended to regard art as a kind of unessential gilding on the practical realities of everyday life, and as having no really fundamental or even significant interaction with social problems. This point of view was much more pronounced among American socialists than among those of Europe because American Marxism at the beginning was more completely a workingman's movement primarily interested in day-to-day economic questions. Until World War I and especially until the Russian Revolution of 1917, the United States—in contrast to England and the Continent—had very few intellectuals who were directly interested in Marxism, and these few were usually regarded with the greatest suspicion by their fellow socialists. Most of them were writers, rather than artists or architects, who had become attracted to some aspects of Marxism through an earlier interest in utopianism and Christian socialism, as in the case of William Dean Howells, or else, like Jack London, Upton Sinclair, and Ernest Poole, had become conscious of social problems during the "muckraking" era. There were, however, a few artists with leanings toward Christian socialism, most of whom were inspired by the writings of John Ruskin; but these men rarely displayed their socialism in their art. Fairly typical is the case of W. J. Linton, the well-known American wood engraver who was a native of England and a friend and disciple of Ruskin, and whose socialism was expressed not in his engravings, but in the tracts and booklets which he wrote and printed at his own Appledore Press.[173]

Probably the first well-known American artist to present "the lower classes" in a deliberately sympathetic vein was William Morris Hunt (1824-1879). Some of Hunt's work (Fig. 44) was directly inspired by that of Millet, the French painter of peasant life of whom Hunt said, "When I came to know Millet, I took broader views of humanity. . . ."[174] And although Hunt was not actually a socialist, some of his work also shows the influence of Courbet,[175] the greatest founder of realism in painting, who had very close connections with French socialism. For Courbet was a close friend of Marx's contemporary and rival, the celebrated socialist-anarchist Proudhon; and, as previously mentioned, Courbet himself participated in the Paris Commune of 1871.

With the spread of naturalism as a literary and artistic movement, an increasing number of American artists began to depict realistic scenes of everyday life among the poorer classes in the cities. Chief of these was Eugene Higgins, who said that the paintings of Millet and the writings of Victor Hugo had largely molded his life: he actually identified himself with Jean Valjean, the hero of Hugo's *Les Miserables*. Higgins also said, "I am painting for men like Gorky," referring to Maxim Gorky, the Russian socialist writer who later was to become the leading literary figure of Soviet Russia; and Higgins himself occasionally depicted Russian subject matter (Fig. 45). In 1907 an article on Higgins was included among the several articles on art which the prominent American socialist, John Spargo, wrote for the *Craftsman*, an American periodical established in 1901.[176] The subtitle of Spargo's article referred to Higgins as "an American artist whose work upon canvas depicts the derelicts of civilization as do the tales of Maxim Gorky in literature." Spargo's own interest in art was partly based on the ideas of William Morris: in 1908 he published a book entitled *William Morris; His Socialism*.

The title of the *Craftsman* itself clearly reflects the influence of Morris, and through Morris, of postutopian socialism. In the first issue of the magazine the editor, Gustav Stickley, spoke of his aim "to extend the principles established by Morris." Stickley was the leading figure in the United Crafts of Eastwood (now Syracuse), New York, a group which not only published the *Craftsman* but designed and built

[173] F. J. Mather, Jr., "The Century and American Art," *The Century, 1847-1946* (New York, 1947), p. 164.

[174] Martha Shannon, *Boston Days of William Morris Hunt* (Boston, 1923), p. 40.

[175] C. H. Sawyer, "Naturalism in America," *Courbet and the Naturalistic Movement*, George Boas, ed. (Baltimore, 1938), pp. 116-17.

[176] For Spargo's article, from which the information herein on Higgins was taken, see the *Craftsman*, Vol. 12, No. 2 (May 1907), pp. 135-46. The *Craftsman* was published from 1901 through 1916.

a simplified kind of furniture inspired chiefly by the simple functional forms of William Morris' own furniture. The influence of the arts and crafts movement was likewise reflected in the similar forms of the Spanish "mission" furniture popularized by Elbert Hubbard and the Roycrofters at East Aurora, New York. Hubbard had visited Morris in 1892 and had been much affected by his artistic doctrines, though not by his socialism.

Morris' emphasis on craftsmanship, combined with his medievalism, also had a profound effect on the work of American artists and architects of the later Gothic Revival, and particularly on American typography of the period. The early typography of Goudy, for example, and that of the Gothic Revivalist architect, Bertram Grosvenor Goodhue, clearly reflect the style of Morris (cf. Figs. 46 and 47), but, as in the case of Elbert Hubbard, the socialist content of Morris' art is largely lacking. Thus, in 1922 Goodhue wrote, "Before the [First World] war I thought of myself as an internationalist, without giving the word any socialistic or radical meaning. . . ."[177]

It was especially through the medium of the *Comrade*, an American socialist periodical published in New York from 1901 to 1905, that the influence of William Morris and his followers was popularized in American book art. For among the able artists contributing to that magazine was the well-known English illustrator, Walter Crane (Fig. 48), who had been converted to socialism by Morris' essay *Art and Socialism*, and had already become widely known among American socialists on a trip to this country in 1891-1892. On this trip (during which he had published in the *Atlantic Monthly* for January 1892 an article entitled "Why Socialism Appeals to Artists") Crane had expressed particular admiration for one of Goodhue's designs.[178] Even though the *Comrade* was compelled to suspend publication after less than three years, it had an enduring effect on the technique of American illustration, an effect reinforced by later socialist periodicals. It is significant that such socialist influence has been so largely restricted to the art of drawing, because drawing is a medium which easily permits large-scale reproduction and thus can become easily available to the masses, whereas painting and sculpture have often been regarded by socialists as "fine arts" dominated by the upper classes in capitalist societies.

The *Comrade* was absorbed by the *International Socialist Review*, founded in 1900, which in turn ceased publication in 1918 during World

[177] C. H. Whitaker, *Bertram Grosvenor Goodhue, Architect* (New York, 1925), p. 40. However, Ralph Adams Cram, the noted Gothic Revivalist architect who was for many years Goodhue's partner, tells (in *My Life in Architecture* [Boston, 1936], pp. 20, 26, 46-47, etc.) of the enormous influence the social as well as the artistic ideas of William Morris and Ruskin had upon young American artists in the 1880's and 1890's.

[178] Whitaker, *op.cit.*, p. 16. The design admired by Crane was a magazine cover.

War I. Like most socialist periodicals this magazine displayed little interest in the arts aside from an occasional cartoon or propagandistic illustration in its later issues, and aside from a special department of literature and art conducted for only two years (1908-1910) by John Spargo who earlier had been editor of the *Comrade.*

In the period of "muckraking," interest in social problems became widely spread even among nonsocialists in this country, and several artists who later were to be famous for their work in socialist periodicals first became known for their contributions to muckraking magazines. At this time, for example, the old *Life,* then a humorous magazine under the editorship of John Ames Mitchell, showed considerable interest in problems of a social nature. Among the artists from whom Mitchell accepted drawings was Art Young, later to achieve renown primarily as a contributor to the *Masses* and other socialist periodicals. Moreover, Mitchell himself wrote a book, *The Silent War* (1906), dealing with the class struggle, and this was illustrated by William Balfour Ker (Fig. 49), who in the years just preceding World War I did much illustration for magazines of social protest, including the *Masses.*

With the *Masses,* founded in 1911 as an artists' and writers' cooperative by a group which included both radicals and nonradicals, the influence of socialism in general and of Marxism in particular greatly increased, and a much larger segment of Americans became aware of socialist content in art. Nevertheless, then and later no consistent socialist aesthetic ever developed in the United States, mainly because of the constant splitting and realigning of the numerous socialist groups. Even at a comparatively late date, relatively few members of the Marxist groups were much interested in the visual arts because there still were relatively few "intellectuals" among American Marxists, and also because neither Marx nor Lenin had found time to develop an aesthetic. Furthermore, Lenin himself rejected modern "isms" in the arts only a short time after the Bolshevik Revolution, and in this was followed by Stalin, with the result that among American Marxists any interest in radically new developments in literature and art was for some years to be chiefly restricted to the followers of Trotsky, reflecting Trotsky's own interest in them. Yet even among the American Trotskyists—who, it will be recalled, were all expelled from the American Communist Party in 1928—considerably more attention has been paid to literature than to the visual arts.

Aside from a few individuals, only later did the American Stalinists, and thus the American Communist Party, begin to urge the need for a consistent aesthetic, in harmony with developments in Russia itself. By background and training Stalin had originally been primarily a practicing revolutionary, rather than a theoretician, in partial contrast to such prominent opponents as Trotsky and Bukharin; consequently, for a long time—in this country as elsewhere—Stalin attracted to his following fewer intellectuals than did those opponents. However, in the process of victoriously combating the philosophies of Trotsky and Bukharin, including their philosophies of art, the Stalinists devoted themselves increasingly to the theoretical aspects of Marxism, and eventually developed a general aesthetic of their own largely based on Stalin's own tastes. But this aesthetic, as we have seen, became victorious in Russia only after Stalin's victory over his chief enemies in 1929, and actually remained relatively ill-defined until after World War II.

In this country, in the years immediately following Stalin's triumph—and at first under the influence and guidance of the revived Proletcult movement in Russia—a very large number of party-line "cultural" organizations and periodicals were soon established, including, among many others, the John Reed Club, the Workers Dance League, the Workers Music League, and Theatre Collective. Particularly important was the John Reed Club, founded in 1929 as the American affiliate of the International Union of Revolutionary Writers, with branches in most large cities. Each of the principal branches had its own periodical of literature and art, the best known being the *Partisan Review*, which was founded as the organ of the New York branch in 1934 but remained under Stalinist auspices only until 1936.

Although the various cultural organizations founded as part of the Proletcult movement exerted considerable influence between 1930 and 1935 (the year in which they either disbanded or obediently shifted their interest from revolutionary proletarian culture and class warfare to the Popular Front against fascism), the scope of these organizations was limited insofar as they tended to restrict their membership to the "proletariat." Writers and artists might be admitted to the "proletariat" because of their value as propagandists for proletarian culture, but members of other professions were ordinarily excluded, so that communist influence in American culture was necessarily somewhat restricted. With the change in the Russian line to support the Popular Front, however, and with the consequent deemphasizing of class warfare, pronounced official efforts could eventually be made to seek the support of Americans in those other professions formerly considered unduly antiproletarian in spirit. Therefore, in September 1938 William Z. Foster published in the *Communist*, then the party's theoretical organ, an article entitled "The Communist Party and the Professionals." In this he emphasized the importance of making use of carefully selected professional men willing to "display a thorough readiness to accept Party discipline"; and insisted that in view of the many "potentialities for service by Communist professionals, any tendencies in our Party to underestimate the importance of these elements should be combatted." Thus in the late thirties, up to the Soviet-Nazi pact of 1939, communist influence in the professions and in American culture in general was particularly strong. However, the fact that at this time the party line was stressing the importance of opposing fascism by means of a Popular Front with non-Marxian parties meant that any specifically Marxian art and art theory was deemphasized.

It was only after the end of World War II that the heaviest official emphasis was to be placed by communists on "art as a weapon" in the class struggle. This old slogan of Proletcult was revived once more in 1946 to accompany the cultural purges, first publicly signalized by Stalin's speech on February 9 of that year. For, with the breaking up of Russia's wartime alliance with "bourgeois" countries against Hitler, revolutionary communism and class warfare had been deliberately revived, and new purges—artistic as well as political—had become necessary because of the sharp change in the party line.

On February 11, 1946, the very day that Stalin's speech first appeared in the New York *Daily Worker*, that newspaper began to publish a series of six articles by Samuel Sillen under the general title of "Which Way Left Wing Literature?" and with such subheadings as Art and Politics, Art as a Weapon, Ideology and Art, and The Path before Us. Taking the form of an attack on an article in the current *New Masses* (written by Albert Maltz and entitled "What Shall We Ask of Writers?"), Sillen's series laid down a firm line for literature and art which was promptly supported in the Communist Party press by such wheelhorses as Mike Gold and A. B. Magil. And when *Mainstream*, a new party-line cultural periodical began publication early in 1947, Sillen was made its editor and later became editor of its successor, *Masses & Mainstream*.

Two months after Stalin's speech of February 9, a still more authoritative indication that art was now to be much more thoroughly emphasized by the party line was made by William Z. Foster (who in the summer of 1945 had replaced Earl Browder as leader of the reconstituted American Communist Party in order to put the whole new postwar line into effect). For on April 18, 1946, Foster was the chief speaker at a symposium in New York on "Art as a Weapon," a symposium jointly sponsored by the *New Masses* and the *Daily Worker*. In an article published in the *New Masses* five days later, Foster wrote ". . . there must be a clear understanding that 'art is a weapon' in the class struggle. Not only is art a weapon, but a very potent one as well."[179] And now he stressed the relative importance of *national* cultures, as opposed to internationalism, in harmony with the changing Russian foreign policy.

[179] W. Z. Foster, "Elements of a People's Cultural Policy," *New Masses*, Vol. 59, No. 4 (Apr. 23, 1946), p. 6.

In the following year a formal and definitive statement of the whole new cultural line was published in a pamphlet entitled *Culture in a Changing World, a Marxist Approach*, written by Victor J. Jerome, chairman of the cultural commission of the American Communist Party. This statement, the pamphlet said, was "based on the text of a major address delivered . . . at a Marxist cultural conference held in New York in June, 1947, under the sponsorship of the magazines, *Mainstream* and *New Masses*" (although, strangely enough, the two magazines and the *Daily Worker* had apparently carried no report of the address). The statement praised the line established by Samuel Sillen's articles in the *Daily Worker* over a year earlier. For the further guidance of party-liners, Jerome's pamphlet was reviewed favorably and at great length by Samuel Sillen himself in the March 1948 number of *Political Affairs*, the theoretical magazine of the American Communist Party, of which Jerome was editor,

In his pamphlet, as Sillen said, Jerome firmly laid down the postwar Stalinist line that socialist "reality in art involves partisanship." And in characteristic Stalinist fashion Jerome called for a two-fold struggle "simultaneously . . . against the vulgar, mechanico-materialist view" and "against the idealist disruption of reality in art . . . by its absolutizing of form" (i.e., by its formalism).

Thus for the first time strong official attempts were now being made by the American Communist Party to arrive at a complete Stalinist aesthetic by slavishly following—as usual—the postwar line laid down in Soviet Russia. As already noted, in Russia itself the development of a detailed official aesthetic had previously been hampered by the primacy given to economic and political problems, by the bitter internal controversies, by purges, and by the fear of capitalism and nazism. During World War II such an aesthetic had again been somewhat held back by the need to avoid discord with Russia's wartime allies; but at the same time the war had brought to those allies an increased interest in all things Russian including Soviet art and art theories.

For all these reasons, most of the few important books on art theory written or published by Americans sympathetic to Stalinism were of recent date. Late in 1945 there was issued by International Publishers—apparently in recognition of the survival of wartime interest in Russia and thus in Stalinist Marxism—an American edition of an able little book entitled, *Marxism and Modern Art; an Approach to Social Realism*. This, written by F. D. Klingender, an English critic sympathetic to the Stalinist point of view, had originally been published in England in 1943. However, most of the books on Marxist art which were soon to be published in this country reflected the dutifully increased interest in art among Stalinists and their sympathizers since Stalin gave a new importance to art by his signal, early in 1946, for the postwar revision of Russian culture. Among the most important of such works were the volume of selections from the writings of Marx and Engels entitled *Literature and Art* (1947), Sidney Finkelstein's *Art and Society* (1947), and Louis Harap's *Social Roots of the Arts* (1949)—all issued by International Publishers. The head of this publishing house was Alexander Trachtenberg, whom one former member of the Communist Party has called "the Red cultural commissar for America."[180]

Of all the books on art criticism published in this country in connection with this new Stalinist emphasis on art, the best is Finkelstein's *Art and Society*, issued when the author was music critic of the *New Masses*, and with a title borrowed from a well-known essay by Georgy Plekhanov, a celebrated father of Russian Marxism and acknowledged teacher of Lenin. Finkelstein's book is one of the ablest and most complete expositions of a theory of art sympathetic to Stalinism ever published anywhere. To non-Stalinists the book may serve to demonstrate the difficulty which those who sympathize with Soviet Russia have in keeping up with the party line, for in it the author highly praised the work of Picasso (who three years earlier had joined the French Communist Party) seemingly just before *Pravda* launched, in August 1947, a sharp attack on Picasso's art as bourgeois and formalist.[181] While *Art and Society* was not published until October 1947, the book was presumably too far along in the press for any revisions to be made after the *Pravda* article had appeared in print.

At first it seemed as if Finkelstein would escape unscathed: the reviews of his book in the American communist press were almost entirely favorable. However, well over two years later, on May 15, 1950, the *Daily*

[180] Budenz, *Men without Faces*, p. 239. Trachtenberg was one of twenty-one leaders of the Communist Party indicted in June 1951 for conspiring to advocate or teach the violent overthrow of the government: see the *New York Herald Tribune*, June 21, 1951, pp. 1, 11, 12.

[181] However, famous foreign artists sympathetic to Russia have often been lauded by Stalinists outside of Russia, and their reputations made use of, even though their art was in disfavor within the Soviet Union itself. This had clearly become the case with Picasso: hence the issue of *Masses & Mainstream* for March 1948 could contain (pp. 6-20) a laudatory article "Picasso at Work," by Louis Parrot. It might be added that in March 1950 Picasso was refused a visa by the Department of State when he sought to visit Washington as head of a European delegation to bring a world peace petition addressed to Congress. The Department of State said that the members of the delegation were stooges for the Partisans of Peace, which it called a communist-line organization: see the *New York Herald Tribune*, Mar. 4, 1950, pp. 1 and 6. As part of his contribution to the communist "peace" campaign, Picasso drew a dove of peace which was widely publicized. It was caricatured by a French anticommunist artist in an even more widely publicized poster of an armored dove, decorated with the Soviet symbol of the hammer and sickle, and labeled "La colombe qui fait boum" (The dove that goes bang).

Worker suddenly published an article by one Barnard Rubin entitled "Serious Errors in Finkelstein's 'Art and Society.'" In this—surprisingly—the book was now attacked as anti-Semitic, and also as "formalistic" because it had praised such "corrupt darlings of imperialism's culture" as T. S. Eliot and James Joyce by venturing to suggest that the writings of Eliot and Joyce could be used as models by progressive cultural workers.

Three days later the *Daily Worker* published Finkelstein's recantation written in the usual abject style of a party-liner attacked in a Russian-type purge (thereby, in the Stalinist view, demonstrating the "self-criticism" which in Russia is supposed to be replacing the class antagonisms of capitalist society). Finkelstein now admitted that his book suffered from a "classless" point of view toward the arts as a consequence of which he had wrongly confused primitive art and folk art, had wrongly interpreted the term "realism," and had failed to distinguish adequately between those national movements based on bourgeois approaches to art and those founded on a true working-class approach. Most humbly Finkelstein accounted for his errors by saying that he had originally written the book before World War II, and that when he had returned from military service he had not succeeded in rewriting it properly. This, being interpreted, means that he had not been successful in taking account of those shifts in the Russian policy and in the party line which had occurred since he wrote the original draft.

In spite of Finkelstein's recantation, from May until August 1950 articles and letters attacking his book appeared frequently in the *Daily Worker*. One letter was written by Louis Harap, author of *Social Roots of the Arts*, but Harap evidently made a bad mistake in thus seeking to demonstrate his orthodoxy for the *Daily Worker* a few days later printed a sharp letter from Samuel Sillen, editor of the party-line monthly, *Masses & Mainstream*, pointing out that Harap's book shared some of Finkelstein's errors.

The discussion in the *Daily Worker* was wound up on August 7 and 8, 1950, by two articles written by no less an authority than V. J. Jerome. As the party's spokesman in cultural matters, Jerome summed up the attack by pointing out that Finkelstein had clearly succumbed to "right-opportunist errors." But Jerome evidently felt that there were some alleviating circumstances and that the discussion had only succeeded in confusing many party-liners, because he called for a "thoroughly critical review" of the book as the next step. This "thoroughly critical review" duly appeared in the September 1950 number of his own magazine, *Political Affairs*. While this review (entitled "Art and Class," and written by Harry Martel and Marvin Reiss) recognized that Finkelstein had made some important contributions, it reiterated that "his work reveals a dominant tendency to a non-class approach," a "formalist" tendency to emphasize "bourgeois esthetics" and novelty, an improper treatment of realism, and a failure to recognize that bourgeois modern art obliterates "national art" and does so "in the cosmopolitan, 'international' bourgeois art jargon which is the same in New York, Hollywood, Paris, or London." He had, in short, failed "to show that the 'innovations' of the 'modernists' are merely the decadent shimmer of moribund capitalism." Significantly, however, the review concluded that "In the world-battle for peace and progress, the Communist Party recognizes that the artist is a key figure." Thus, at long last the importance of the artist was now fully accepted by the American Communist Party.

But if Finkelstein's book—notwithstanding all these delayed assaults leveled against it by the party—is outstanding in quality among writings on art by American party-liners, it seems all the better by comparison with the art criticism written by other American Marxians. For most of this has appeared in the form of articles which present not only second-hand but often inadequate versions of some phase of Russian Marxist art theory, whether of the current orthodox party line or some "deviation." And most of these articles have appeared in relatively obscure periodicals read chiefly by the fanatic few of the particular Marxist sect. Because the art theories contained in such periodicals so directly reflect, in secondary form, the Russian prototypes already discussed, no attempt will be made to treat them in detail here. Suffice it to say that most of the better-grade art criticism sympathetic to Stalinism has appeared in the pages of the *Partisan Review* in its brief Stalinist period (1934-1936), in the *New Masses* (1926-1948), and especially in *Masses & Mainstream. Dialectics: a Marxist Literary Journal*, edited by Angel Flores and published in New York by the Critics Group during the late 1930's, contained occasional articles on art from a similar point of view; and the Critics Group also issued at this time a number of important Russian Marxist documents on art, including a translation of Plekhanov's *Art and Society* (1937), and of Mikhail Lifshitz's *The Philosophy of Art of Karl Marx* (1938). In spite of the fact that during the Popular Front the party line regarded serious Marxian inquiry of this sort as "sectarian" (i.e., as too likely to stir up trouble between Soviet Russia and its non-Marxian allies in opposing fascism), the Critics Group managed to publish *Dialectics* until 1939.

Some of the best of all the Marxian art criticism written in this country has been printed in periodicals sympathetic to Trotskyism, notably the *Partisan Review* during the Trotskyist phase which occurred immediately after its revival in 1937. Valuable articles also appeared during the middle 1930's in the *Modern Monthly*, an independent periodical that published all those shades of leftist—including Trotskyist—opinion which were not Stalinist and not social democratic. The "Right deviationist" group, led by Jay Lovestone, paid less attention to the arts than did the American Trotskyists. Nevertheless, from the time that his faction was expelled from the Communist Party in 1929 until it voted to disband late in 1940, its members tended to uphold the doctrines of Bukharin concerning the unripeness of capitalism for revolution, doctrines with implications for art as well as for economics and politics.

Thus all the major points of view and all the chief changes in the party line which have been represented in the art theories and criticism of Soviet Russia itself have had protagonists in the United States. But because the writings of these protagonists have mostly been restricted to periodicals of small circulation, their direct influence on the actual practice of art has ordinarily been restricted to relatively small groups.

However, in addition to actual members of such groups there has long existed in the United States a much larger body made up of liberals, or even radicals, of various shades of opinion who have been interested in the arts, and whose opinions and theories have frequently been more or less colored—often unconsciously, and in widely different ways—by those of the various Russian factions and their American representatives. Because less subject to any party line, both the art theory and the practice of such liberal-radicals have tended to be more original. Most of them have had strong equalitarian, humanitarian, or collectivistic inclinations, often derived from earlier American currents of thought, but which have made them sympathetic to some aspects of Marxism and have frequently led them to collaborate with Marxians. Many have been artists stirred to social protest against capitalism partly, at least, by their first-hand knowledge of the difficulties and injustices which beset the artist within a primarily business and industrial civilization. Some of these artists had also served as staff artists on newspapers and in this way had become very much aware of everyday social problems and injustices. This was particularly true of several members of the group of artists known as "The Eight," formed in 1908 under the leadership of Robert Henri. This group became known to its detractors as the "Ash-can School," because several of its members—notably John Sloan (Fig. 50) and George Luks—particularly liked to paint scenes of lower-class urban life. It is significant that George Luks had already been the subject of a laudatory article in the *Craftsman*[182] written by the well-known socialist John Spargo, and that John Sloan was later to become art editor of the *Masses* and a member of the Socialist Party.[183] Significantly, also, Robert Henri, the leader of the

[182] *Craftsman*, Vol. 12, No. 6 (Sept. 1907), pp. 599-607.
[183] According to Max Eastman, *Enjoyment of Living* (New York, 1948), p. 549.

group, was not unsympathetic to philosophical anarchism. From 1912 to 1918 he taught art at the Modern School of the Ferrer Center where for a time his celebrated pupil, George Bellows, and his friend, John Sloan, also taught. The Ferrer Center was the headquarters of the Francisco Ferrer Association, named for Francisco Ferrer Guardia, a Spanish anarchist and libertarian educator who had been executed at Barcelona in 1909 for allegedly leading a military rebellion.[184]

The socially radical spirit of such men as these was in part, at least, the result of their artistic radicalism, for they all sharply opposed academic traditions in art while upholding modernism of one sort or another. Indeed, it was largely friends of Henri and members of "The Eight"— especially Arthur B. Davies—who were chiefly to be responsible for putting on the celebrated Armory Show, held at the 69th Regiment Armory in New York in 1913, which first introduced Americans to the modern movement in art on a large scale.

Artistic radicalism of this kind has often made some American artists willing to collaborate with Marxists in attacking capitalism largely because they looked upon conservative art as a product of a philistine civilization which happened to be capitalistic. In contributing their services as illustrators or cartoonists to periodicals of social protest, many

[184] Leonard D. Abbott, "Francisco Ferrer and the Modern School," *Critic & Guide* (Girard, Kan.), Oct. 1949, pp. 10-12; and information generously furnished by Mr. Abbott, Carl Zigrosser, and Manuel Komroff. Among the sponsors of the Ferrer Center, which attracted many leading radicals and libertarians, were Mr. Abbott, the anarchists Emma Goldman, Alexander Berkman, and Hippolyte Havel, Hutchins Hapgood, and the muckraker socialist, Charles Edward Russell. Ferrer's followers also established a colony at Stelton, N.J., and published a periodical, the *Modern School*, to which Rockwell Kent and other now noted artists contributed, and of which Carl Zigrosser was at one time editor. The Ferrer Association in New York started at 6 St. Mark's Place in the fall of 1910. In October 1911 it moved to 104 East 12th Street, and a year later to 63 East 107th Street where it reached the peak of its activities. There were classes in various subjects. Will Durant taught in the children's school and gave evening talks in philosophy. Leonard Abbott lectured on literature; and Clarence Darrow and Joseph McCabe were also lecturers. Speakers at the Saturday night discussions included Alexander Berkman, Emma Goldman, Elizabeth Gurley Flynn, W. E. Walling, Lincoln Steffens, Hutchins Hapgood, Upton Sinclair, Edwin Markham, Hubert H. Harrison, Christian Brinton, and Harry Kemp. Mr. Abbott stated that Henri began his art class at East 12th Street in the winter of 1911-1912 and continued it until the New York association broke up in 1918. Bellows taught at East 12th Street and at East 107th Street where Abbott and Emma Goldman said Sloan also taught, though Van Wyck Brooks has said Sloan denied this. Henri's class, with a model, was held two evenings a week and supervised alternately by himself and Bellows. The class was radical only in involving no systematic teaching: desired, a procedure commonplace today but then considered revolutionary. The following artists frequented the class at some time or other: Man Ray, Manuel Komroff, Ben Benn, Helen West Heller, Paul Rohland, Harry Wickey, and Adolph Wolff. The Ferrer Association came under attack during World War I because of its pacifist tendencies. In 1915 the children's school moved to Stelton. Activities at New York ended in 1918, and at Stelton (now Piscataway) early in 1952.

of them have simply been registering a protest against conservatism. In most cases, being artists, they have been temperamentally too individualistic to accept the Marxian creed in its entirety: Marx's emphasis on liberty as the goal of the class struggle has appealed to them, but not the Marxian belief in impersonal "scientific" procedure toward that goal.

This was the case with most of the more prominent artists who at one time or another contributed to the *Masses*, relatively few of whom were actually practicing political socialists. Among the contributors were well-known painters and draftsmen such as its art editor, John Sloan, also Eugene Higgins, Robert Henri, George Bellows, Arthur B. Davies, Glenn Coleman, Maurice Becker, Hugo Gellert, H. J. Glintenkamp, Boardman Robinson, and Stuart Davis; the sculptors, Jo Davidson and Mahonri Young, who submitted drawings; and various able cartoonists including Art Young and Robert Minor. With the help of such highly competent artists, the *Masses*—which is said to have marked the first appearance of "realism"[185] in an American magazine—was the best illustrated periodical in the country, at least until 1916 when John Sloan and four other staff members resigned in a dispute with Max Eastman,[186] the editor since 1913.

Before this dispute took place, the *Masses* had already begun to oppose American participation in World War I: in fact, of all the contributing artists, George Bellows was the only important one who actively supported participation. As a result of its antiwar stand, in 1917 the *Masses* was finally forced to cease publication when seven members of the staff were accused of obstructing the draft. These seven—including two artists, Art Young and H. J. Glintenkamp—were indicted under the so-called Espionage Act, and most of the group—including Art Young—were twice brought to trial. "Exhibit F" at the trial was a cartoon by Art Young entitled *Having Their Fling* (Fig. 51) in which he depicted his idea of the forces responsible for the war by showing bankers and clergymen dancing wildly in a shower of gold to the music of the devil's orchestra of cannon. Only after two juries had disagreed were the defendants finally freed, and by a very narrow margin.

Among those who deplored the attack on the *Masses* and who likewise opposed the entry of the United States into World War I were the members of the staff of a literary and artistic journal called the *Seven Arts*. This periodical had a wide influence in spite of its very brief life (it was published only from November 1916 until October 1917 when its financial sponsor refused to support the antiwar stand of the editors). Most of the

---

[185] Eastman, *op.cit.*, p. 411.
[186] *Ibid.*, pp. 548-56; also J. J. Sweeney, Museum of Modern Art, *Stuart Davis* (New York, 1945), pp. 11-12.

staff—which included Van Wyck Brooks, Randolph Bourne, Waldo Frank, and the unpolitically-minded music and art critic, Paul Rosenfeld—were socialists or liberals who, like Ruskin and Morris rather than Marx, were interested both in craftsmanship and in the arts as forces for achieving the good society. The dominant figure of the group was the socialist Van Wyck Brooks, among whose chief idols were William Morris and John Ruskin.

One young American much influenced by the *Seven Arts* was Lewis Mumford, destined to become a leading American critic of the arts, an international authority on housing and city planning, and a widely known liberal. At the age of twenty Mumford had been profoundly affected by the writings of the Scottish bio-sociologist and city planner, Patrick Geddes, whom Mumford himself had described as "a scientific interpreter of Ruskin." Because of his Ruskinian point of view derived from Geddes, Mumford was also attracted by the similar ideas of Van Wyck Brooks and other members of the *Seven Arts* group. Indeed, when the *Seven Arts* ceased publication it merged with the *Dial* of which Mumford became associate editor in 1919. Significantly enough Mumford's first book, *The Story of Utopias* (1922), was written, the preface tells us, at the suggestion of Van Wyck Brooks and under the influence of the ideas of Patrick Geddes. The stimulation of Geddes' ideas also led Mumford to become one of the founders of the Regional Planning Association of America after World War I, and to publish several important books on city planning, and on social and cultural history.

After the *Masses* stopped publication in 1917, several attempts were made to establish successors. Art Young, one of the defendants in the famous trial, was responsible for at least two of these. He first sought to establish a monthly magazine of artistic satire, entitled *Good Morning* (1919-1921), and when that failed, Young tried again with the likewise unsuccessful *Art Young's Quarterly*.

The chief successor of the *Masses* was the *Liberator*, founded in 1918 under private control[187] but under joint socialist and liberal auspices. This took up pretty much where the *Masses* had left off. Many of the artists who had contributed to the *Masses* also worked for the *Liberator*, including Young, Bellows, Robinson, and Minor (Fig. 52), who in 1918 went to Russia as the *Liberator's* foreign correspondent;[188] but now an increasingly important part was also played by younger artists, especially

[187] According to Eastman, *Enjoyment of Living*, p. 415, note 1, the *Liberator* was founded under the joint ownership and control of Eastman and his sister. Eastman, who was the first editor, resigned in 1922.

[188] He also represented the *New York World* and the *Philadelphia Public Ledger*: see Benjamin Gitlow, *The Whole of Their Lives* (New York, 1948), p. 70.

William Gropper (Fig. 53). In 1922 the *Liberator* became a completely communist-line periodical and almost immediately began to pay less attention to art except for extremely propagandistic and party-line cartoons. Two years later it ceased publication when it merged with two other left-wing periodicals to form the *Workers Monthly*.

In 1926 the *New Masses* was established by a partly different group of writers and artists, and, until lack of funds compelled it to close down early in 1948, was for most of its life a periodical sympathetic to revolutionary communism of Stalinist persuasion, even though shortly after its founding the editorial board had decided that the magazine would not be one "of communism or Moscow, but a magazine of American experiment."[189] Among the many artists who at one time or another contributed to the *New Masses* were John Sloan and Hugo Gellert (two of the six editors in the first days of the magazine), also Glenn Coleman, Adolf Dehn, Waldo Frank, Miguel Covarrubias, Art Young, Gropper, Maurice Becker, and Louis Lozowick. Of these artists several were outspoken radicals, notably Becker, Gropper, Louis Lozowick, and Hugo Gellert,[190] the last of whom painted a series of murals in the cafeteria at 30 Union Square, the building which in 1927 had become the headquarters of the *Daily Worker*.[191] Several of the contributors to the *New Masses* drew direct inspiration from European leftist art of the period. For example, the art of the then antibourgeois German satirist George Grosz (Fig. 25) seems to have had direct influence on the thin linear style and satirical subject matter of Adolf Dehn. It has also apparently helped to inspire some of the subject matter of William Gropper,[192] who until the Popular Front liked to satirize "bourgeois" legislators (Fig. 53). The art of Soviet Russia early had an especially profound effect on Louis Lozowick, who had been in Berlin in 1922 and had seen the great exhibition of modern Russian art held in that year.[193] Because of Lozowick's leftist views and because he was one of the first American artists to depict industrial scenes, his work was much admired in the Soviet Union, and an exhibit of his drawings was held in Moscow in 1928.[194]

[189] Joseph Freeman, *An American Testament* (New York, 1936), pp. 381-82. The *New Masses* was reorganized in 1928 under the editorship of Michael Gold, "and now for the first time an attempt was made to create a popular literary magazine with an explicitly Marxist policy," according to Bernard Smith, *Forces in American Criticism* (New York, 1939), p. 369.

[190] M. W. Brown, *American Painting (1913-1929)*, (unpublished Ph.D. thesis, New York University, 1949), p. 275.

[191] Benjamin Gitlow, *I Confess* (New York, c. 1940), pp. 307-9.

[192] Brown, *op.cit.*, pp. 276-77.

[193] While in Berlin, Lozowick talked with many modern artists: see László Moholy-Nagy, "Abstract of an Artist," *The New Vision; and Abstract of an Artist* (New York, 1946), p. 74. A few years later Lozowick published a book on Russian painting since the October Revolution entitled *Modern Russian Art* (New York, c. 1925).

[194] Brown, *op.cit.*, p. 372.

DONALD DREW EGBERT

Lozowick, Becker, and Dehn were among nearly fifty artists, writers, architects, and educators who, during the presidential campaign of 1932, issued a statement calling for the formation of committees throughout the country to furnish "support in the national elections of the Communist Party and its candidates, Wm. Z. Foster and James W. Ford." According to the *Daily Worker* for September 14, 1932, the statement signed by the fifty said "that the only effective way to protest against the chaos, the appalling wastefulness, and the indescribable misery inherent in the present economic system is to vote for the Communist candidates," a point of view that many of the signers have long since repudiated. This was the first time in this country that the communists had made such direct use of writers and artists for immediate political purposes, employing now a technique of mass pressure said to have first been developed in this country by the I.W.W. in an effort to obtain amnesty for jailed "Wobblies" in 1923.

However, it is important to note that relatively few of the artists contributing to the *New Masses* in its early period were active communists or fellow travelers. Even though the editorial policy of the *New Masses* was always sympathetic to communism and closely followed the Communist Party line, one former party member on the staff wrote that of fifty-six artists and writers grouped around this periodical in the early days, only two were actually members of the party and less than a dozen were even sympathetic to it.[195] As time went on, those artists who were neither party members nor fellow travelers increasingly fell away. Some withdrew their names from the long list of contributing editors (a list carried until the magazine suspended publication as a monthly in September 1934), while others failed to do so although inactive. Of the few remaining well-known artist contributors, nearly all were to turn away from the *New Masses* in 1939 when it supported the Russo-German pact.

After the pact the *New Masses* gradually declined in circulation until, in January 1948, it appeared for the last time as a weekly, although two months later it was to be combined with another periodical and resurrected as a monthly under the title *Masses & Mainstream*. The last issue of the *New Masses* had contained an open letter from twelve Russian communist writers addressed to their colleagues in the United States, the gist of which was: Whose side are you on? In the third issue of *Masses & Mainstream*, thirty-two American writers, painters, and musicians published their reply. Said they: "We want to share . . . responsibility with you. . . . On this May Day we grip your hand. . . ." Among the signers

[195] Freeman, *op.cit.*, p. 379. Although Freeman's statement was published as late as 1936, it apparently applies only to the early days of the *New Masses*.

100

were Sidney Finkelstein, the critic, and such well-known American painters as Philip Evergood, Raphael Soyer, and Max Weber.[196] It might be added that Evergood, Weber, and Soyer, along with Hugo Gellert, Gropper, Louis Lozowick, Stuart Davis, and Joe Jones, had been among the nearly 150 signers of a letter which was prominently published in the *New Masses* and praised by the *Daily Worker* for April 28, 1938, as upholding "the verdicts in the recent Moscow trials of the Trotzkyite-Buckharinite traitors." The letter was an answer to the commission of inquiry headed by John Dewey which had investigated the Moscow trials, had interviewed Trotsky in Mexico, and had absolved him from the Moscow verdict that he had conspired with other defendants and with Fascist nations to overthrow the Soviet government and to assassinate its leaders. Weber, Gellert, and Gropper together with Art Young, Maurice Becker, Rockwell Kent, and several other artists were among the 400 signers—some of them neither communists nor fellow travelers—of a letter published in the *Daily Worker* on August 14, 1939, denying that "the U.S.S.R. and the totalitarian states are basically alike." This letter (a reply to charges leveled by John Dewey's Committee for Cultural Freedom) was published just nine days before the Nazi-Soviet pact.

It must be emphasized, however, that many of the American artists who have joined in signing statements like those cited above have kept their art largely separate from their political views even when those views have coincided with the party line. For instance, this was long the case with Max Weber. In spite of a record of frequent sympathy for Soviet Russia and for aspects of the party line as supported by such periodicals as the *New Masses* or *Masses & Mainstream*, so little was this ever reflected in the subject matter of his paintings that he was reprimanded in the columns of *Masses & Mainstream* itself.[107]

Most of the artists who, unlike Weber, have more completely subordinated their art to Marxism or to a Marxian party line have usually expressed themselves by means of the cartoon. For example, several highly talented cartoonists contributed to the *Daily Worker*. Among them were Art Young, Robert Minor, Abraham Redfield, Fred Ellis, and Jacob Burck, most of whom worked in a very simple and forceful lithographic style apparently inspired by that of Minor, a style which has also in-

[196] *Masses & Mainstream*, Vol. 1, No. 3 (May 1948), p. 6. The Russian letter had appeared in *Literaturnaya Gazeta* for Sept. 20, 1947. Another English translation is in *Soviet Press Translations*, Vol. 2, No. 21 (Dec. 15, 1947), pp. 287-89. Finkelstein and Evergood were to be listed for some time as contributing editors of *Masses & Mainstream*, as was William Gropper. Weber was chairman of the Manhattan Committee of Artists for Wallace in 1948. Raphael Soyer's brother, Moses Soyer, was art editor of the *New Masses* in 1944-1946.

[107] See W. T. Burger, "Max Weber," *Masses & Mainstream*, Vol. 2, No. 4 (Apr. 1949), p. 87.

fluenced leading cartoonists on "capitalist" papers.[198] Minor himself—the only artist of the original *Masses* group to become a founder of the American Communist Party—eventually gave up his cartooning because, as a convinced member of the party, he came to believe that direct participation in communist political and economic activities is more important than cartooning for bringing about the revolution of the proletariat. Among many other activities, Minor served in Moscow as the representative of the American Communist Party to the Communist International; was imprisoned for several months in 1930 for participating in a "hunger demonstration" in New York's Union Square, a demonstration calling for a general strike; and went to Spain in 1937 to oppose Franco in the Spanish Civil War. He was the Communist Party's candidate for various political offices, including governor of New York and United States senator. After Earl Browder was jailed for passport fraud in 1939, Minor was made acting secretary of the American Communist Party, usually considered the most important party post. Although Minor fell into disfavor with Moscow and with the party in 1945, when Browder was demoted and later expelled, he remained listed in *Who's Who in America* as an editor of the *Daily Worker*, and in 1950 on the occasion of his sixty-sixth birthday the *Daily Worker* reported that he "was honored by the Communist Party with the warmest greetings."[199]

The fact that Minor gave up art in favor of political and economic activity reflects the comparative lack of interest in the arts characteristic of Stalinists everywhere until after World War II. As already noted, of all the socialist and communist factions, the Trotskyist groups have from their beginnings been particularly interested in the theory and criticism of art because of Trotsky's own interest in such matters. And because Trotsky, unlike Lenin and Stalin, considered that the more abstract forms of modern art could express the spirit of the Marxist revolution, American Trotskyists have lent their support to modern movements in art which were long opposed by Lenin and Stalin and which therefore have also been generally opposed by American Stalinists.

One particularly important factor in spreading, even among nonsocialists, modern art forms that originally, at least, were regarded by some artists as possessing socialist or communist connotations, has been the influence of artists who came to this country from abroad. It will be remembered, for example, that when leftism in art—including futurism,

[198] According to Freeman, *op.cit.*, p. 304, the style of Minor (who once was a cartoonist on the *St. Louis Post-Dispatch* and the *New York World*, among other papers) influenced Fitzpatrick of the *Post-Dispatch* and Rollin Kirby of the *World*. Minor, a former anarcho-syndicalist, had been stimulated by French anarchist artists.

[199] *Who's Who in America* (1950-1951), and the *Daily Worker*, July 17, 1950, p. 5. For an account of Minor's extraordinary career, see Gitlow, *The Whole of Their Lives*, especially pp. 70-82, 323-25.

constructivism, and the other "isms"—felt the weight of Lenin's disapproval in 1920, many artists who were not willing to devote their art entirely to the revolution left Russia. One of the artists who migrated from Russia about this time made his way to the United States via Siberia. This was David Burliuk, who, according to his biography in *Who's Who in America*, regarded himself as the founder of Russian futurism.

But since those artists who have left Soviet Russia have almost invariably been those *unwilling* to devote themselves to the revolution, the strongest Marxian influences on American painting have not come directly from Russia itself. They have come, indeed, from Mexico, mainly as a result of the influence of the communist painter, Diego Rivera. Rivera—together with Siqueiros, also a communist, and with José Orozco, a Mexican revolutionary who sympathized with some aspects of Marxism—was chiefly responsible for a great revival of mural painting in fresco. This began on a large scale in 1922-1924 with the frescoes executed in the National Preparatory School at Mexico City by a group of leading radical artists, a group which included Siqueiros, Rivera, and Orozco. Fresco as a medium could be particularly approved by all communists because, it will be recalled, Lenin had praised it as so well suited to Marxist propaganda in warm countries; but it was also approved by many noncommunists interested in its expressive possibilities for modern art. Although none of the leading Mexican artists executed major works in this country until 1930, the influence of this revival of fresco had already reached the United States. Among the first Americans to use the medium was Boardman Robinson, previously a contributor to the *Masses* and the *Liberator*, who painted his first frescoes in 1927.

Because the Mexican fresco painters have so greatly affected art in the United States, the story of the two most influential communists among them, the former anarchists Siqueiros and Rivera, is worth noting. In 1922 Siqueiros, the most violently revolutionary of all the Mexican artists, was a leader in founding what became known as the Revolutionary Syndicate (i.e., Union) of Technical Workers, Painters, Sculptors, and Allied Trades, of which Rivera and Orozco were also members. This was in part inspired by Spanish syndicalism and Russian communism. Siqueiros early joined the Mexican Communist Party, in 1923 was elected a member of its executive committee, and soon became an ardent Stalinist. He first came to the United States in 1932, and at Los Angeles executed in automobile paint (as a new and revolutionary material expressive of the industrial age) a series of murals in a workers' settlement. So revolutionary and inflammatory was the content of these paintings that he was shortly compelled to leave the country. In 1934, however, he held a successful exhibition in New York, returned to New York early in

1936 as a delegate to the first American Artists' Congress, and at that time was "active more or less officially as court artist to the Communist Party until he left in 1937 to join the Government [Loyalist] military forces in Spain."[200] On May 24, 1940, he is said to have led the band of Mexican communists who, disguised as policemen, made an abortive attempt to assassinate Trotsky three months before he was murdered.[201]

In contrast to Siqueiros, who had comparatively little influence within this country outside of communist circles, Rivera for a time had a tremendous vogue with many North American "capitalist" patrons to whom his beliefs, and hence the content of his art, were really anathema. And this was true also of the Mexican revolutionary Orozco.

Rivera, who had joined the Mexican Communist Party in 1922 and, with Siqueiros, had been made a member of its executive committee the following year, first entered the United States in 1930. After a trip to Russia in 1927-1928 he had fallen out with the Stalinists and had become an ardent follower of Trotsky. For, as Rivera said later, he too believed in "complete freedom for art";[202] and this point of view was opposed by the Stalinists as art for art's sake. It was Rivera who in 1936 secured asylum for Trotsky in Mexico, and Trotsky once praised Rivera as the greatest of all the interpreters of the October Revolution.[203] Certainly Rivera never concealed the fact that he believed in violent revolution: for example, in 1932 he wrote in an American periodical, "I want to be a propagandist of Communism. . . . I want to use my art as a weapon."[204] And in a manifesto which he issued in 1938 jointly with André Breton, the French poet and founder of surrealism, Rivera stated: "We believe that the supreme task of art in our epoch is to take part actively and consciously in the preparation of the revolution."[205]

It is significant that this manifesto was issued by Rivera, then a Trotskyist, in collaboration with a surrealist because many of the chief surrealists, under Breton's leadership, in theory frequently supported Marxist communism. Like Marxism, surrealism seeks to discredit bourgeois ideology, which it does by attempting to destroy all existing conservative and academic conceptions in art. Thus Dali, the celebrated surrealist painter—who first visited this country in 1934, moved here to live in

[200] L. E. Schmeckebier, *Modern Mexican Art* (Minneapolis, 1939), p. 162. See also Elliot Clay, "Siqueiros: Artist in Arms," *Masses & Mainstream*, Vol. 4, No. 4 (Apr. 1951), pp. 60-73.

[201] Gitlow, *The Whole of Their Lives*, p. 343. See also L. A. Sánchez Salazar and Julián Gorkin, *Murder in Mexico* (London, 1950), *passim*.

[202] André Breton and Diego Rivera, "Manifesto: Towards a Free Revolutionary Art," *Partisan Review*, Vol. 6, No. 1 (Fall 1938), p. 51.

[203] Trotsky, "Art and Politics," *op.cit.*, p. 7.

[204] Diego Rivera, "The Revolutionary Spirit in Modern Art," *Modern Quarterly*, Vol. 6, No. 3 (Autumn 1932), p. 57.

[205] Breton and Rivera, *op.cit.*, p. 52.

1940, and has had an immense vogue which has especially affected American advertising art—once said, "The whole Surrealist faction is rapidly evolving towards a complete acceptance of the Communist cultural platform."[206] However, insofar as surrealists woo the irrational by seeking to express the individual's subconscious existence, rather than—like Marx —the realistic aspects of social existence including conscious action in a material world, surrealism was not accepted by Stalinists. In fact, when once the surrealists offered their services to the Soviet Union, Stalin promptly declined the offer as "impractical," whereupon Breton and most other surrealists became Trotskyists although a few other prominent surrealists (including Tristan Tzara, founder of the earlier art movement known as dada) became active Communist Party members in their respective countries.[207] Yet even if in theory many surrealists are communists of one variety or another, in actuality they tend toward a kind of anarchistic individualism which they inherited from dadaism, a movement in which Breton as well as many other surrealists had participated and which, as already noted, had communistic connections.[208]

But to return to Rivera and his vogue in the United States even among anti-Marxist circles: in 1929, the year before Rivera first came here, he had been awarded a gold medal by the relatively conservative American Institute of Architects. Two years later the Arts Commission of Detroit, of which Edsel Ford was chairman, awarded him a commission for a series of frescoes in the Detroit Institute of Fine Arts. Much controversy was aroused by these and still more by the frescoes soon commissioned for Rockefeller Center in New York. A portrait of Lenin (Fig. 54), which Rivera insisted on placing in a fresco at Rockefeller Center in 1933, caused the Rockefeller management to interrupt the work, pay off the artist, and eventually to have the fresco destroyed, thereby stirring up a tremendous furor in the art world.[208a]

One of Rivera's assistants at Rockefeller Center was the American

[206] Quoted by T. H. Robsjohn-Gibbings, op.cit., p. 225. Dali was later attacked by the surrealist leader André Breton as having revealed Fascist tendencies by painting a portrait of one of Franco's ambassadors: see Wallace Fowlie, Age of Surrealism (Denver, Colo., 1950), p. 106. Breton, a former member of the French Communist Party who eventually underwent a sharp revulsion against communism, came to the United States during World War II.

[207] Robsjohn-Gibbings, op.cit., pp. 192-93. In its emphasis on the subconscious, surrealism has, of course, Freudian implications. While Freudianism had some supporters in Russia until the middle 1930's, it has since been completely rejected as bourgeois doctrine: see Joseph Wortis, Soviet Psychiatry (Baltimore, 1950), especially pp. 71-102 and 120.

[208] See Barr, Cubism and Abstract Art, p. 17; also Herbert Read, The Politics of the Unpolitical (London, 1943), p. 129.

[208a] With the proceeds from this fresco, Rivera painted a Marxist version of American history in the Lovestoneite New Workers' School in New York.

artist Ben Shahn, who had attracted the attention of Rivera by a series of paintings of Sacco and Vanzetti (Fig. 56). Shahn himself had become interested in socialism partly through the Sacco-Vanzetti case itself and, earlier, by reading Ernest Poole's novel of social reform, *The Harbor*.[209] Drawings by Shahn appeared in early issues of *Masses & Mainstream*.

According to many opponents of communism, some of the boldest attempts made by communists or their sympathizers to influence Americans by means of art have been made through the medium of the motion picture, which, it will be recalled, Lenin had praised as the most significant weapon of propaganda. In the 1920's—and later—Charlie Chaplin was only the most prominent of several movie actors accused of sympathy for radical causes. In 1930 a considerable uproar was aroused by the fact that the great Soviet Russian director, Eisenstein, signed a contract with Paramount Pictures at $3,000 a week. Six months later, after a violent campaign against Eisenstein in which he was repeatedly assailed as a "Red Dog," the famous director was dismissed by Paramount without being allowed to begin a picture. All he had accomplished was to prepare two scenarios— one of them made from Theodore Dreiser's *An American Tragedy* with the hearty approval of the author, who much later was to become a communist himself. After the Paramount episode, Eisenstein conceived the idea of making a picture in Mexico and obtained the backing of Upton Sinclair, the famous socialist writer. Sinclair raised the money, took charge of editing the immense amount of film sent back from Mexico by Eisenstein, and had it condensed into a motion picture issued in 1933 under the title of *Thunder over Mexico*. This was disapproved by Eisenstein, whose supporters maintained that Sinclair had carefully edited out all revolutionary implications.

One of the most violent of the public discussions on the question of communism in Hollywood was stirred up during the autumn of 1947 when several actors, directors, and others in the motion-picture industry testified before the Committee of the House of Representatives on Un-American Activities that communists or fellow travelers were dominating the Screen Writers' Guild. Various members of the Guild were brought before the Committee, and several of them were cited for contempt of Congress on refusing to state whether or not they were or had been members of the Communist Party, and were eventually jailed. One of them was Albert Maltz who had been made a scapegoat among American party-liners in February 1946 because he had the bad luck to write for the *New Masses* an article entitled "What Shall We Ask of Writers?" just before Stalin signaled for the post-war cultural purges.

[209] J. D. Morse, "Ben Shahn: an Interview," *Magazine of Art*, Vol. 37, No. 4 (April 1944), pp. 136-37. Sacco and Vanzetti were anarchists.

In 1951 the Committee on Un-American Activities likewise subpoenaed a number of prominent actors and other important figures in the film industry. Some of them—including actors Larry Parks and Sterling Hayden—testified that they were former members of the Communist Party but had broken off their communist connections.

Also well known in Hollywood was Hanns Eisler, the German-born composer against whom a writ of deportation was issued early in 1948 when he was accused of having joined the German Communist Party in 1926. Eisler (whose brother, Gerhart Eisler, was denounced by the Committee on Un-American Activities as the number-one communist agent in the United States and was later to jump bail and flee as a stowaway on the Polish motor ship *Batory*) had come to this country in 1940. He had soon made a reputation for his motion-picture scores and other music, and according to various ex-communists was prominent in spreading communist propaganda in the musical world.[210] Charged with being an undesirable alien, Hanns Eisler left the United States while his case was pending, and soon turned up in communist East Germany.

Such direct, or allegedly direct, connections as the above between Marxism and the arts in America have, however, been relatively limited in number and influence. As everyone knows, there are fundamental differences between Marxism and the American tradition, differences which so far have prevented Marxism from having a very wide appeal in this country, certainly in any direct way. Not the least of these differences is the characteristic American insistence on the political freedom of the individual now, and not just later in some future classless society. And this emphasis on individual freedom now (which if anything has more in common with aspects of anarchist theory than with Marxism) has usually had a particular appeal for artists, who almost by definition are exceptional individuals more or less individualistic by temperament. Consequently, Americans in general and American artists in particular, even those who feel that adequate economic freedom from want is lacking in this country, are likely to resent the kind of political and social regimentation which Marxians themselves ordinarily consider to be inherent in Marxism until the Marxian goal of the classless society has been achieved, and which is so pronounced in the "democratic centralism" of the Communist Party.

[210] *New York Herald Tribune*, Feb. 13, 1948, p. 21. Hanns Eisler wrote the music for the dramatization of Gorky's *The Mother*, which played in New York in 1935 and which has been called "unadorned Communist propaganda" by Ruth Fischer. *Stalin and German Communism*, p. 615. According to Budenz, *Men without Faces*, p. 241, Eisler had "served since 1935 as head of the International Music Bureau, connected with the Communist International, the purpose of which was to spread pro-Soviet allegiance among musicians, musical critics and composers the world over."

But although the *direct* effects of Marxism have been relatively limited in American art taken as a whole, there have been important factors helping to spread the *indirect* influence of Marxist, and especially of Russian Marxist, art in this country. In some cases this indirect and often unconscious influence has resulted from efforts within the American democratic tradition to meet the threat of Marxism by seeking to overcome various economic problems of capitalist society which have aroused the sharpest Marxist criticism, problems which in some cases, according to some critics of capitalism, have been better solved in Soviet Russia. Much art of social protest in the United States has been of this nature.

In other cases, the indirect impact of Marxism on non-Marxist art in America has been made possible by the fact that there are certain characteristics common to Marxism and the American democratic tradition which therefore encourage similar tendencies in the arts. Thus, both Marxism and American democracy, in theory if not in practice, tend to emphasize the virtues of a classless society, although the one stresses economic equality in the ownership of the means of production, the other political equality combined with equality of economic opportunity. Largely as a result of this jointly equalitarian spirit, in both cases (though much more so in Russia) the artist is under heavy pressure from the society in which he lives to conform to the prevailing mores. Moreover, both Marxism and the American tradition share an optimistic belief in progress and in the special importance of industrial and technological progress. Both, therefore, have tended to glorify the engineer and the manager of industry as "practical" men of action, rather than the "impractical" artist, and have tended also to regard art which does not serve some directly utilitarian purpose as irrelevant to "real" life. Like most working-class and middle-class people of our twentieth-century industrial civilization, the average proletarian Russian and the average middle-class American have both generally preferred relatively literal and "realistic" storytelling in art. It was no doubt largely for this reason that the superlatively realistic acting of the Moscow Art Theater not only was enthusiastically received when its troupe came to the United States in 1923, but brought to that Theater special recognition from the Soviet government under Stalin.

Besides the characteristics common to Marxism and the general American democratic tradition which have indirectly made it easier for some aspects of Marxist art to influence art in America, there are also, of course, Marxist characteristics which for several different reasons have appealed to special groups in the United States, many of them not socialist or communist sympathizers. Thus the high degree of contemporaneity, of "modernness," emphasized by much Marxist art—for example, by Soviet futurism and constructivism in the years immediately following the Revolution of 1917, and by the early Soviet films such as Eisenstein's *Potemkin*[211]—has had an appeal not only to American faddists and cultural snobs, but at the same time to many sincere artists, critics, and collectors interested in new means of expression often quite apart from any Marxist content. Then, too, the international spirit of this early Soviet art and of that of the Trotskyists has attracted many Americans with a cosmopolitan point of view, including many sincere and well-educated people who believe that true culture, true civilization, must transcend national boundaries. The Marxian emphasis on the common people has been sympathetically received by many democratic Americans, including many artists, some of them communists or socialists and some not, who have come to believe that most American art has lost touch with the everyday realities of American life. This point of view, for example, was characteristic of John Sloan and other members of the group of artists known to their detractors as the "Ash-can School": it is clearly reflected in the subject matter of Sloan's painting, "Backyards, Greenwich Village" (Fig. 50), executed in 1914 when Sloan was art editor of the *Masses* as well as a member of the Socialist Party. The tendency to regard art as a form of social expression rather than solely the product of an individual temperament achieved its widest currency in the United States during the great depression of the 1930's. It is the point of view reflected in the then widely popular "social-protest" painting of such artists with leftist sympathies as Gropper, Philip Evergood, and Mervin Jules. It was reflected also in the attitude of Stuart Davis toward his seemingly abstract paintings. And to a somewhat lesser degree it could be seen in the subject matter of works by Henry Billings, Moses and Raphael Soyer, and many other socially conscious painters of the period. In those days, indeed, it was the point of view accepted by many average Americans who had no real interest in Marxism *per se* but whose attention had been newly focused on economic and social problems by the depression.

Thus it must be remembered that aspects of Marxist art have appealed to many Americans and to American institutions for reasons that are not necessarily Marxist at all. Among such American institutions may be cited the Museum of Modern Art and the New School for Social Research in New York. The New School, for example, in 1930-1931 helped to popularize the Mexican fresco painters by giving wall space to Orozco (who, as noted above, was in sympathy with many aspects of Marxism)

[211] *Potemkin* was first shown in New York during the autumn of 1926. It (together with Pudovkin's *Mother*) had been highly praised by Mary Pickford and Douglas Fairbanks when they returned from a trip to Russia in the previous summer. Only one or two minor Russian films had circulated earlier in the United States. See J. Freeman, "The Soviet Cinema," in *Voices of October*, p. 217.

for his mural, *Russia* (Fig. 55), depicting Lenin, Stalin, and other Soviet leaders. Yet at the same time the authorities of the New School had Thomas Benton, the developing American regionalist, paint his murals of New York life entitled *City Activities*; so that the New School, although somewhat left of center in its approach to many educational and social problems, could scarcely be accused of being deliberately "communistic" or "socialistic" in any political sense.[211a]

More important has been the New York Museum of Modern Art, which since its founding in 1929 has necessarily been concerned with all new art movements, including those of Soviet Russia as well as others influenced by Soviet Russia. But the Museum of Modern Art has been interested primarily in new artistic *media* and *forms* rather than in any one specific kind of content, so that in most of its exhibition catalogues all mention of the political sympathies of even the most politically minded artists has been omitted. Because of its focus on modern art forms, particular attention has had to be paid to the more abstract and expressionistic kinds of art, including surrealism and including also the International Style in architecture, which was actually given its name by members of the Museum's staff.[212] Among the examples of modern art exhibited at the Museum have been many derived from, or influenced by, those varieties of early Soviet art which Lenin and Stalin condemned as too abstract and as therefore lacking in proper Marxist content. Thus, one of the American artists most favored by the Museum has been Alexander Calder, noted for his "mobiles" and "stabiles" constructed in wire and sheet metal. Yet the mobile, or construction that moves, had largely been developed by the great Russian constructivist Naum Gabo, who, inspired by the constructions of Picasso, had executed as early as 1920 a moving construction which he called *Kinetic Model*.[213] The close relation between the forms of some of Calder's earlier works and this kind of Russian constructivism seems particularly obvious if *Kiki's Nose* (Fig. 57), one of Calder's stabiles (or nonmoving constructions) made in 1931, is compared with the painting *Abstraction* (Fig. 58), executed by the Russian constructivist Lissitsky about 1922.[214] But although some of Calder's

[211a] It is true that Benton's work was included in an exhibition on "The Social Viewpoint in Art," organized by the John Reed Club of New York in 1933, a fact suggesting that his regionalism was then not so pronounced as it later became.

[212] P. C. Johnson, Museum of Modern Art, *Mies van der Rohe* (New York, 1947), p. 43. It was so named by H.-R. Hitchcock and Johnson at the insistence of Alfred H. Barr, Jr.

[213] See Ruth Olson and Abraham Chanin, Museum of Modern Art, *Naum Gabo; Antoine Pevsner* (New York, 1948), p. 18; also J. J. Sweeney, Museum of Modern Art, *Alexander Calder* (New York, 1943), p. 33. The latter rightly points out that Calder developed the mobile beyond Gabo (who was anticipated by Duchamp).

[214] Calder was trained as an engineer and thus not unnaturally tended to be sympathetic to the constructivists' glorification of "the Machine." In his mobiles Calder

works (especially before he came under the influence of the surrealist Miró) do show the influence of some elements of constructivism, this does not mean that they therefore necessarily reflect a Russian Marxist content. For that matter, it will be recalled that Gabo, one originator of mobiles (who with his brother, Antoine Pevsner, was given a special exhibition at the Museum of Modern Art in 1948), had left Russia with those constructivists who were *not* willing to devote the subject, form, and content of their art solely to the revolution.

While special attention has been devoted by the Museum to many abstract tendencies in modern painting and sculpture and to that related movement in architecture which it named the International Style, it has, of course, by no means restricted itself to these. For one thing, like the New School for Social Research, it has helped to encourage that modern revival of relatively realistic mural painting in fresco which, though it happened to originate with Mexican communist and revolutionary artists, spread far beyond revolutionary circles and was accepted by many who had no connection whatever with socialism or communism. The Museum has similarly shown much interest in the arts of South America simply for their contributions to modern art. The fact that—along with the works of numerous South American noncommunist artists—the Museum of Modern Art, like other American museums, has exhibited the paintings of the Brazilian communist Candido Portinari[215] is thus essentially irrelevant, the more so because Portinari's communism had not been very specifically expressed in his art aside from his interest in subjects dealing with the laboring man.

The Museum of Modern Art has also encouraged interest in folk art, partly because folk art, like other "primitive" arts, has been glorified by admirers of abstraction for its expressive simplification and distortion of the forms of nature. Thus the Museum's approach to folk art is very different from that of the Soviet Union, where this point of view would be attacked as "formalistic." Moreover, in the Soviet Union, in contrast to the United States, a distinction is drawn between primitive art and folk art because Marxians look upon primitive art as the product of a prehistoric classless society, whereas folk art, they say, is produced in societies

---

also reflects the influence of Mondrian, the Dutch De Stijl painter: he was led to enter the field of abstract art by a visit to Mondrian's Paris studio in 1930. See Sweeney, *op.cit.*, p. 28, and the *Museum of Modern Art Bulletin*, Vol. 18, No. 3 (Spring 1951), p. 8.

[215] The exhibition was held in 1940. In 1941 Portinari painted four frescoes on the walls of the Hispanic Foundation of the Library of Congress at Washington, frescoes paid for with funds appropriated by the Brazilian government and the Office of the Coordinator of Inter-American Affairs headed by Nelson Rockefeller. Portinari was one of the leading Brazilian communists who fled to Montevideo early in 1948: see *Time*, Jan. 19, 1948, p. 40.

with class divisions and will therefore disappear when the forthcoming classless society is achieved. Nevertheless, in both the United States and Soviet Russia, folk art can to some degree be admired as an expression of the "common man" everywhere as well as an expression of regionalistic nationalism. The great exhibition of folk art held at the Museum of Modern Art in 1932 was entitled *American Folk Art: the Art of the Common Man in America, 1750-1900*. And it is significant that this exhibition, which foreshadowed the revival of folk art under the New Deal, was held during the depths of the depression when interest in the problems of the common man was being partly, if indirectly, aroused by Marxist criticism of capitalism as the cause of those problems. In the years that followed, also, the Museum helped to foster certain kinds of art (notably those connected with public housing and large-scale planning) by means of which the New Deal was seeking to solve some of the economic and social problems that had come to a head during the depression, problems that in some cases had been encountered also in the U.S.S.R.

Everyone knows how under the New Deal the federal government, and to a lesser degree the state governments, undertook a much greater responsibility for the welfare of citizens of lower than average income. Although the question is still occasionally debated as to whether the New Deal was "socialism," most authorities now seem to agree than in Franklin D. Roosevelt's view the New Deal was engaged not in fostering socialism but in tiding capitalism over a series of crises—that it was, indeed, not a single over-all plan but a series of extemporizations[216] in the form of state capitalism. Certainly the Communist Party had at first sharply opposed Roosevelt, and continued to do so after the American recognition of Soviet Russia in 1933. Late in 1935, however, the Communist Party reversed itself and began to support the New Deal, including its art projects, in harmony with the changing Russian foreign policy. For with the Seventh World Congress of the Communist International, held at Moscow in July 1935, the new Russian policy of a Popular Front against fascism had finally been defined.[217] Once this shift in the party line had taken place, the American Communist Party—though under attack from the Special House Committee for the Investigation of Un-American Activities as set up in 1938 under the chairmanship of Martin Dies—continued to support Roosevelt until October 1939. In that month its leader, Earl Browder, was arrested for passport fraud, some two months after the Nazi-Soviet nonaggression pact. Following the Nazi attack on

216 For example, this view of the New Deal was expressed by Miss Frances Perkins, Roosevelt's Secretary of Labor, in a speech before the Program in American Civilization, Princeton University, Mar. 8, 1950.

217 The policy of the Popular Front had, however, been tentatively formulated as early as 1933. See Gitlow, *The Whole of Their Lives*, pp. 257-58.

Russia, Roosevelt again received communist support, but this was once more withdrawn from the Democrats after World War II.

Yet even though the New Deal was originally opposed by American communists, its emphasis on social welfare, as opposed to individualistic laissez faire, had early helped to pave the way for some indirect Marxist influence in this country largely because many of the problems of the New Deal were somewhat similar to those already met by Soviet Russia. In particular, Russia had already developed a very concentrated organization for centralizing both the national and social aspects of planning on a huge scale. Such planning—which in Russia was based on the Marxian doctrine that man differs from other animals in consciously planning to achieve social goals[218]—had commenced when Lenin formed a state planning commission as early as 1920, but had greatly increased in importance with the Five Year Plans, the first of which began in 1928. Since the New Deal felt the necessity of developing a much greater amount of large-scale planning than had ever before been known in this country, the Russian example doubtless was something of a spur to the United States as well as to many other countries hit by the depression.[219]

When bitter controversy arose over the degree of centralization that might be permitted in the United States, at first the tendency under the leadership of the more radical elements within the New Deal was for a considerable amount of centralization. As time went on, however, partly as a kind of reaction against the ever increasing centralization of power that was taking place in Soviet Russia under Stalin, it gradually became evident that the American planners who in the long run received the approval of large numbers of their countrymen were those who held that neither large-scale planning nor its administration should be too completely centralized. The Tennessee Valley Authority, for example, with its vast engineering and architectural works, was finally carried through successfully under the direction of David Lilienthal, who believes in a multiple economy in which centralized planning under government auspices is restricted to a limited number of certain kinds of problems, and who even then urges that the administration of all plans be decentralized.[220] And Robert Moses, New York City's great planner of parks and parkways who has had so profound an effect on American landscape and highway design, has always insisted that regional and local decentralization of governmental authority in planning is necessary if the American democratic tradition is to be preserved.

[218] For a summary of Marx's views on planning, see especially Vernon Venable, *Human Nature: the Marxian View* (New York, 1946), particularly p. 78 and pp. 155ff.

[219] For the relation of socialism and of Soviet Russia to planning, see Edward H. Carr, *The Soviet Impact on the Western World* (New York, 1947), pp. 20ff.

[220] D. E. Lilienthal, *T.V.A.—Democracy on the March* (New York and London, 1944), chaps. 14, 15, 18.

During the New Deal, as part of its large-scale plans for combating the depression, the federal government, with the encouragement of President Roosevelt himself, first faced the problem of enabling artists to survive by giving them government commissions.[221] Late in 1933 the Department of the Treasury set up a relief program under which nearly 4,000 needy artists executed some 700 murals in public buildings as well as over 15,000 other works of art before the project closed in the following summer. The Treasury then launched a somewhat different project aimed less at relief than at the decoration of public buildings by the most competent artists available. Meanwhile, the Federal Art Project of the Works Progress Administration was established in 1935 to take over relief for other artists, enrolling at its peak over 6,000 persons. Before it came to a close in 1939 the members of the project had developed an enormous Index of American Design, had conducted free art classes averaging 60,000 students a month, and had painted many additional murals in public buildings, besides carrying on numerous other activities.

Because the Mexican fresco painters, and especially the communist Diego Rivera, had begun to have a great vogue in this country just before the New Deal began, it is not surprising that the influence of these men was felt in many of the mural paintings executed under the various New Deal projects, most of them by artists who were not socialists, communists, or fellow travelers. The influence of the Mexicans sometimes manifested itself directly in the use of the revived fresco technique, and less directly in helping to foster subject matter with more conscious "social significance," more criticism of economic and social conditions, than had previously been found in American art. Fairly typical examples of this socially-conscious subject matter—although particularly well executed—are the murals which Henry Varnum Poor painted in 1935 under the second art project of the Department of the Treasury for the Department of Justice Building in Washington (Fig. 59). In one of them entitled *T.V.A. Worker*, the chief figure is depicted with a kind of halo, apparently because he is engaged in working on a great social project and is therefore considered to be especially worthy of canonization by mankind. Whereas in the companion mural, *Pleading the Gold Case*, the lawyer who pleads for the retention of the gold standard is represented as thin-lipped and sharp-faced presumably because he was believed to place the value of gold above that of humanity.

One mural sponsored by this second phase of the Treasury Department's program aroused particular controversy. This was one of the two

---

[221] The original suggestion is said to have come from Roosevelt's friend and former schoolmate, the artist George Biddle, who had been impressed by hearing that the Mexican government had hired Rivera, Orozco, and other artists to paint murals in public buildings at mechanics' wages.

murals painted by Rockwell Kent for the Federal Post Office Building in Washington, and installed in 1937. Part of the painting, the subject of which was the delivery of mail to Puerto Rico by airplane, depicted a colored woman holding a letter on which was an inscription in a strange language. When eventually the language was recognized as Eskimo, the inscription was translated by the Arctic explorer Stefansson as follows: "To the peoples of Puerto Rico, our friends. Go ahead, let us change chiefs. That alone can make us equal and free." Whereupon Kent was accused of urging revolt.[222]

Not very long thereafter, in 1939, an investigator for the Committee on Un-American Activities stated before it that Kent was a communist, presumably because Kent was known to be a member of a considerable number of organizations usually considered as part of the Communist Front.[223] Kent promptly wrote to Martin Dies, the chairman of the Committee, maintaining that he was not a member of the Communist Party, that his opinions and public actions had never been influenced by the party and that he had never held or advanced views to any degree inconsistent with our American democracy.[224] It would seem, therefore, if Kent's own repeated statements are accepted, that he is one of the considerable number of American artists who sympathize with many of the social aims of Marxian communism, but who are too individualistic ever to conform completely to the rigid control of the Communist Party. Yet, among other activities, he has been a contributing editor of the *New Masses*, served as chairman of a conference supporting the *Daily Worker* in April 1945, and was president of the International Workers Order, a fraternal insurance agency founded in 1930 which has been described as "organized by Communists and . . . under the control of Communists from the beginning. . . ."[225]

It was natural for many of the artists who participated in the art projects of the New Deal, especially those who worked for the W.P.A., to develop a new interest in the point of view of the workingman, for

[222] See Rockwell Kent, *This Is My Own* (New York, 1940), p. 307.

[223] In 1949 and in 1951 the House Committee on Un-American Activities listed Kent as having been "affiliated with at least eighty-five Communist-front organizations": see the *New York Times*, Apr. 19, 1949, p. 6, and the *New York Herald Tribune*, Apr. 5, 1951, p. 39.

[224] Kent, *op.cit.*, pp. 356-57.

[225] See Budenz, *Men without Faces*, pp. 211 and 191. In April 1951 Kent, as president of the International Workers Order, was a witness before the New York Supreme Court in a suit brought by the State Insurance Department in an effort to have the I.W.O. dissolved on the ground that it was communist dominated: see the *New York Herald Tribune*, Apr. 4, 1951, p. 19, and Apr. 5, p. 2. Late in June 1951 a justice of the New York Supreme Court ordered the "dissolution and liquidation" of the I.W.O. as a "political front for a revolutionary group": *ibid.*, July 1, 1951, section 2, p. 3.

like workingmen and unlike most artists, W.P.A. artists were paid according to a fixed scale of wages. Understandably, therefore, they too formed trade unions to protect their common interests, and in some cases these trade unions and similar organizations of artists were no doubt partly inspired by prototypes which existed in Mexico and also in Soviet Russia, and which there had been founded under the auspices of members of Communist parties. Among the most prominent of the American organizations were the Artists' Union, which was established in 1933; the United American Artists, which became an affiliate of the C.I.O.; and the American Artists' Congress, founded in 1936 to combat war and fascism and to defend the individual artist's civil rights through collective action.[226] The Artists' Union for three years (1934-1937) published a magazine, *Art Front*, to which such well-known radical artists as Gropper, Lozowick, and Maurice Becker contributed, and of which Ben Shahn and Stuart Davis were editors. Not only did communists found some of the artists' organizations of this kind, but within some of them they greatly helped to encourage the spread of proletarian subject matter already popularized among leftist artists by the John Reed clubs. Moreover, in some cases communists made every effort to take over artists' organizations, and members who declined to follow the party line were driven out. For example, several leading members of the American Artists' Congress, including the painters George Biddle and Niles Spencer, the sculptor William Zorach, and the critic-historians Lewis Mumford and Meyer Schapiro, resigned from the congress because they refused to approve the Russian attack on Finland.[227] As a result of occasional episodes of this kind, many conservatives and some middle of the roaders became convinced that not only the artists' organizations founded during the New Deal but the art projects of the New Deal itself were all helping to lead directly to the triumph of communism in the United States. Thus, shortly after the House Committee on Un-American Activities had reported in January 1939 that "a rather large number of the employees on the Federal Theater Project are either members of the Communist Party or are sympathetic to the Communist Party," Congress cut off all appropriations, and the project was forced to close.

In addition to penetrating many of the art organizations under the New Deal, American communists and their sympathizers also often supported

[226] H. M. Kallen, *Art and Freedom* (New York, 1942), II, pp. 895-96.
[227] *Art Digest*, Vol. 14, No. 15 (May 1, 1940), p. 14. The American Artists' Congress and the United American Artists joined with the League of American Writers in running an Artists' and Writers' Congress which met early in June 1941, and which passed a resolution condemning the European war as "a brutal shameless struggle," two weeks before Germany invaded Russia. A few weeks later most of these organizations were calling for the utmost aid to Soviet Russia.

the efforts of American minorities, and particularly the Negro minority, to achieve equal rights in the arts as well as in other aspects of American life. This was part of a large-scale attempt to win Negroes to communism, and during the early years of the depression was carried on under the slogan "Self-Determination for Negroes in the Black Belt" in accordance with a program laid down in 1928 by the Sixth World Congress of the Comintern. In 1925 communists had been responsible for organizing the American Negro Labor Congress, later called the League of Struggle for American Rights. In 1936 they had helped to establish the National Negro Congress. This was captured completely by the communists in 1940, but by 1947 was dissolved, according to some authorities because the communists had decided to devote their full attention to infiltrating and capturing the National Association for the Advancement of Colored People—an attempt which failed.

As long as the revolutionary slogan, "Self-Determination in the Black Belt," prevailed, American communists often sought to foster revolutionary Negro art. However, in 1935 the communist line changed as part of the change in world communist strategy. For now, with the Popular Front against fascism, the communists subordinated the idea of revolution to that of democratic resistance to fascism. In American Negro affairs this meant that the party line now for a time supported the position of the National Association for the Advancement of Colored People, which had formerly been attacked as "reformist." Following the Nazi-Soviet pact, moreover, the communists ceased to emphasize the importance of the American Negro and Negro art because of the Nazi notions of race. And even after Nazi Germany attacked the Soviet Union in 1941 all agitation for Negro rights (and, correspondingly, for Negro art) continued to be played down, but for a different reason. For now the communists feared that self-conscious militancy on the part of American Negroes would destroy national unity: at a time when the primary goal of the Soviet Union was to win the war, other aims had to be postponed. But once World War II had ended and postwar tensions began to increase between Russia and her wartime allies, the communists once more revived the program of "Self-Determination in the Black Belt," and in 1951 even moved their national party headquarters to Harlem. Again some attempt was made to foster Negro art.

One of the most important Negroes won over to sympathy with Soviet Russia and important aspects of the party line was Dr. W. E. B. Du Bois, the educator and writer who eventually became a contributing editor of the *New Masses* and *Masses & Mainstream*. A founder of the National Association for the Advancement of Colored People (in which he was a major figure until asked to resign in 1948), Dr. Du Bois had begun to urge as early as 1915 that due recognition be given to Negro artists in the United States.[228] And this movement had been aided by a growing interest in African Negro sculpture which as early as 1907 had inspired Picasso in the experiments leading to the development of cubism and other phases of the modern movement in art. Interest in the arts of the Negro had also been fostered by the increasing vogue for jazz, which at times has been praised by communists, among others, as an important American folk art. However, among communists the party line has varied in its point of view toward jazz, depending on the attitude toward folk art prevailing within the Soviet Union at the given time, on the prevailing party line toward minorities and the race problem, and on the attitude of Russia toward the United States.

In Russia itself, American jazz had first become widely known in 1925 when a small jazz band made up of American Negroes visited Moscow. With the extreme proletarianization of art under the first Five Year Plan, jazz fell into disfavor as a "bourgeois" product, but was revived in 1932 in connection with Stalin's new slogan, "Life is better, Life is gayer." In the middle thirties Russia even established a state jazz band. However, with the Nazi-Soviet pact of 1939, jazz began to decline once more; and under the anti-Americanism which dominated Russian foreign policy after World War II, jazz so completely lost official favor for a time that the once enormously popular state jazz band was abolished.

In those periods when jazz has been in favor in Russia, or else when the party line in the United States has especially sought to foster "Self-Determination in the Black Belt," the American Communist Party has usually upheld jazz either as a Negro "folk" art, or as a product of a minority downtrodden under "capitalism." During the 1930's, after the revival of jazz in Russia at the end of the first Five Year Plan, the party line in this country usually made a distinction between those aspects of jazz regarded as Negro folk music, and therefore considered good, and the more "commercial" varieties of jazz, which were looked upon as "capitalistic," and therefore bad. A somewhat different line was to prevail after World War II, with jazz now regarded as derived from the music of a laboring people, the American Negroes, and as representing a struggle led by Negro musicians to liberate music from the conditions imposed upon it by an evil "monopolized commodity production system." Bebop was thought to exemplify this contradiction and struggle within jazz in a

[228] See J. A. Porter, *Modern Negro Art* (New York, 1943), p. 98. Du Bois, besides being a founder of the N.A.A.C.P., was its director of publications and research from 1910 until 1934, and its director of special research from 1944 until 1948 when he was asked to resign at a time when he was active in behalf of Henry Wallace and of the Progressive Party. See Shirley Graham, "Why Was Du Bois Fired," *Masses & Mainstream*, Vol. 1, No. 9 (Nov. 1948), pp. 15-26; also Wilson Record, *The Negro and the Communist Party* (Chapel Hill, N.C., 1951), especially p. 264, note.

heightened form—as possessing "rich imaginative and inventive . . . qualities" on the one hand, and yet as also tending toward mere "barren formalistic experiment" because of the conditions of modern life under capitalism. But even at its worst, bebop was said to have the great advantage of encouraging whites to collaborate with Negroes.[229]

According to some authorities on Negro art, it was the Federal Art Project of the W.P.A. which gave many Negro artists their first real chance to work on an equal basis with white men.[230] Certainly some of the artists' organizations founded during the period of the New Deal gave particularly strong support to the campaign for equal rights for Negro artists. This was notably true of the Artists' Union, whose magazine, Art Front, published articles on the problems of race, nationality, and art, including one by the well-known art historian and critic, Meyer Schapiro. In this article Schapiro subscribed to the more or less Marxian view that social class rather than race or nation in the last analysis determines "the conception of what is or should be American."[231]

One of the chief problems which faced the New Deal was the question as to how far the federal government should enter the field of housing. As everyone knows, the New Deal eventually encouraged government-subsidized housing as the only way of securing adequate shelter for the economically lowest third of the nation. However, so powerful was the American tradition of private initiative in the building industry, so strong the general opposition to "the government in business," that the only way in which sufficient public support could be gained for housing legislation was by putting it before the people not on its merits as a housing program but as giving employment to workmen in the building trades.

For some time during the New Deal the communists were silent on the housing question, both because they opposed Roosevelt until late in 1935, and because "orthodox" Marxians, following Engels, have at times opposed any alleviation of the workers' lot in an effort to avoid possible postponement of the proletarian revolution. However, in September 1936, the *Communist*, then the most authoritative party magazine in this country, finally came out in support of a housing program in an effort to win working-class support and thereby gain control of the whole program.

The government-subsidized housing erected under the New Deal was

[229] For jazz in Russia see Jelagin, *op.cit.*, especially pp. 255ff. The party line in this country was reflected in Sidney Finkelstein's discussion of jazz and bebop in "What About Bebop?" *Masses & Mainstream*, Vol. 1, No. 7 (Sept. 1948), pp. 68-76; also his book, *Jazz: a People's Music* (New York, 1948).

[230] Porter, *op.cit.*, p. 127.

[231] Meyer Schapiro, "Race, Nationality and Art," *Art Front*, Vol. 2, No. 4 (Mar. 1936), pp. 10-12. For Schapiro's views on art as an expression of class also see his previously cited article in the *Marxist Quarterly*, "Nature of Abstract Art," especially p. 88.

mostly of two chief types, both of which were derived ultimately from European prototypes originally developed, in part at least, under socialist influence, mainly because socialists were among the first to become interested in the housing problem. One of the two was that superblock type of row house oriented to the sun, and placed on the extra large city-block upheld in various writings of the Fabian socialist, Raymond Unwin. As already indicated, this type of housing had been further developed in Austria and in Germany—both by socialists and by liberals such as Gropius—especially during the period of the Weimar Republic when social democracy had been particularly strong (Figs. 30 and 31). In the United States it has been much used for government-subsidized urban housing, such as the Williamsburg development in Brooklyn (Fig. 60), built in 1936-1937 under the Emergency Housing Division of the Public Works Administration but financed through private contracts. And more recently some of the principles—but some only—underlying this type of housing have been followed in real-estate developments built under private auspices, including Stuyvesant Town in Manhattan, erected after World War II by the Metropolitan Life Insurance Company.

The other variety of housing much used by the New Deal was the English garden city, "invented" by Ebenezer Howard and fostered by Fabianism and guild socialism. The actual buildings of the garden cities laid out under the New Deal (Fig. 61) show, however, some influence from German architecture of the International Style. These garden cities of the New Deal were also partly inspired by an earlier American garden city, Radburn, New Jersey, designed in 1929 under the influence of the English examples and like them built under private auspices. The garden-city type of government-built housing is best exemplified by the "Greenbelt" towns, four of which were projected, and three—Greenbelt, Maryland (Fig. 61), Greendale, Wisconsin, and Greenhills, Ohio—were carried out. Promoted by Rexford Tugwell as head of the Resettlement Administration primarily on the grounds of making work for building trades, they actually were in large part built by P.W.A. labor. Tugwell himself warmly believed in the ideas of Ebenezer Howard, while Clarence Stein, the able architect of Radburn who also served as adviser for the Greenbelt towns, is an avowed disciple of Howard and of Raymond Unwin, and likewise acknowledges the inspiration of his friend Lewis Mumford.

Although the Greenbelt towns followed the precedent of the English garden cities in being run as cooperatives, in them one of the most essential elements of the English garden city—namely, local industry—was not planned for. The result was that the towns almost inevitably became housing not for workingmen and their families but for members of the white-collar class with sufficient means to be able to commute to work in the nearest city. And with the return of prosperity and the decline of the New Deal, American suspicion of any business not conducted by individual private initiative once more increased in strength, so that in 1947 the cooperative stores at Greenbelt were being sharply assailed as monopolistic, while the houses of the town were eventually sold to private owners. However, the new contributions to town planning made at Radburn and at the Greenbelt towns have exerted great influence abroad, and particularly in social democratic Sweden, communist Poland, and socialist Britain. Even in the United States more planned communities of this general type are being laid out under private initiative than is commonly supposed. Many of them are built or underwritten by great insurance companies as a form of investment—for example, Fresh Meadows (on Long Island in the outskirts of New York) and Park Forest (near Chicago), both begun in 1946.

The world-wide depression that gave rise to the New Deal in this country was, of course, also largely responsible for bringing the Nazis to power in Germany, and consequently for the migration of so many German artists to other countries including the United States. Because of their exaggerated nationalism, the Nazis violently opposed all modern abstract art, including the International Style in architecture, as being insufficiently national and Germanic. Thus some varieties of art important during the mildly socialistic Weimar Republic were now most sharply attacked. As already mentioned, the famous Bauhaus, like other centers of modern art in Germany, was closed as "bolshevistic" and "degenerate," in spite of the historical fact that the so-called "bolshevistic" art which it encouraged had long been proscribed in Soviet Russia itself.

It was during this period that several leading members of the Bauhaus group left Germany, notably Walter Gropius, Ludwig Mies van der Rohe, László Moholy-Nagy, and also Joseph Albers, Marcel Breuer, and Herbert Bayer. After only a brief stay in England, Gropius was called to Harvard, where he became chairman of the department of architecture in the Graduate School of Design, and where he called Breuer to join him for a time. Mies van der Rohe was made chairman of the department of architecture at Illinois Institute of Technology (then called Armour Institute); while Moholy-Nagy became the first head of the New Bauhaus in Chicago (later refounded and renamed the Institute of Design), of which he was still director at the time of his death in 1946. It will be recalled that Moholy-Nagy, with Albers, was responsible for developing at the Bauhaus a pedagogical method based in part on Russian constructivism, though with any specifically Russian or communist content omitted. This method of teaching he brought with him to the New Bauhaus and the Institute of Design at Chicago; and to a lesser degree, also, it was to be introduced at Harvard by Gropius, at Black Mountain College and Yale by Joseph Albers, and by Mies van der Rohe at the Illinois Institute of Technology with which the Chicago Institute of Design combined after Moholy-Nagy's death.

Most of the modern artists who left Germany when the Nazis were gaining power, and who migrated to the United States, were not socialists in any formal or active political sense even though often artistically radical. This became true even of the painter George Grosz who, although he had participated in leftist political agitation in Germany immediately after World War I, had withdrawn from politics in the thirties after he came to this country to live. Nevertheless, many of these German architects and artists, like Gropius, regard themselves as stimulated by the artistic tradition of William Morris (who, it will be remembered, subscribed to some of the social and political principles of Marxism, though not to its materialism) so that they too believe in the close relationship of art to life, and thus to economic and social problems. However, their approach to such problems—like that of Morris himself—has usually had an ethical basis rather than the fundamentally economic basis characteristic of Marxism.

Of these émigré artists, Moholy-Nagy was to exert an especially strong influence on modern art in the United States, mainly through his books. We have already seen how as a youth in Hungary after World War I, Moholy-Nagy had come to consider himself a social, as well as an artistic, revolutionary, but his revolutionary art had been disapproved by the Hungarian Communist Party as too abstract and individualistic. Yet in spite of his almost anarchistic revolutionary individualism, Moholy-Nagy, like most other members of the Bauhaus group, was always deeply interested in social improvements and admired all who worked for social reform. That he regarded Marx and Lenin merely as two of those who had sought such reform is indicated in one of his books published in this country in which he wrote: "Under the pressure of new needs openminded resolute individuals emerged with fervent hopes for a better social order and for which they were ready to fight and sacrifice. . . . From the encyclopedists and Voltaire and Rousseau, the way led to Fourier, Proudhon, Marx, Bakunin, Kropotkin, Lenin. . . ." Nor did Moholy-Nagy limit himself to the socialists, anarchists, and communists just cited but went on to include in this list of social reformers scientists such as Einstein and Pavlov; several nonsocialist musicians, writers, and architects (including Gropius, Le Corbusier, and Frank Lloyd Wright); and several painters (among them Kandinsky, Picasso, the Russian suprematist Malevich, and the Dutch artist Mondrian).[232]

[232] László Moholy-Nagy, *Vision in Motion* (Chicago, 1947), p. 61.

Nevertheless, in certain respects Moholy-Nagy's point of view resembled that of Marx and apparently reflected in an indirect way the influence of Marxism. Like Marx, he maintained that "the so-called 'unpolitical' approach of art is a fallacy," and insisted that "the artist has a formative ideological function."[233] Like Marx, he attacked capitalism as a system imposed on labor, without plan in its social aspects, and with the end of squeezing out profits to their limit. Like Marx, again, he deplored the separation of fine and applied art and held that technological progress, in art as in everything else (Fig. 32), should be exploited for the benefit of all people and all peoples. But although he subscribed to the Marxian concept of the revolution, Moholy-Nagy—like the anarchist Bakunin, whom he greatly admired—sharply differed from Marx in his concept of the nature of the revolution. For he wholeheartedly agreed with Bakunin's statement that "a revolution must be social, not political,"[234] insisting that "the revolutionist should always remain conscious that the class struggle is, in the last analysis, not about capital, nor the means of production, but in actuality it concerns the right of an individual to a satisfying occupation, work that meets the inner needs, a normal way of life, and a real release of human powers."[235] In short, Moholy-Nagy rejected the primarily economic and political basis of Marxian materialism for an emphasis on the freedom of the individual now, rather than in some future classless society, a point of view also in sharp opposition to the authoritarian "democratic centralism" of Soviet Russia and of the Communist Party. And it was a point of view not only in sympathy with the anarchism of Bakunin or Kropotkin and the socialism of William Morris, but also with the individualism of the American democratic tradition. It is interesting to note in this connection that Moholy-Nagy's regard for democratic individualism seems to have increased during his years in the United States, doubtless as a result of the influence of the American environment upon him.[236]

Moholy-Nagy has been discussed at some length in this book primarily because of his sympathy with some aspects of anarchism and socialism, and because through his writings and his teaching he exerted such unusually wide influence on the arts of design in the United States. It must be remembered, however, that while other influential members of

[233] *Ibid.*, p. 29.   [234] Sibyl Moholy-Nagy, *Moholy-Nagy*, p. 234.

[235] L. Moholy-Nagy, *The New Vision* (New York, 1938), p. 16.

[236] See Moholy-Nagy, *Vision in Motion*, p. 48, where he interprets the word democracy, as he says, "in its essential original meaning, culminating in the philosophy of the best of the American revolutionaries, such as Jefferson, Paine and Whitman." While it is true that these great Americans have also been glorified by communists, particularly during the Popular Front, as exemplifying "democracy" in the Russian sense of the word, Moholy-Nagy's admiration for them seems to have been based on their individualism as well as on their democratic spirit.

the Bauhaus group have largely shared Moholy-Nagy's views in regard to design, many of them have not agreed with his political ideas. For example, we have seen that the political views of Walter Gropius, the founder of the Bauhaus, are those of a liberal and democrat who in art stresses the kind of cooperation and collective effort previously found in the medieval guild system and the ideas of William Morris. So important to Gropius is this kind of cooperation that the noted firm of American architects of which he is a member is actually called the Architects Collaborative, and all of the members are considered to be on an equal footing.

Clearly, then, while some aspects of Moholy-Nagy's philosophy could appeal to American democratic individualism, the point of view of Walter Gropius and other former members of the Bauhaus staff could in major respects appeal to that equalitarianism which is also such an important factor in the American tradition. It is thus not surprising that the Bauhaus group has been able to exert so profound an influence on the arts and on the education of artist and architect in the United States. Moreover, the theories of design held by the group have been fostered in the field of art criticism by the popularity in this country of the writings and lectures of Herbert Read, the famous English anarcho-socialist critic of art and literature. For like the Bauhaus, Read reflects in many ways the influence not only of William Morris but of constructivism as well; and his theory of art education has even been described by a friend as "based on a frank acceptance of the principles of the Bauhaus school to which he is attached by a natural predisposition."[237]

Because all of these men have to a considerable degree been interested in the social aspects of art and architecture they could be particularly influential during the 1930's when the depression had brought the United States to a new consciousness of social problems. At the same time, the cosmopolitanism of many of their theories of art could appeal to the increasing number of Americans who were becoming convinced that only through international cooperation can aggressor nations be controlled and further world wars prevented. Also the close attention that they have paid to solving local climatic problems in architecture could prove attractive to American regionalists. In thus appealing to American audiences on several different grounds, these artists, architects, and critics have been able to exert an enormous influence on American art and art education. And through the medium of their principles and beliefs perhaps the strongest indirect influence of some aspects (but some aspects only) of Marx's critique of capitalism has affected the art of the United States.

[237] See E. H. Ramsden, "Herbert Read's Philosophy of Art," in Herbert Treece, ed., *Herbert Read, an Introduction to His Work by Various Hands* (London, 1944), p. 48.

Yet because their social awareness, their collectivism, is fundamentally artistic rather than economic or political, they cannot justly be called Marxians. And because these men—whether socialists or liberals or simply artists—do not stress any specifically nationalistic spirit in art, they were far from having any basic sympathy for the variety of Marxism then most powerful, the relatively nationalistic Russian Marxism characteristic of Stalin and his followers including those communists in the United States who followed the Communist Party line.

Thus it is clear that attacks on *all* "modern" art as "Communistic" or "Socialistic"—attacks like that leveled by Representative Dondero of Michigan in speeches delivered before the House beginning in 1949[238]—cannot be accurate: the problem is not so simple as all that. For one thing, such attacks too often forget that before World War II many thoroughly patriotic Americans, disturbed by the rising power of nazism, joined organizations of the Popular Front which only later were to be considered subversive. Similarly, during World War II many loyal Americans, including many artists, considered it patriotic to admire the Russian stand and counterattack against the Nazis, and therefore innocently joined organizations to forward Russian-American friendship, some of which, however, were under communist control. Still other Americans, simply interested in fostering honest liberalism, joined groups later said to have been taken over by communist sympathizers, groups such as the Independent Citizens Committee of the Arts, Sciences and Professions, of which Mrs. Franklin D. Roosevelt was a member for a time. This committee, founded in 1944 as the Independent Voters Committee of Arts and Sciences to support the reelection of President Roosevelt, closely followed the Communist Party line and ended up

---

[238] For Dondero's speeches see the *Congressional Record*, Mar. 11, 1949, pp. 2364-65; Mar. 25, 1949, pp. 3297-98; May 17, 1949, pp. 6487-90; Aug. 16, 1949, pp. 11811-14. In his speech of August 16, Dondero attacked nonacademic art as communistic in the following words: "The human art termites, disciples of multiple 'isms' that compose so-called modern art, [are] boring industriously to destroy the high standards and priceless traditions of academic art. . . ." He went on to accuse all defenders of modern art of upholding the "party-line." Mr. Dondero apparently knew that the "isms" to which he objected were attacked by Lenin as early at 1920 and largely expelled from Russia, and that Stalin had continued to attack them as "formalistic" or "mechanistic."

For replies to Dondero, made by Representatives Plumley of Vermont and Javits of New York, see the *Congressional Record* for June 16, 1949, and August 23, 1949. In March 1950 the directors of the Museum of Modern Art in New York, the Institute of Contemporary Art, Boston, and the Whitney Museum of American Art, New York, issued "A Statement on Modern Art" in which they declared, "We . . . reject the assumption that art which is esthetically an innovation must somehow be socially or politically subversive, and therefore un-American. We deplore the reckless and ignorant use of political or moral terms in attacking modern art. We recall that the Nazis . . . and . . . the Soviets suppressed modern art. . . . and that Nazi officials insisted and Soviet officials still insist upon a hackneyed realism saturated with nationalistic propaganda."

among the backers of Henry Wallace. By that time many of the original noncommunist members had already resigned.[239] For American opposition to the communists had enormously increased, partly as a result of evidence uncovered by the House Committee on Un-American Activities in 1947, and especially as a result of communist activities in Greece, Italy, and France, and of the communist coup in Czechoslovakia early in 1948. On July 20, 1948, eleven of the leaders of the Communist Party were arrested by the F.B.I. and indicted under the Smith Act, passed in 1940, for conspiring to teach the overthrow of the United States government by force or violence. And on June 20, 1951 a year after the beginning of communist aggression in Korea, twenty-one additional leading communists were indicted under the same act. Among them was V. J. Jerome, the head of the cultural commission of the party.

For the purpose of counteracting this change in the American attitude, in 1948 the Kremlin had begun to place a renewed emphasis on propaganda for world peace, and communists began to foster a whole series of "peace congresses" in various parts of the world. In so doing, they were at first able to secure the support of a considerable number of liberals, including American liberals. The earliest of these congresses, held at Wroclaw, Poland (formerly Breslau, Germany) in August 1948, was attended by an American delegation, which included representatives of the arts who joined in praising Russian "peace" policies while attacking "American imperialism and its plans for war." Among the later congresses was one known as the Cultural and Scientific Conference for World Peace, which met in New York under the sponsorship of the National Council of Arts, Sciences and Professions in March 1949. This was on the eve of the Atlantic Pact against which the communist peace drive was partly directed. Among those who sponsored the conference were such famous noncommunists as Thomas Mann and Albert Einstein. One of the speakers was the left-wing American painter, Philip Evergood; another was Shostakovich, who attended as a member of a large Soviet Russian delegation. Some of the foreign delegates, including the Mexican painter Siqueiros, were prevented from attending because the Department of State refused them visas on the grounds that they were active members of a Communist party.[240]

One aspect of this campaign for peace was the World Peace Appeal, or so-called "Stockholm peace petition," which was circulated for signa-

[239] See Budenz, *Men without Faces*, p. 219, also Billy Rose's column, "Pitching Horseshoes," *New York Herald Tribune*, Feb. 24, 1950, p. 19. According to Rose, Mrs. Roosevelt was herself responsible for the decline of the committee when she resigned and attacked it after discovering that it had been taken over by communist sympathizers.
[240] *New York Times*, Mar. 24, 1949, p. 3.

tures in many countries and which Secretary of State Dean Acheson attacked as Moscow-inspired. The principal clearinghouse and distributor for the petition in the United States was the Peace Information Center, headed by W. E. B. Du Bois, the widely-known Negro whom we have already mentioned for his activities in fostering Negro art and artists. In August 1950 the Peace Information Center and its officers, including Du Bois, were instructed by the Department of Justice to register as foreign agents, and in February 1951 were indicted by a federal grand jury for failing to do so.[241]

Among the numerous American endorsers of the World Peace Appeal, many of them noncommunists, were Rockwell Kent, the painter, and the noted Negro singer, Paul Robeson, as well as no less than five Protestant bishops.[242] In the summer of 1950 the Department of State refused to validate the passports of both Kent and Robeson. Kent was accused of violating passport regulations on a trip abroad earlier in the year, a trip which had included a visit to Moscow with a delegation representing the World Committee of Peace Partisans, denounced by the Department of State as a communist-line organization. When told of the invalidation of his passport, Kent is reported to have said, "Anything that the Communists say about peace sounds good to me," and "I would work for peace with anyone, Communists or non-Communists."[243]

Paul Robeson (who had decided in the middle 1930's that the Negro had a better chance of advancing under Russian communism than in the United States) had also participated in the peace campaign from the beginning, and at home and abroad had repeatedly assailed the Marshall Plan, the Atlantic Pact, and the American defense of Korea. In November 1950 a communist-line World Peace Congress in Warsaw divided its International Peace Prize for Arts between Robeson and Picasso.[244] Robeson had once said, "It is unthinkable that [American Negroes] would go to war on behalf of those who have oppressed us for generations" against a country, the U.S.S.R., "which in one generation has raised our people to the full dignity of mankind."[245]

[241] New York Herald Tribune, Aug. 25, 1950, p. 5, and Feb. 10, 1951, p. 1. See also W. E. B. Du Bois, "I Take My Stand," Masses & Mainstream, Vol. 4, No. 4 (Apr. 1951), pp. 10-16. Later in 1951 the defendants were acquitted.

[242] New York Herald Tribune, Aug. 25, 1950, p. 5.

[243] See Time, Aug. 28, 1950, p. 17; New York Herald Tribune, Aug. 19, 1950, p. 3, and Mar. 4, 1950, pp. 1 and 6. In 1951, while a witness before the New York Supreme Court, Kent was asked if he believed that the only way social error could be remedied was through communism. He replied "If you mean, do I believe in Russian communism for America, I do not. I do believe in socialism. . . ." See the New York Herald Tribune, April 4, 1951, p. 19.

[244] See Time, Dec. 4, 1950, p. 38.

[245] Ibid., Aug. 14, 1950, p. 12. In 1949 the House Committee on Un-American Activities listed Robeson as affiliated "with from fifty-one to sixty Communist-front

However, while it is certainly true that some of the American artists who participated in the peace petition, as well as in other activities discussed above, have either been members of the Communist Party or fellow travelers, it is important to remember that many others have been neither party members nor sympathetic to the party. In short, it cannot be too strongly emphasized that the artistic radicalism or liberalism which leads some American artists to sympathize with radicals in other fields may at times have a thoroughly American—if often naive—basis. For often it is an expression of a characteristically American spirit of individualistic nonconformity and thus of private enterprise.[246]

Conclusion

Since a work of art is an expression of human life, it in some way reflects the conscious or unconscious philosophy of life of the artist (or group of artists) who produces it. But it cannot be denied that this philosophy in turn is in part necessarily affected by the environment and social beliefs of the artist. Consequently, in spite of sharp differences all the varieties of socialism share many of the same beliefs, so that the artists who subscribe to these different kinds of socialism have much in common in their approach to art: as might be expected, they tend to emphasize those kinds of art which seem to lend themselves to social expression and social usefulness. Yet, however interested in social problems they may appear to be, great artists are, almost by definition, unique individuals whose creative individuality does not easily lend itself to any form of economic or political collectivism. And it must also be remembered that the great majority of artists, when left to themselves, are not politicians of any kind, but just artists. Thus revolutionary art and revolutionary politics are frequently dissociated to a very considerable degree—they may or may not be combined in the same person—although (to repeat) radicalism

organizations": see the *New York Times*, Apr. 19, 1949, p. 6. He was a contributing editor of *Masses & Mainstream*.

[246] See Peyton Boswell's editorial, "A Plea for Tolerance," *Art Digest*, Vol. 23, No. 17 (June 1, 1949), p. 7. One might add that this frequent spirit of nonconformity, and hence of private enterprise, in the arts has often been looked upon with considerable suspicion by American private enterprise in business through fear of being accused of harboring radicals such as Communist Party members or fellow travelers. A possible case in point is that of actress Jean Muir, who in the summer of 1950 was paid off and dropped from a television show as a "controversial person" by the sponsor of the show in spite of Miss Muir's insistence that she is an anticommunist. Her name had been listed in a booklet, *Red Channels*, published under the aegis of the weekly newsletter, *Counterattack*. *Red Channels* "purports to catalogue radio and television personalities who have allegedly been sympathetic to Communist-front organizations." The dismissal of Miss Muir was denounced by the Council of Actors Equity Association, the A.F.L. theatrical union, which at the same time "'unequivocally' condemned Communism and Fascism." See the *New York Herald Tribune*, Sept. 13, 1950, p. 17.

in art often predisposes the artist to regard radical social doctrines favorably.

Even in the Marxian view, however, there is no necessary one-to-one relationship between the development of the economic foundation of society and the ideological superstructure which rests upon it and which includes art. Art and economics and politics do not necessarily have to develop equally in the same society, or for that matter in the same human being. Hence although it is often easy to distinguish the arts of economic and political radicals from those of conservatives (who, unlike both radicals and liberals, prefer the status quo to either revolutionary or evolutionary change), it is, as we have seen, frequently difficult to distinguish between the kinds of art admired by radicals and those admired by socially-minded liberals. Historically, liberalism and socialism have tended to overlap, as they overlapped in the life of William Morris or even in the history of the Bauhaus, with the result that it has been relatively easy for socialists and many liberals to influence one another in the arts and to do so both consciously and unconsciously.

As this book has endeavored to show, by implication at least, this question of the relation of radicalism in art to social radicalism is also part of a problem which every artist has to face, the problem of achieving adequate originality while still retaining an adequate relationship with his fellow men. For if the artist is not artistically radical at all, his work may well lack the element of significant originality and individuality fundamental to all worthwhile art. If, on the contrary, he is so radical that no one can understand or appreciate his work—if, in short, his art lacks every kind of social significance—not only will artistic survival become difficult or impossible for him but he will fail (as socialists insist) to take his proper place in society. Yet if political radicalism leads him instead to devote his art *entirely* to fostering social aims so that works of art are nothing but a means to nonartistic ends, art then becomes nothing but a kind of propaganda. Each different form of society has its own particular dangers for the arts, and this tendency to reduce art to sheer propaganda, to sheer social utility, is the chief danger to which the arts of a socialist society may succumb, as developments in Soviet Russia have so clearly indicated. However, one must add in fairness that, with all its limitations, it is a tendency which in theory causes art to be considered an official necessity in the Soviet Union, and not a mere unessential luxury, as it is so often regarded in the United States.

It is true that in this country from early colonial times to the present, radical movements of a socialist nature have always been endemic, primarily because tendencies toward equalitarianism have always been characteristic of American democracy as they have also to some degree

129

been characteristic of all forms of socialist theory. But in spite of the more-or-less equalitarian spirit of American democracy, socialism has never been able to gain in any direct way a really strong place in American civilization and art because American individualism has customarily been so suspicious of anything that might smack of collectivistic regimentation. Moreover, the Marxist belief in the class struggle and the triumph of the proletariat has never been very widely accepted in the United States, where so many of those whom Marx has labeled proletarians do not ordinarily think of themselves as members of any class, but if pressed to do so are likely to say that they consider themselves part of the middle class. As a result, very few of the varieties of socialism which have been found in the United States have originated there. And the few native groups which, like the Oneida Community, have adopted a communistic existence independent of foreign influence have usually been compelled to withdraw from ordinary American society and to adopt a communal way of life at least partly against their will, and mainly because their neighbors objected to some of their customs.

For all these reasons, from the seventeenth century to at least the middle of the twentieth century, socialist influences on art, as on other aspects of life in the United States, have been chiefly indirect. In this indirect way they have had considerable importance. But even indirectly they have ordinarily been strong only when some of the aims, ideals, and needs of the American democratic tradition have happened to coincide with some of the principles characteristic of socialism. Thus in the art of the United States, as in other aspects of American life, any imported socialist content has usually been retained only when it reinforces already existing American tendencies. Otherwise, except for the art of small, if vociferous, socialist and communist minorities, the socialist and especially the Marxian content has customarily been dropped out. Usually in the American version of an imported socialist style either there is little or no content other than that which may reside directly in the very nature of the medium and of the form given to that medium, resulting in what Russian Marxism today decries as formalism, or else—as is so often the case—the socialist content has been modified in a characteristically American direction.

Yet as is so often implied in this book, it cannot be said with truth that there is any *single* direction which can be called truly American. And American art helps to document this fact by indicating the existence in the United States of an ever prevailing yet ever varying tension between individualism *and* equalitarianism, a tension in which, unlike most socialism, the individual is considered primary *now* and not merely in some future society. The author believes that in this very tension (which socialist criticism helps to keep vital, and which in important respects is also not unrelated to the Christian tradition) lies hope for further efforts to overcome both the economic injustices that frequently accompany irresponsible individualism, and the bureaucratic or technocratic tyranny so often characteristic of large-scale collectivism. It is this tension, in short, which may offer particular hope for achieving a higher degree of individual and social justice not only in American life but throughout the world.

Epilogue (for the 1967 Edition)

At the time the previous parts of this book were originally published early in 1952, Joseph Stalin dominated the communist world except in Yugoslavia, and the cold war was at its height. On March 5, 1953, Stalin died—and the "thaw" (as Ilya Ehrenburg named it) promptly began not only in the Soviet Union but in nearly all of the other communist nations and parties throughout the world, making the communist attitude toward the arts, as toward other aspects of life, somewhat less dogmatic. In July of that year an agreement between the United States and its United Nations allies, on the one hand, and the communists of North Korea and their Chinese allies, on the other, brought to an end the Korean War. But communist aggression in the war itself had led more Americans, including some artists, away from their former sympathy for communism.

In 1950 Senator Joseph McCarthy had become the leading American anti-communist of the Radical Right, and early in 1953 he reached the peak of his power when he was made head of the Senate Permanent Subcommittee on Investigations after the Republicans took control of Congress. Even though McCarthy was finally condemned by his fellow Senators late in 1954, the anti-communism he had done so much to stir up did not cease to affect many artists and their art adversely for several years thereafter. And "modern" artists were particularly affected because Republican Representative Dondero continued that campaign against modern art as being "subversive" and "Communistic" which he had begun in 1949. As late as 1956, for instance, Dondero spoke in the House on "Communism under the Guise of Cultural Freedom—Strangling American Art."[247]

Artistically conservative artists also played an important part in attacking "modern" artists as "Communistic." In 1952,[248] for example, a committee of the conservative National Sculpture Society, with the whole-hearted encouragement of its three-term president, an academic sculptor named Wheeler Williams, protested the awards made in a national sculpture competition sponsored by the Metropolitan Museum of Art. The committee declared that "thousands of dollars in prizes" had gone "to work not only of extreme modernistic and negative tendencies but mediocre left-wing work at that."[249] New York's Museum of Modern Art, the Whitney Museum of American Art, and other leading art organizations sprang so forcefully to the defense of the Metropolitan Museum that the chairman of the Sculpture Society's committee tried to claim that the

[247] For this speech of Dondero on June 14, 1956, see the *Congressional Record*, 84th Cong., 2d Sess., pp. 10419-10425.
[248] This was shortly after all work on my essay in *Socialism and American Life* had been completed.
[249] *New York Times*, Feb. 10, 1952, Section 2, p. 9.

word "left-wing" had been used with "no reference to political aspects in America."[250]

Meanwhile, since 1948 artistic and sociopolitical rightwing organizations together had been making strong efforts to bring about the destruction of twenty-nine mural panels on the history of California in San Francisco's Rincon Post Office Annex. These had been painted between 1940 and 1948 by Anton Refregier, who had won a competition conducted under the auspices of the National Fine Arts Commission for this last large government art project of Franklin D. Roosevelt's administration. Although on completion the murals were officially approved, they were promptly attacked by organizations of the Right both as artistically offensive and as un-American and subversive. One chief evidence cited for the latter charge was the fact that in a panel showing representatives of the various allied nations seated around the peace table after World War II, the Soviet flag, with its hammer and sickle, was included along with the flags of other major allies of the United States. It is true, however, that the painter of the murals, the Russian-born Refregier, was—and remained—sympathetic to the Soviet Union and had long participated in leftist causes. A resolution calling for the removal of the murals was introduced into the House of Representatives in 1953, that year when McCarthyism reached its peak, with the eventual result that the matter was referred to a subcommittee of the Committee on Public Works which was headed by none other than Representative Dondero. Even so, the murals were ultimately saved by the many protests from art organizations and individuals who maintained that the paintings should be judged on their merit as art rather than on the politics of the artist, and also that liberty of expression is one of the foundations of a democratic society.[251]

Anti-communism of the Right had particularly adverse effects on the selection of works of art for exhibition abroad under the auspices of the State Department and the United States Information Agency, organizations which are, of course, dependent upon grants from Congress. In 1952 a high official of the Information Agency felt it necessary to declare that "our Government should not sponsor examples of our creative energy which are non-representational." He added, "We are not interested in purely experimental art,"[252] thereby arousing a storm of protest from many avant-garde Americans. Furthermore, the Information Agency found it advisable to practice a silent political censorship—as was finally revealed by the *Washington Post and Times Herald* on March 6, 1955,

[250] *New York Times*, Apr. 26, 1952, p. 18.

[251] For the story of these paintings see especially Aline Louchheim, "The Case of a Criticized Mural," *New York Times*, May 10, 1953, Section 2, p. 13.

[252] Quoted in a letter by Alfred H. Barr, Jr., in the *College Art Journal*, Vol. 15, No. 3 (Spring 1956), p. 184.

three months after Senator McCarthy had been condemned by his colleagues. In practicing its censorship, not only did the U.S.I.A. decline to exhibit "works of avowed Communists," but also those of "persons who publicly refuse to answer questions of congressional committees regarding connection with the Communist movement"[253]—entirely without reference to the nature or artistic quality of the works of art themselves.

By 1956, however, the Information Agency felt secure enough to sponsor the idea of sending to Australia, during the Olympic games there, an exhibition entitled *Sport in Art*. The exhibition, originated by *Sports Illustrated* (a Time, Inc., periodical far from being on the Left) and prepared under its auspices, had been assembled by the respected and apolitical American Federation of Arts. Before the exhibition was scheduled to leave for Australia, it was sent on a tour of various American cities without incident until it came to Dallas, Texas. There it was sharply attacked by rightwing Texans, including conservative artists, chiefly on the ground that the exhibition included works by artists accused of having been aligned with "the Communist-socialistic international group of subversives." This was also the culmination of a long series of attacks made in Dallas on the entire modern movement in art. So violent was this particular assault, even though none of these pictures in any way reflected communist influence in subject matter or content, that the Information Agency backed down and cancelled the scheduled tour to Australia.[254] And so jittery was the Agency that it also cancelled the European tour of 100 paintings of the twentieth century, ranging in style from nonobjective to realistic, which had been selected and were being assembled by the American Federation of Arts at the Agency's own request. A spokesman for the Agency stated that ten (later increased to twelve) of the chosen artists had been found to be "social hazards." When the American Federation of Arts refused the Agency's request to withdraw the works by these artists, on the ground that the Federation could make selections only on the basis of artistic merit, the U.S.I.A. cancelled the entire show in accordance with a decision from the White House. In July 1956, the director of the U.S.I.A. declared before a Senate Foreign Relations subcommittee that it had become the Agency's policy to include no works by politically suspect artists in exhibitions overseas;

[253] Quoted in *ibid.*, p. 185, from the *Washington Post*.
[254] For the story of these events in Dallas see especially Charlotte Devree, "The U.S. Government Vetoes Living Art," *Art News*, Vol. 55, No. 5 (Sept. 1956), pp. 34-35 and 54-56; *New York Times*, Feb. 12, 1956, Section 2, p. 15; *Time*, Vol. 67, No. 11 (Mar. 12, 1956), p. 70, also Vol. 65, No. 18 (May 2, 1955), pp. 80-81. As late as 1961 some members of the Dallas Junior League prevented a showing of works—for charity—by Pablo Picasso, since 1944 an avowed member of the French Communist Party, even though the works in question had nothing specifically "communistic" in subject matter or content. See *Time*, Vol. 78, No. 23 (Dec. 8, 1961), p. 24.

and it was now indicated that there would be no further government-sponsored exhibitions abroad of paintings executed since 1917, the year of the Bolshevik Revolution.

Nevertheless, in 1959 the U.S.I.A. did sponsor an exhibition of American art of the last thirty years at an American fair held that summer at Moscow's Sokolniki Park with the approval of the Senate Foreign Relations Committee. (A parallel Russian fair was to be held in New York's Coliseum.) The chairman of the House Un-American Activities Committee then declared that thirty-four of the sixty-seven artists included in the American show had records of affiliations with communist front organizations and causes, and demanded that the works of twenty-four of them be removed. However, President Eisenhower flatly refused to censor the exhibition, even though he expressed his own repudiation of cubism and its descendants as well as of expressionism; and he called a painting in the show by Jack Levine, one of the artists cited by the chairman of the Un-American Activities Committee, a "lampoon." He also several times made clear his own liking for "realistic" art—once indirectly in a conversation at the Soviet exhibit in New York with Frol Koslov, Deputy Premier of the Soviet Union.[255]

Interestingly enough, official Soviet critics found the American show at Moscow disappointing for much the same reasons as President Eisenhower. They, too, much preferred "realistic" art, though where Eisenhower preferred it from the essentially "bourgeois" point of view of an artistically average American, the Soviet critics insisted upon it in harmony with the official Soviet aesthetic of socialist realism. After all, Khrushchev had continued to uphold that originally Stalinist aesthetic, even though only his own non-Stalinist doctrine of "peaceful coexistence" between "socialist" and "capitalist" countries made possible the exhibition of American art at Moscow and the Soviet exhibition at New York, as well as many other cultural exchanges.

It was in his speech at Moscow on February 14, 1956, before an open session of the Twentieth Congress of the Communist Party, that Khrushchev had publicly emphasized the softer foreign policy accepting "different roads to socialism" including parliamentary democracy, along with "peaceful coexistence"—a policy which in the United States was to

[255] On President Eisenhower's opinions see Frederick S. Wight, *Jack Levine* (New York, 1955) pp. 5 and 6; and the *New York Herald Tribune*, June 30, 1959, p. 12. After President Eisenhower had thus openly expressed his views, the director of the U.S.I.A. hurriedly announced that, "based on the President's feeling," over twenty-five American paintings from earlier (and consistently representational) periods of American art would be added to the exhibition. See the *New York Herald Tribune*, July 8, 1959, pp. 1 and 13; also *Time*, Vol. 74, No. 3 (July 20, 1959), pp. 16-17. At the time of the dispute over the art in the American exhibition for Moscow, Jack Levine was in Greece, having been cleared by the F.B.I. and given a passport.

weaken the appeal of the violent anti-communism of the American Radical Right. At the same party congress, on February 24 and 25, 1956, Khrushchev delivered the long speech in which he savagely attacked Stalin's reputation and the "cult of personality." Although this speech was given before closed sessions of the congress and was supposed to be kept secret, rumors about it were soon circulating. On June 4 the American State Department released the text of the entire speech, obtained from a source that has never been made public. The resulting confusion among communists everywhere was enormous. On June 27 *Pravda* even carried a long article by the American communist leader Eugene Dennis containing the most far-reaching criticism of Stalin that had ever come out of the Soviet Union.

The further "thaw" among communists resulting from Khrushchev's attack on Stalin and Khrushchev's doctrine of "different roads to socialism" made it possible for Palmiro Togliatti, the leading Italian communist, to enunciate in June 1956 the doctrine of "polycentrism." According to this doctrine the Soviet Union and its Communist Party should no longer be regarded as constituting the one single center for world communism; instead, according to Togliatti, the other communist nations and parties should be relatively independent and separate centers of communist power. So rapidly and widely did this doctrine spread throughout the communist world that, in 1960 at a congress of communist parties held in Moscow, when a proposal was made under Soviet leadership for a world communist secretariat, the proposal met with so much opposition that Khrushchev felt compelled to disown it and even to renounce the Soviet party's position of leadership in the communist movement. And in 1964 that position was at last officially renounced by the Soviet party itself, for the ever more bitter ideological dispute with Red China had made it obvious to Khrushchev and finally to the Soviet party that the U.S.S.R. must seek all possible support from other communist parties against Peking.

The communist world, already fragmented in 1956 by Khrushchev's attack on Stalin and Togliatti's promulgation of "polycentrism," was fundamentally split later in that year by the Red Army's brutal repression of the Hungarian Revolution even though that Revolution was supported by most Hungarian communists. Consequently, on November 5, 1956, the New York *Daily Worker* ran an editorial denouncing the Soviet action.[256] Under the leadership of William Z. Foster, always utterly faithful to Soviet policy, the stalwarts of the American Communist Party

---

[256] See John Gates, *The Story of an American Communist* (New York, 1958), pp. 179-80. According to Gates, who was editor of the *Daily Worker* when the editorial was published, that paper was the only communist paper in the world to attack Soviet repression of the Revolution.

succeeded in repressing such "revisionism" within a little over a year; but, because so many of the revisionists, including the editor of the *Daily Worker* and most artists and "intellectuals," either had been expelled from the party or had left it in disgust, the party was gravely weakened. Early in 1958 the *Daily Worker*, whose cartoons had so long maintained an exceptionally high artistic level, suspended publication, and resumed only as a weekly paper (later appearing twice a week). In 1958, too, the American Communist Party was reduced to only about 5,000 members. Since that time it has never even claimed to number more than 13,000, partly because it was weakened again in the 1960's when it expelled those members who had become "deviationists" in favor of Red China and Albania. (Yet it has never become as impotent as the Socialist Party, whose candidate for President had polled so few votes— less than 2,500—in 1956 that beginning in 1960 it ran no Presidential candidate.)

Even apart from the widespread alienation from communism caused by the political events mentioned above, many socially radical American artists and others interested in the arts were also alienated by the fact that the Soviet regime and party continued to cling to the Stalinist aesthetic of socialist realism. It is true that the dogmatism with which socialist realism was imposed on artists in the Soviet Union itself, or under Soviet dominance elsewhere, tended to vary with the political situation in the U.S.S.R. and abroad. And some great artists, Picasso among them, continued to be accepted as members of communist parties of noncommunist countries, even if they refused to practice socialist realism, simply because of their propaganda value to world communism. But this did not mean that their art was necessarily acceptable within the Soviet Union itself; the most artistically radical works of Picasso, for instance, have not been exhibited in the Soviet Union to this day.

It should be noted, however, that although under Khrushchev and his successors socialist realism has remained the official Soviet aesthetic, Khrushchev did make possible a new version of socialist realism in architecture. Well before he attacked Stalin's reputation in February 1956, he had already assailed Stalinist architecture: late in 1954 he had given a speech to an All-Union Congress of Builders, Architects, and Workers in the Building Materials Industry,[257] denouncing Soviet architects for using so much steel (needed for heavy industry and munitions) and for refusing to adapt their work to new materials (especially reinforced concrete, less wasteful of steel). He also censured the Soviet architects' preoccupation with ornament, urging simple, honest expression. All this was ob-

[257] See *Pravda*, Dec. 28, 1954, for this speech. As the speech had been delivered on December 7, the three-week delay in publishing it suggests that Khrushchev's new point of view had won out within the Soviet regime only with difficulty.

viously an attack on the expensive, elaborately ornamented skyscrapers, such as that for Moscow University, designed and built during Stalin's last years as the most prominent Soviet architectural productions. In the same speech, however, Khrushchev was careful to assail form divorced from content—that is (in the official Soviet view), the abstract kind of form so prevalent in the modern arts, including the modern architecture, of the "capitalist" West.

A little over a year later, in his first, or open, speech before the Twentieth Congress of the Soviet party, Khrushchev declared that technology is independent of ideology, and that therefore the U.S.S.R. must study "all the best that science and technique yield in the world of capitalism" so as to make use of it for the Soviet brand of "socialism."[258]

Thus, under socialist realism a modern architecture like that of the "bourgeois" architects of the West became possible, but only provided that its content was in some way "socialist." Still, as long as communist architects devoted themselves to architectural programs such as city planning, mass housing, or other types of design and building that could satisfy Soviet national and social needs as determined by the regime, they could be regarded as achieving socialist content. And if they did so by making use of advanced technical methods and of forms, however abstract, characterized by economy of means, they could meet the requirements of socialist realism in architecture. But this obviously was a kind of architectural socialist realism very different from that which had prevailed under Stalin.

It is true that this development in socialist realism as applied to architecture could have little or no direct effect upon American architects, so few of whom have ever been sympathetic to communism largely because it is especially difficult for an overtly radical architect to get clients. And since the American Communist Party was so soon to dwindle drastically following the Hungarian Revolution, the chance of finding socially radical clients would become even less than before. However, this new kind of socialist realism in architecture made possible by Khrushchev was primarily responsible for the development of a flourishing modern architecture in the Soviet "satellites." As a consequence—and thanks also to Khrushchev's doctrine of "peaceful coexistence" and to the spread of "polycentrism"—some modern architects from the satellite countries have in recent years had notable success in the United States. For example, since 1958 the modern Polish architect Jerzy Soltan has taught for part of each year at Harvard in the Departments of Architecture and Urban Design; since 1962 he has taught periodically at the architectural school of Carnegie Institute of Technology; and in 1966-1967 he was for a time a visiting critic in architecture at Princeton and

[258] *Pravda*, Feb. 15, 1956, p. 5.

also at Yale, where over the previous five years he had frequently served on juries for the work of advanced students. Likewise noteworthy is the fact that in 1965 two talented young Bulgarian architects, Ivan Tzvetin and his wife Angela Danadjieva, won an international competition for designing the Civic Center Plaza in San Francisco from a field of 316 other competitors.

Meanwhile, by continuing to demand in Soviet arts other than architecture a socialist realism like that of Stalin's day, Khrushchev and his successors were losing the support of nearly all foreign artists and intellectuals interested in modern art. Yet they were being impelled by an overriding political necessity; for otherwise, in the ideological dispute with Red China (of which American communists first heard rumors in 1959 but which became thoroughly public only in 1961), the Russians would have given the Chinese further opportunity to brand them as "revisionists" of true Marxism-Leninism. It was primarily for this reason that for some eight months in 1962-1963, Premier Khrushchev personally led a campaign in the Soviet Union violently attacking abstract art. And after Khrushchev's downfall, his successors bluntly announced early in 1965 that they intended to carry on the same general policies with regard to the arts—and they have done so.

Thus the Soviet dispute with Red China has resulted in a further split between Soviet domestic policy and Soviet foreign policy, a split therefore profoundly affecting communist arts in the U.S.S.R. itself very differently from those abroad. For while at home the Soviet leaders have had to maintain socialist realism in order not to give the Red Chinese an additional reason for calling them "revisionists," they have had to accept "polycentrism," including "polycentrism" in the arts, in order to retain the support of most Communist parties abroad both in the "satellites" and in noncommunist countries. As a consequence, outside the Soviet Union not only artists with communist sympathies but communist leaders of the West have increasingly abandoned socialist realism in all the arts, at first tacitly and then sometimes explicitly.

It was foreseeable that the first pronounced reaction against socialist realism in painting or sculpture in any "socialist" country would begin in Yugoslavia while Stalin was still alive (for Tito had broken with Stalin as early as 1948, though the break did not affect Yugoslav art for some years). In the "satellites" the reaction, appearing first in Poland, set in during the "thaw" after Stalin's death. It became much stronger in Poland after the new and more national Polish communist regime under Gomulka, made possible by Khrushchev's de-Stalinization speech, successfully stood up to Khrushchev and the other Soviet leaders in October 1956 shortly before the Hungarian Revolution. (In Poland the peak of freedom for artists and especially for writers was to come in the years from 1961 to 1964. Since that time Gomulka's regime has somewhat tightened the censorship in arts other than architecture.)

As early as 1955, during the "thaw," a painter of Cracow named Tadeusz Kantor led the movement in Poland away from socialist realism and toward abstract art after a trip to Paris. There he had been stirred by avant-garde art from many countries, especially by works of the American abstract expressionist Jackson Pollock, who earlier, like so many other leading abstract expressionists, had been involved with leftwing political art.[259] Kantor, in 1960, at a time when not only "peaceful co-existence" but "polycentrism" had swept so much of the communist world, and the power of the Radical Right had dwindled in the United States, had a one-man show at New York's Saidenberg Gallery. In the following year the Museum of Modern Art in New York displayed his work and that of fourteen other Polish painters almost all of whom were painting in a nonobjective style.[260]

Meanwhile, some Polish composers were becoming known as leaders of the more "abstract" varieties of contemporary music in Europe. As a consequence, the Polish composer Witold Lutoslawski was invited to teach at Tanglewood, Massachusetts, by the great American avant-garde composer Aaron Copland (who in the 1930's and 1940's had been strongly sympathetic to the political and social Left). When Lutoslawski arrived in the United States in 1962, he mentioned that there was a thriving studio for electronic music in Warsaw. He said that in 1961 he himself had "made . . . a new beginning" with a work that "makes a considerable use of the techniques of chance, or aleatoric music," and that he was "working solely in that direction."[261] It is significant that abstract expressionist painters such as Jackson Pollock, who inspired Tadeusz Kantor, have similarly made aesthetic use of chance. And in view of the artistic radicalism of both electronic music and the music of chance, it is likewise significant that the leading American practitioners of each, Milton Babbitt and John Cage respectively, "subscribe to the political

[259] The noted American art critic, Harold Rosenberg, wrote in *Art News*, Vol. 59, No. 10 (Feb. 1961), p. 58, in a review of a book on Jackson Pollock: ". . . Pollock himself, I have been told, joined the Communist Party [in the 1930's]." More recently Rosenberg has pointed out, in an article entitled "From Pollock to Pop . . ." (*Holiday*, Vol. 39, No. 3 [Mar. 1966], p. 99) that "Almost all the originators of America's abstract [expressionist] art had been steeped in the political art of the Depression. Pollock had been influenced by left-wing Mexican mural painting; Rothko had composed tableaux of the city poor; de Kooning had executed constructions for Artists Union demonstrations; Reinhardt and Motherwell had dabbled in Marxism—the latter was to cling to the Spanish Civil War as his major theme in the years that followed." By 1955, however, when Kantor saw Pollock's paintings at Paris, the abstract expressionists had essentially given up direct sociopolitical interests.

[260] See Peter Selz, *15 Polish Painters* (Garden City, N.Y., 1961), the catalogue of the exhibition.

[261] *New York Times*, Aug. 12, 1962, Section 2, p. 9.

implications of their musical thought, Cage being an anarchist and Babbitt a conservative with anarchist sympathies."[262]

In short, the more recent artistically radical movements abroad are often related to what the Russians officially regard as some kind of Marxist revisionism, in which elements of anarchism as well as of philosophical idealism are likely to be found. And on spreading to the United States, such movements tend to become associated with anarchism of a more individualistic kind which in this respect reflects American individualism, as the anarchism of Thoreau had done long before.

It was only to be expected that Premier Khrushchev's defense of socialist realism and his corresponding violent attack on abstract art in 1962-1963 would bring adverse criticism from many artists once sympathetic to Soviet communism. And, indeed, his views also brought criticism from some leaders of communist parties once regarded as wholly subject to the hegemony of Moscow. Significantly, the political leader who led the way was the originator of the doctrine of "polycentrism," the Italian communist Togliatti, who in 1963 declared: "Tolerance is essential in cultural matters. Nobody can impose on an artist how to write a poem, how to create music, how to paint."[263]

It was also only to be expected that such attacks on Khrushchev and Soviet socialist realism by prominent communists outside of the Soviet Union would have an effect on some American communists. Indeed, Khrushchev's interpretation of art split American communists so thoroughly that it apparently brought about the demise in 1963 of the Communist Party's cultural magazine, *Mainstream* (which had changed its name from *New Masses* to *Masses and Mainstream* in 1948 largely as a reflection of the cold war line, and then to *Mainstream* in 1956 as a consequence of Khrushchev's de-Stalinization speech). In July 1963, Sidney Finkelstein, that leading American communist art critic, who had been an editor of *Mainstream* and its predecessor for some fifteen years, and whose books on the arts had been published in at least ten countries including the Soviet Union, ventured to oppose Premier Khrushchev in the pages of *Mainstream* itself with the support of his fellow editors. He criticized Khrushchev for taking "for granted," in attacking freedom of expression in the arts, "an absolute identity" between art and ideology, "as if art were [nothing but] an ideological statement expressed in artistic techniques." In the next issue of *Mainstream*, V. J. Jerome, still a kind of cultural commissar for the American Communist Party, sought

[262] Richard Kostelanetz, "Milton Babbitt and John Cage Are the Two Extremes of Avant-Garde Music," *New York Times*, Jan. 15, 1967, Section 6, p. 64.
[263] Quoted by Eldon Griffiths, "Mr. K's Turn toward Stalinism," *Saturday Evening Post*, Vol. 236, No. 21 (June 1, 1963), p. 70. Fidel Castro in Cuba was another communist leader who expressed his displeasure with Khrushchev's art policy.

to rebut Finkelstein in an article entitled "Towards the Marxist Theory of Ideology."[264] However, so obvious and deep was the split among leading American communists on the subject of ideology and art that in that same August 1963 number of *Mainstream* (in which artists Anton Refregier and Hugo Gellert were listed as contributing editors) it was announced that the magazine would cease publication until the following January. But in fact publication was never resumed.

Meanwhile, as we have mentioned, most American artists once sympathetic to the U.S.S.R. and to communism had long before given up their social radicalism for reasons artistic, political, or both. A noted exception was Rockwell Kent, who in 1960 presented an extensive collection of his works to the Soviet Union as a "peace prize," and, like the Mexican communist painter Siqueiros, was awarded one of the Lenin Peace Prizes announced in Moscow on April 30, 1967, with special praise for his attacks on American policy in Vietnam. But other American artists, particularly avant-garde artists, who had retained their interest in social radicalism, had almost all become disgusted with the continuing Soviet insistence on socialist realism. They had therefore nearly all turned to the New Left in their social views, while executing their works of art as they pleased without any directly social subject matter or content.

The New Left, which in the political spectrum lies in a broad and varying area between communism and social democratic socialism, became influential in the United States quite belatedly. In Europe its origins go back especially to the early 1950's and to efforts by leftwing intellectuals and communist dissidents to form a movement with a "revisionist" Marxian ideology. Philosophically, the movement was very largely based on Marx's early *Economic-Philosophical Manuscripts of 1844*, which had been brought to light and fully published only in the 1930's.[265] In this Marx had maintained an essentially aesthetic point of view largely derived from the utopian socialist Saint-Simon, who in his last writings regarded the artist as the true leader of the good society. Marx held that voluntary productive activity is man's element, and that in this activity he expresses himself as an artist because in producing he "creates in accordance with the laws of beauty."[266]

---

[264] *Mainstream*, Vol. 16, No. 8 (Aug. 1963), pp. 43-50. Jerome quoted and criticized on p. 44 the statement I have quoted from Finkelstein's article in the July issue of *Mainstream*, p. 36. Finkelstein himself was specifically attacking Khrushchev's chief speech against freedom of expression in art even while indicating his own lack of sympathy for abstract art. A translation of Khrushchev's speech, which had been delivered on March 8, 1963, was published in the same July number of *Mainstream*.

[265] The first complete edition, in the original German, was published in 1932. An incomplete Russian translation had appeared in 1927.

[266] Karl Marx, *Ökonomisch-philosophische Manuskripte aus dem Jahre 1844*, in *Karl Marx, Friedrich Engels; Historisch-kritische Gesamtausgabe* (Moscow, etc., 1927-

EPILOGUE

In this early work of Marx there thus remained a degree of emphasis on "idealism" and on the self that, much more than the complete materialism of Marx's mature "scientific socialism," reflected elements of utopianism and anarchism. Hence, whereas Marx and especially Engels later tended to equate materialism with realism in art, the New Left, in relying on this early work of Marx, was led by elements of anarchism and of philosophical idealism to be more likely to accept abstraction in the arts. After all, the great anarchist Peter Kropotkin had indicated in his *Paroles d'un révolté* (1885) that realism was inadequate for expressing the revolutionary idea still lacking in the art of his own day.[267] Furthermore, many of the symbolists, who did so much to pave the way for modern abstract art, were anarchists stimulated by Kropotkin, among others. The symbolists, in turn, influenced such founders of the modern movement in art as the young Picasso and his friend the poet and critic Guillaume Apollinaire, both of whom were strongly sympathetic to anarchism.[268] And even though Picasso became a communist in 1944, he has never given up his relatively abstract art for Soviet socialist realism.

In some countries, notably France and England, specific New Left political parties were founded. These gained momentum especially as a consequence of the Hungarian Revolution of 1956, which, like the treatment of the Russian poet and novelist Boris Pasternak, who in 1958 was brutally compelled by the Soviet regime to refuse a Nobel Prize, disillusioned so many artists, among others, once sympathetic to communism.

However, the New Left which developed belatedly in the United States during the 1960's has never established a New Left party, but has consisted of a kind of popular front of heterogenous protesters mainly among students and bohemians possessed of a rebellious anarchic streak. Its chief periodical, *Studies on the Left*, of which Lee Baxandall, historian of Marxist aesthetics, is an editor, first appeared late in 1959. The movement has been fostered by a variety of leftists including the largely communist-inspired W. E. B. Du Bois Clubs (named for that Negro leader interested in the arts who in 1961 finally joined the Communist Party), the Maoist Progressive Labor Party, and some Trotskyists, notably the Young Socialist Alliance and the Spartacist splinter group. Abroad, the New Left has especially stood for nuclear disarmament and in this has opposed both

1935), Pt. I, Vol. 3, p. 88. For the influence of Saint-Simon, see my article "The Idea of 'Avant-Garde' in Art and Politics," in the *American Historical Review* for December 1967.

[267] Peter Kropotkin, *Paroles d'un révolté*, Elisée Reclus, ed. (Paris, 1885), pp. 58-60.

[268] As a young anarchist in Barcelona, Picasso in 1901 had been a founder and art editor of an essentially anarchist magazine called *Arte Joven*: see Anthony Blunt and Phoebe Pool, *Picasso; The Formative Years* (New York, 1962), p. 11 and Fig. 60. Symbolism as a literary movement had begun in 1885-1886 and was taken up by the painter Gauguin, who had been inclined toward anarchism, in 1887.

American and Soviet policy. But it also has supported Castro in Cuba and has further opposed American foreign policy as represented by NATO, by American intervention in the Dominican Republic, and especially by the war in Vietnam. Opposition to the last, combined with agitation for the civil rights and free speech movements, has been particularly strong in the American New Left. But about the only American artists to devote their art directly to supporting the New Left have been folk singers such as Joan Baez, and also the veteran Pete Seeger, whose inspiration, according to Joan Baez, all folk singers must recognize. Seeger has for years been accused of sympathy for communist causes; and Joan Baez, a convinced pacifist, has refused to pay income taxes, in this recalling the anarchistic civil disobedience of Thoreau.[269] The Radical Right has reacted sharply. Thus, "Life Line," backed by the rightwing Texas millionaire H. L. Hunt, and broadcast from over 400 stations, has declared that folk singing is a "Red weapon."[270]

Much recent American art, mostly apolitical, has been influenced by art movements abroad which themselves to some degree have reflected New Left, and so essentially "revisionist," kinds of Marxism, though ordinarily in a nonparty way. For instance, many of the ideas of Victor Vasarely—the Hungarian-born artist and socialist living in France, who has been the chief founder of Op Art, so widely practiced among avant-garde artists in the United States—have distinct parallels with Marxist theories of art. Like Marx, Vasarely has rejected the idea of the apolitical artist. He has attacked contemporary society for failing to "derive a collective conception of art that comes up to its needs"; and in 1950 he declared, "I dream of a social art."[271] In a somewhat Marxian way Vasarely has sought to develop a kind of science of art collectively produced, suited to the modern age of mass production in industry; and he has insisted on an organically architectonic integration of all the arts. But Vasarely's point of view is "revisionist" in urging a nonobjective art, an art in which, therefore, Marxian materialism and realism are not equated.

In calling for an integration of the arts adapted to and expressive of

[269] In 1961, for instance, Seeger was convicted of contempt of Congress as a result of invoking the first amendment in 1955 and refusing to answer questions of the House Committee on Un-American Activities; however, the conviction was reversed by a U.S. Circuit Court of Appeals in May 1962. Joan Baez was one of 300 Americans who, in protest against the war in Vietnam, declared in the spring of 1966 that they would refuse to pay all or part of their 1965 income tax: see the *New York Times*, Apr. 10, 1966, p. 14.
[270] *Newsweek*, July 4, 1966, p. 81.
[271] See "Vasarely, the Pop of Op," *Réalités*, No. 176 (July 1965), p. 66; and Victor Vasarely, *Plastic Arts of the 20th Century*, intro. by Marcel Joray (Neuchâtel, Switzerland, 1966), p. 64.

the industrial age, Vasarely clearly has much in common with the old Bauhaus. And in fact he was trained at a school generally known as the Budapest Bauhaus, founded by a painter who had recently come from the Bauhaus in Germany.

After World War II the ideas of the original Bauhaus were deliberately revived and developed further by a new school in Germany, the Hochschule für Gestaltung (or College of Design) at Ulm, which has exerted a wide influence among modern architects and industrial designers. Founded by Inge Scholl in memory of her brother and sister executed during World War II by the Nazis for leading an anti-Nazi movement among German students, the Hochschule began operation in 1953, though it was officially opened only in 1955. Its first director and the designer of its building at Ulm was the Swiss-born, Bauhaus-trained, artist, Max Bill, who in being a painter, sculptor, architect, typographer, and industrial designer himself, represents the Bauhaus' ideal of an organic fusion of the arts. Bill, however, believes that he has moved beyond that unification of art, craft, and technology which was the ideal of the Bauhaus, toward more of an integration of art and mathematical science. Nevertheless, he left the Hochschule für Gestaltung in 1957 after a dispute with younger members of its faculty who rejected the Bauhaus' interest in the crafts and considered that Bill failed to stress objective science sufficiently.

Not only has the Hochschule stood for a radical point of view toward design, but—as could be expected of an institution anti-Nazi in origin—its social and political attitude has been anti-conservative and thus necessarily on the radical side. The result has been that, like the Bauhaus earlier, the Hochschule has suffered severely from repeated attacks by political as well as artistic conservatives. Yet like the Bauhaus, too, the political attitudes of its faculty and student body represent a wide range of views from democratic and liberal through a sort of utopian socialism to Marxism—though Marxism primarily of a "revisionist," more-or-less New Left but nonparty kind. Of the faculty members the one farthest to the Left is Claude Schnaidt, author in 1965 of a highly sympathetic biography of Hannes Meyer,[272] the communist architect who had briefly been head of the Bauhaus between Gropius and Mies, and who, not unlike the Hochschule für Gestaltung, had emphasized the relation of design in the arts to science.

The influence of the Hochschule für Gestaltung has been felt on both sides of the "Iron Curtain"—in Yugoslavia, Poland, England, Argentina, Japan, and also the United States, where members of its faculty have taught and lectured frequently since the late 1950's, with significant impact on the teaching of architecture and industrial design. As early as

[272] Claude Schnaidt, *Hannes Meyer; Bauten, Projekte und Schriften* (Teufen AR, Switzerland, 1965).

1957-1958, Otl Aicher and his wife, Frau Aicher-Scholl, founder of the Hochschule, were visiting critics in design at Yale. Especially important have been the frequent visits of Tomás Maldonado and other members of the faculty of the Hochschule to the Department of Architecture at Carnegie Institute of Technology. There, for instance, at various times since 1961 Maldonado has lectured, been a critic of design, and participated in faculty seminars on the development of the curriculum. After giving a lecture before the School of Architecture of Princeton University early in 1966, Maldonado returned as a visiting faculty member in the fall term at a time when the school was revising its curriculum in partial harmony with his ideas: he was appointed Lecturer in Architecture for the succeeding academic year.[273]

Much as at the Bauhaus earlier, internal difficulties had arisen at the Hochschule für Gestaltung. Maldonado, disappointed by its failure to teach total environmental design, resigned in 1967. Previously, though he had opposed Max Bill as too unscientific, he had, by 1964, successfully led a group of the faculty regarding themselves as "humanists" in a controversy with their more "mechanistic" colleagues. The "humanists," who felt that politically the "mechanists" inclined too far to the Right, had in turn been criticized as being too far Left.

Back in 1961 the influence of the Hochschule had been felt at Zagreb, Yugoslavia, where there was held an exhibition of art representing movements growing largely out of Op Art, and thus partly reflecting the stimulation of Vasarely. The exhibition was organized by a young Yugoslav art critic named Matko Meštrović with the help of a Brazilian-born painter, Almir Mavignier, who a few years before had been a student at the Hochschule für Gestaltung. This exhibition and two similar ones organized by Meštrović and others at Zagreb in 1963 and 1965 gave their name to the international art movement known as the New Tendency, whose influence has now been felt widely in Europe and somewhat in the United States.

Significantly, at the Zagreb exhibition of 1963 (which was likewise shown at Venice and at Leverkusen, West Germany) a Marxist interpretation of abstract art was offered by Meštrović and also jointly by two artists from Paris representative of tendencies largely deriving from Vasarely

[273] With further regard to the influence of specific faculty members of the Hochschule für Gestaltung in the United States, one might mention that Herbert Ohl, who in 1961 had lectured in New York, was briefly a lecturer at Carnegie Institute of Technology in 1963 and in the following year was a critic there for a short program in prefabricated structures. Otl Aicher was scheduled to be a visiting critic at the same school in 1965, but illness compelled him to curtail his program. In March 1966 Ohl conducted a guest course at Texas A. and M. University. Meanwhile, Gui Bonsiepe had given a lecture at New York in 1964 under the auspices of the American Institute of Graphic Arts. In the summer of 1966 Maldonado participated in a program at Aspen, Colorado.

and Op Art.[274] All three maintained, in contrast to official Marxist-Leninist critics of the Soviet Union, that a good abstract art is possible—with the implication that the Russians in espousing socialist realism had misunderstood Marx and Lenin. In making such a declaration, Meštrović represented what the official Russian art critics under socialist realism would at least tacitly disapprove of as Yugoslav "revisionism" of true Marxism, while the two Parisian artists could be regarded as reflecting an aspect of the New Left in France, "revisionist" but independent of any party control over art. All three were prominent again in the New Tendency exhibition held at Zagreb in 1965, at which for the first time a group of Soviet artists participated, all of them constructivists not allowed to exhibit their work publicly in the U.S.S.R.[275] So also for the first time Americans exhibited—members of the "Anonima Group," whose name suggests a de-emphasis of the personality of the artist, like that for which Marxian artists have so often stood, and which is one of the principles of Vasarely. Nevertheless, although the group believes in working as a team to investigate aspects of visual perception, and values the results of collaborating more than the individual distinction of the collaborators, it rejects the artist's political protests as utterly irrelevant. Furthermore, it insists that "*Anonima* does not mean anonymity within the group [itself]. It means, on the contrary, the recognition of individual differences (temperamental as well as ideological) among its members."[276] And in this the group reflects a spirit of pluralism and individualism in harmony with the pluralism and individualism that, in theory at least, have been so characteristic of the American tradition.

Thus at the time this Epilogue was written in 1967, the influence on American art of the orthodox Marxist-Leninist aesthetic of socialist realism was minimal—far less than the political and social influence of the very small American Communist Party. The tiny Socialist Party, running no candidates, was emphasizing education. The Marxist influences that were still affecting American artists were coming mainly from the New Left, whose Marxist elements were essentially "revisionist," and

[274] One of the two artists from Paris was the Hungarian-born artist François Molnar; the other was François Morellet, a member of the *Groupe de recherche d'art visuel*, another member of which is Vasarely's son, known as Yvaral.

[275] The actual works of this Soviet constructivist group named *Dvizheniye* (Russian for "Movement") were not exhibited at Zagreb either, only photographs of them. According to Douglas MacAgy these artists had been inspired by photographs of works from the 1930's by the famous Russian-born constructivist Naum Gabo, who had left Soviet Russia in 1922. I am grateful to Mr. MacAgy and to Matko Meštrović for information concerning the New Tendency movement.

[276] *Anonima Group Statement for the Foksal Exhibition, Warsaw, June 1966* (mimeographed), p. 1. The Anonima Group consists of three artists—Ernst Benkert, Francis Hewitt, and Edwin Miecszkowski—who first came together in 1958-1959.

therefore touched by philosophical idealism and anarchism. But even these New Left ideas affected the form rather than the content of much contemporary American art; for they were taken over mostly by American artists who looked upon them as artistically avant-garde, and who thus adopted them for their artistic, rather than their social, radicalism.

After all, by 1967 the long struggle of Western artists, particularly avant-garde artists, to survive in a "bourgeois" society, that struggle which in the great Depression of the 1930's had led so many American artists to identify themselves with the "proletariat" and therefore to adopt Marxist social views along with socialist realism in art, had become far less acute than ever before. And with the struggle abated, any inclination to regard social realism in the arts as avant-garde essentially disappeared. Furthermore, by the mid-1960's, in the United States as in other Western nations, even the abstract and nonobjective currents of contemporary art, so long considered by their practitioners as the only truly avant-garde kinds, had become accepted by the "Establishment." This was largely because the continuing reactionary attitude of the Soviet regime toward such art had increasingly driven noncommunist politicians toward the view that the artistic radicalism of the avant-garde might be a symbol of democracy in the "free" world. As a consequence, the artistic avant-garde was being sought out and supported in the noncommunist Western world as part of official culture to a degree never before even remotely approximated. In the United States this had become especially true after John F. Kennedy was elected President in 1960, largely because Mrs. Kennedy had more interest in, knowledge of, and respect for contemporary art and artists, as well as for those of the past, than any previous inhabitant of the White House with the possible exception of Thomas Jefferson. Also, some leading American businessmen were decorating their offices with artistically radical contemporary art, some of them because they liked it,[277] others because they considered it either a good investment or else a symbol of their own progressiveness, still others as a symbol of freedom.[278]

With the acceptance of avant-garde contemporary art by some leaders of the business world, the Radical Right was on the whole much less

[277] For instance, David Rockefeller, president of the Chase Manhattan Bank, the second largest in the United States, has adorned the bank's headquarters in New York with $900,000 worth of paintings and *objets d'art*, many of them "modern"—to the disgust of the chairman of the board, George Champion, an old-line banker, conservative in his views about art as well as about money matters. See *Newsweek*, Apr. 3, 1967, p. 74.

[278] In 1967, a professor of business named Richard Eells published a book called *The Corporation and the Arts* (one of a series of studies of the modern corporation issued jointly by the Columbia University Graduate School of Business and Macmillan) in which he foresaw a future of fruitful cooperation between business and the artist as two of "the forces of society that can man the bulwarks of freedom at home and abroad."

impelled to attack practitioners of such art as "Communistic" or "subversive." After all, in the affluent American society of the 1960's, at a time when the concept of liberty itself had become little more than a doctrine of self-expression, the American avant-garde artist to whom personal expression rather than social expression had become so important could be regarded as an individualist in the arts—much as the members of the Radical Right are economic individualists. And if much avant-garde art has been in some way touched by an anarchist spirit, the Radical Right itself has been essentially anarchistic in its distrust of the State.[279] As for those American artists believing deeply in the other side of the American coin, equalitarianism (as manifested, for instance, in the civil rights movement), nearly all were keeping such social interests separate from the subject matter of their art. Hence, even though that tension between individualism *and* equalitarianism in American life—which was emphasized in 1952 at the end of the original version of this book—certainly was continuing to flourish in 1967, most artistically radical artists now were not socially radical; and nearly all of those who remained radical were not expressing their social radicalism directly in the subject matter of their art.

Clearly, within the varying tension between individualism and equalitarianism demonstrated by American history, a wide range of artistic expression and of artistic quality has been possible. Furthermore, it is clear that the quality of any given work of art has not been inevitably determined by the specific social attitude of the artist (or artists) who created it. For the history of art has shown again and again that if some great artists have been socially radical, and have even expressed their radicalism in their art, others equally great have deliberately eschewed social radicalism or, indeed, any conscious interest at all in social or political matters. Therefore, while it is true that the greatness of the artist himself can be fostered or gravely hindered by the society in which he lives, the relation between artistic merit and society is a complex one. It becomes simple only when an artistic style is imposed upon artists for nonartistic ends, to the inevitable detriment of the arts because of the ultimately personal nature of artistic talent, imagination, and insight, and thus of great art itself.

[279] The slogan selected for the far-Right John Birch Society by its founder, Robert Welch, "Less government, more responsibility, and a better world," would surely satisfy most acknowledged anarchists.

CREDITS FOR ILLUSTRATIONS

The author wishes to thank the publishers, institutions, and individuals who granted permission to reproduce illustrations used in this chapter. The sources of the illustrations are as follows: FIG. 1, from Philip B. Wallace, *Colonial Churches and Meeting Houses* (New York: Architectural Book Publishing Co., 1931), p. 117; FIG. 2, from Edward D. Andrews, "Communal Architecture of the Shakers," *Magazine of Art*, Vol. 30, No. 12 (Dec. 1937), p. 712; FIG. 3, from the *Peg Board*, Vol. 4, No. 3 (June 1936), p. 65; FIG. 4, from Edward D. and Faith Andrews, *Shaker Furniture* (New Haven: Yale University Press, 1937), Pl. 27; FIG. 5, from Edward D. Andrews, *The Gift to Be Simple* (New York: J. J. Augustin, 1940), Fig. 6, opp. p. 36; FIG. 6, from *Leslie's Popular Monthly* (1885), but reproduced from Edward D. Andrews, *The Gift to Be Simple*, Fig. 16, opp. p. 100; FIG. 7, from Charles Nordhoff, *The Communistic Societies of the United States* (New York: Harper and Brothers, 1875), opp. p. 40; FIG. 8, from the *American-German Review*, of the Carl Schurz Memorial Foundation, Vol. 7, No. 1 (Oct. 1940), p. 7; FIG. 9, from Richard F. Burton, *The City of the Saints* (New York: Harper and Brothers, 1862), frontispiece; FIG. 10, from *American Architect and Building News*, I (Feb. 12, 1876), preceding p. 53; FIG. 11, photo. courtesy of Ewing Galloway; FIG. 12, from Pierrepont Noyes, *My Father's House* (New York: Farrar and Rinehart, 1937), frontispiece; FIG. 13, from an article by Isaac G. Reed in *Frank Leslie's Illustrated Newspaper* (1870), but reproduced from Frederick B. Adams, Jr., *Radical Literature in America* (Stamford, Conn.: Overbrook Press, 1939), p. 25; FIG. 14, from M. R. Werner, *Brigham Young* (New York: Harcourt Brace and Co., 1925), opp. p. 350; FIG. 15, from the *Cooperative Magazine and Monthly Herald*, No. 1 (Jan. 1826), but reproduced from George B. Lockwood, *The New Harmony Movement* (New York: D. Appleton, 1905), opp. p. 70; FIG. 16, from Walter Creese, "Fowler and the Domestic Octagon," *Art Bulletin*, Vol. 28, No. 2 (June 1946), p. 97, Fig. 22; FIG. 17, from the lithograph *Un Phalanstère* by Arnoux, which accompanied Victor Considérant's *Description du Phalanstère* (2nd ed., Paris, 1848); FIG. 18, from Jules Prudhommeaux, *Icarie et son fondateur Étienne Cabet* (Paris: Édouard Cornély & Cie., 1907), opp. p. 588; FIG. 19, from an old print reproduced in George B. Lockwood, *op.cit.*, opp. p. 210; FIG. 20, photo. courtesy of the *Red Bank Daily Register*; FIG. 21, from W. R. Lethaby, *Philip Webb and His Work* (Oxford: Oxford University Press, 1935), opp. p. 4; FIG. 22, from Catherine Bauer, *Modern Housing* (Boston and New York: Houghton Mifflin Co., 1934), Pl. 8-C; FIG. 23, from *Moderne Bouwkunst in Nederland*, No. 1 (Rotterdam: W. L. & J. Brusse N.V., 1932), p. 24; FIG. 24, from Tony Garnier, *Une Cité industrielle* (Paris: Vincent, 1917), Pl. 64; FIG. 25, from George Grosz, *Das Gesicht der herrschenden Klasse*, Kleine revolutionäre Bibliothek, Band IV (Berlin: Malik-Verlag, 1921), Pl. 19; FIG. 26, from H. Bayer, W. Gropius, I. Gropius, eds., *Bauhaus, 1919-1928* (New York: Museum of Modern Art,

1. Ephrata, Pa., Sisters' House (1743).

2. New Lebanon, N.Y., Shaker meetinghouse (1824).

3. New Lebanon, N.Y., North Family dwelling.

4. New Lebanon, N.Y., South Family, Shaker furniture in the brethren's retiring

5. New Lebanon, N.Y., page from a
Shaker hymnal (1839).

6. Watervliet, N.Y., Shaker dance in the second meetinghouse.

7. Amana, Iowa, an old view of the village.

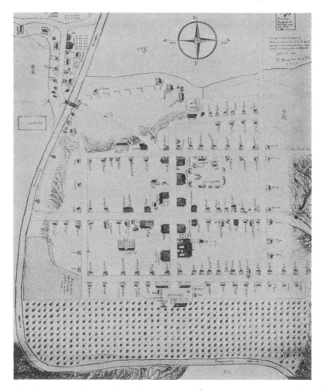

8. Harmony, Pa., plan of the Rappite settlement in 1833.

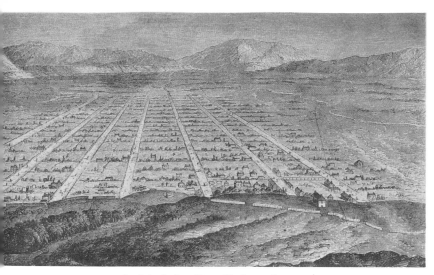

9. Salt Lake City, Utah, early view.

10. Nauvoo, Ill., Mormon temple (1841-1846).

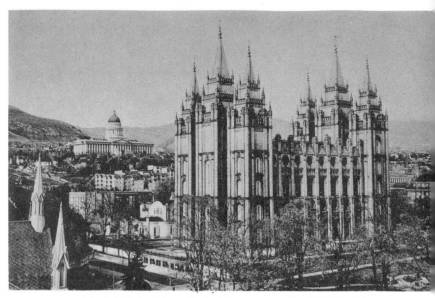

11. Salt Lake City, Utah, **Mormon temple** (1853-1893).

12. Oneida, N.Y., the Mansion House (1860-1871) of the Oneida Community.

13. Oneida, N.Y., the Mansion House, assembly room.

. Salt Lake City, Utah, an old view of Brigham Young's residence (1853-   )
showing the Lion and Beehive houses with the church office between.

15. Robert Owen, project (1825) for a communal settlement at New Harmony, I

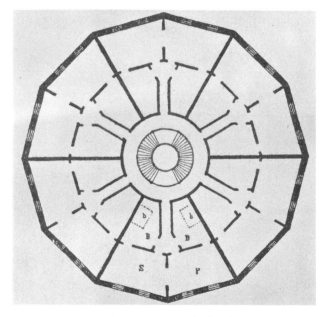

16. Project for a socialistic "palace," from the
Harbinger, Nov. 11, 1848.

17. Victor Considérant, project for a Fourierist phalanx.

18. New Icaria (near Corning, Iowa) the community of the Old Icarians (1879-   )

19. New Harmony, Ind., in the time of Robert Owen.

20. Red Bank, N.J., the North American Phalanx in 1850, from a painting made from a daguerreotype.

21. Bexley Heath, Kent, Red House (1860) by Philip Webb for William Morris.

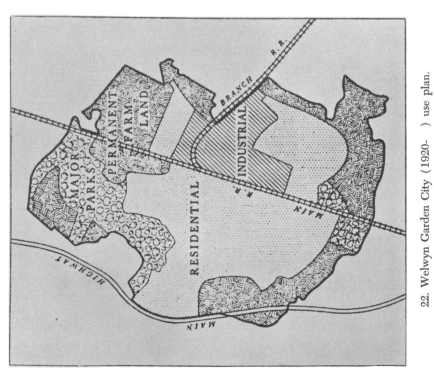

22. Welwyn Garden City (1920-   ) use plan.

23. Amsterdam, Stock Exchange (1898-1903) by H. P. Berlage.

24. Project for the station of *Une Cité industrielle* (1901-1904) by Tony Garnier.

25. "The Communists Fall—and the Exchange Rises" by George Grosz, from his *Das Gesicht der herrschenden Klasse* (1921).

26. Weimar, memorial (1921) to those killed in the Kapp *Putsch*, by Walter Gropius

27. Berlin (near) monument to Karl Liebknecht and Rosa Luxemburg (1926, now destroyed) by Mies van der Rohe.

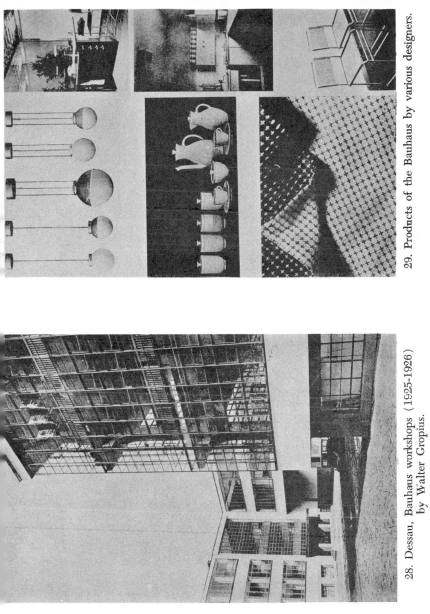

29. Products of the Bauhaus by various designers.

28. Dessau, Bauhaus workshops (1925-1926)
by Walter Gropius.

30. Berlin, Siemensstadt, housing (1929) by Walter Gropius.

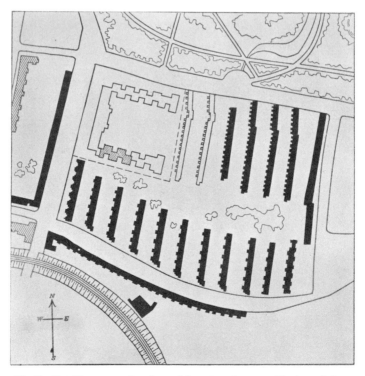

31. Berlin, Siemensstadt, plan of housing (row in black at left is that by Gropius illustrated in Fig. 30).

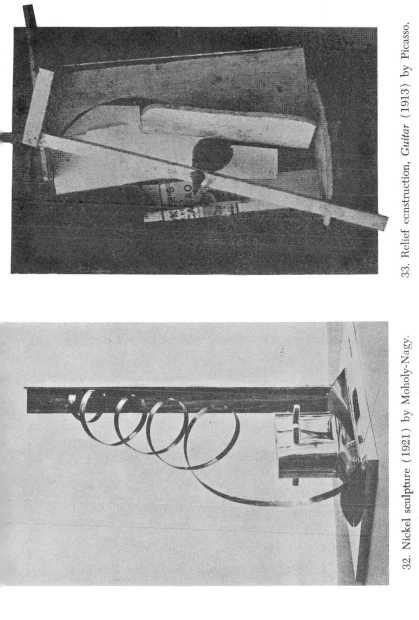

32. Nickel sculpture (1921) by Moholy-Nagy.

33. Relief construction, *Guitar* (1913) by Picasso.

24. Project for a monument to the Third International (1919)

25. Moscow. People's Ministry of Light Industry

36. Moscow, Transport Workers' Club (1929) by **Melnikov**.

37. Moscow, apartment house (1928) by Ginzburg
and Milinis.

38. *Lenin at the Smolny Institute* (1931) by Isaac Brodsky.

39. *Worker and Woman Collective Farmer*, by Vera Mukhina, on the Russian pavilion, World's Fair of 1937 at Paris.

40. Kiev, House of the Government of the Ukrainian Republic (ca. 1933).

41. Moscow, Palace of the Soviets, model by Yofan,
Helfreich, and Schuko.

42. Kiev, winning project (1947) for the Kreshchatik Street, by Vlassov (secon from left), Elizarov, and Zavarov.

43. Moscow, All-Union Agricultural Exposition of 1937, part of the pavilion of the Uzbek Republic.

44. *The Belated Kid* (1857) by William Morris Hunt, Collection Museum of Fine Arts, Boston.

45. **Russian Peasants**, etching by Eugene Higgins.

46. Typography by William Morris, a page from the Kelm-
scott edition (1892) of Caxton's The Golden Legend

47. Typography by Bertram G. Goodhue, a page from
Sonnets from the Portuguese (printed 1896)

48. "The Capitalist Vampire," by Walter Crane, from the *Comrade*, October 1903.

49. "From the Depths," by **William Balfour Ker,** illustrating John Ames Mitchell's *The Silent War* (1906).

50. *Backyards, Greenwich Village* (1914) by John Sloan, Collection Whitney Museum of American Art, New York.

51. "Having Their Fling," by Art Young, from the *Masses*, September 1917.

52. "Cain," by Robert Minor, from the *Liberator*, April 1918.

53. *The Senate* (1935) by William Gropper, Collection Museum of Modern Art, New York, gift of A. Conger Goodyear.

54. *Lenin* (1933, now destroyed) by Diego Rivera, Rockefeller Center, New York.

55. *Russia*, detail of fresco (1930-1931) by José Clemente Orozco, New School for Social Research, New York.

56. *Bartolomeo Vanzetti and Nicola Sacco* (1931-1932) by Ben Shahn, Collection Museum of Modern Art, New York.

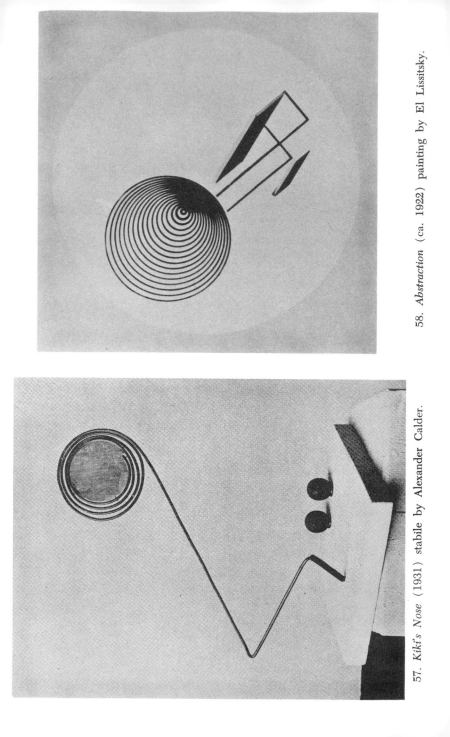

58. *Abstraction* (ca. 1922) painting by El Lissitsky.

57. *Kiki's Nose* (1931) stabile by Alexander Calder.

59. (a) *T.V.A. Worker and Family* and (b) *Pleading the Gold Case* (1935) by **Henry Varnum Poor**, Department of Justice Building, Washington, D.C.

60. Brooklyn, Williamsburg Housing (1936-1937).

61. Greenbelt, Md. (1935-   ).

1938), p. 203; Fig. 27, from Philip C. Johnson, *Mies van der Rohe* (New York: Museum of Modern Art, 1947), p. 37; Fig. 28, from Walter Gropius, *The New Architecture and the Bauhaus* (New York: Museum of Modern Art, n.d.), Pl. 7; Fig. 29, from *ibid.*, Pl. 5; Fig. 30, from Bauer, *op.cit.*, Pl. 1-A; Fig. 31, from *ibid.*, p. 179; Fig. 32, from László Moholy-Nagy, *The New Vision* (4th rev. ed., New York: Wittenborn, Schultz, Inc., 1947), p. 44, Fig. 23; Fig. 33, from Alfred H. Barr, Jr., *Cubism and Abstract Art* (New York: Museum of Modern Art, 1936), Fig. 98; Fig. 34, from El Lissitzky [L. M. Lissitsky], *Russland* (Vienna: Anton Schroll and Co., 1930), Abb. 38; Figs. 35-43, photos. courtesy of Sovfoto; Fig. 44, courtesy of the Museum of Fine Arts, Boston; Fig. 45, supplied by Department of Art and Archaeology, Princeton University; Fig. 46, from Gerald H. Crow, *William Morris, Designer* (London: The Studio, 1934), p. 101; Fig. 47, from Bertram G. Goodhue, *A Book of Architectural and Decorative Drawings* (New York: Architectural Book Publishing Co., 1914), p. 112; Fig. 48, from the *Comrade*, Oct. 1903; Fig. 49, from John Ames Mitchell, *The Silent War* (New York: Life Publishing Company, 1906), opp. p. 200; Fig. 50, courtesy of the Whitney Museum of American Art; Fig. 51, from the *Masses*, Sept. 1917, p. 7; Fig. 52, from the *Liberator*, Apr. 1918, p. 1; Fig. 53, Collection of the Museum of Modern Art, New York, gift of A. Conger Goodyear; Fig. 54, from Diego Rivera, *Portrait of America* (New York: Covici, Friede, 1934), text by Bertram D. Wolfe, copyright 1934 by Bertram D. Wolfe, used by permission of Crown Publishers; Fig. 55, from Justino Fernández, *José Clemente Orozco* (Mexico City: Libreria de Porrua Hnos. y Cia., 1942), Pl. 67, Fig. 63; Fig. 56, Collection of the Museum of Modern Art, New York; Fig. 57, from James J. Sweeney, *Alexander Calder* (New York: Museum of Modern Art, 1943), p. 23; Fig. 58, from J. L. Martin, B. Nicholson, N. Gabo, eds., *Circle* (London: Faber and Faber, 1937), Pl. 15; Fig. 59, from Peyton Boswell, *Modern American Painting* (New York: Dodd, Mead and Co., 1940), opp. p. 83, courtesy of *Life* magazine and of the artist; Fig. 60, from Werner Hegemann, *City Planning and Housing* (New York: Architectural Book Publishing Co., 1938), Vol. 3, p. 141, Fig. 1024; Fig. 61, from Lewis Mumford, *The Culture of Cities* (New York: Harcourt Brace and Co., 1938), opp. p. 452.

INDEX

ASNOVA (Association of New Architects [U.S.S.R.]), 65n, 70n
Abbott, Leonard D., 96n
Academy of Architecture (U.S.S.R.), 84
Acheson, Dean, 127
Aicher, Otl, 146, 146n
Aicher-Scholl, Inge, 145, 146
Alabyan, K., 84, 84n
Albers, Josef, 48, 49, 121
Aleatoric music, 140
Alfaro Siqueiros, David, *see* Siqueiros, David Alfaro
All-Russian Society of Proletarian Architects, *see* VOPRA
All-Union Congress of Builders, Architects, and Workers, 137
Amana and art, 6 8
American Artists' Congress, 104, 116, 116n
American Federation of Arts, 134
American Negro Labor Congress, 117
Anarchism, 4, 33, 102n, 103, 141, 143, 143n, 148
Andrews, Edward D., 4n
Andrews, Faith, 4n
"Anonima Group," 147, 147n
Apollinaire, Guillaume, 143
Art and socialism, 3-131; in America, 85-131; in England, 30-34; in Germany, 34-49; in Soviet Union, 49-85; Art Nouveau, 38; Bauhaus, 40-49; city planning, 33-34; housing, 26, 33-34, 37, 47; International Style, 44-48; Marxist art theory, 16-30; "die neue Sachlichkeit," 39-40; organicism, 23-24; utopianism, 5-16
Art Front, 116, 119
Art Young's Quarterly, 98
Arte Joven, 143n
Artists' and Writers' Congress (1941), 116n
Artists' Cooperative (U.S.S.R.), 83
Artists' Creative Union (U.S.S.R.), 84
Artists' Union, 116, 119, 140n
"Ash-can School," 95, 109
Association of New Architects (U.S.S.R.), *see* ASNOVA
Atlantic Pact, 127
Aveling, Eleanor Marx, 31

Babbitt, Milton, 140-141, 141n
Baez, Joan, 144, 144n
Bakunin, Mikhail, 122; on revolution, 123
Balzac, Honoré, 54
Barr, Alfred H., Jr., 39n, 59n, 133n

Bauhaus, 38, 40-49, 59, 121-122, 124, 129, 145, 146
Baxandall, Lee, 143
Bayer, Herbert, 49, 121
Becker, Maurice, 97, 99, 100, 101, 116
Behrendt, Walter C., 36n
Behrens, Peter, 41n, 45
Bellamy, Edward, 33
Bellows, George, 96, 96n, 97, 98
Benkert, Ernst, 147n
Benn, Ben, 96n
Benton, Thomas H., 110, 110n
Berkman, Alexander, 96n
Berlage, Hendrik P., 37
Bestor, Arthur E., Jr., 13n
Biddle, George, 114n, 116
Bill, Max, 145, 146
Billings, Henry, 109
Bismarck, O. E. L., 34-35
Blake, William J., pseud., *see* Blech, William J.
Blech, William J. (William J. Blake, pseud.), 23n
Blunt, Anthony, 143n
Bonsiepe, Gui, 146n
Boswell, Peyton, 128n
Bourdelle, Antoine, 76
Bourne, Randolph, 98
Breton, André, 104, 104n
Breuer, Marcel, 49, 121
Brinton, Christian, 96n
Brodsky, Isaac, 69
Brooks, Van Wyck, 96n, 98
Browder, Earl, 71, 78, 90, 102, 112
Brown, Ford Madox, 32
Brown, Milton W., 99n
Budapest Bauhaus, 145
Budenz, Louis F., 50n, 74n, 107n
Bukharin, Nikolai, 62-63, 73; on art, 66-68
Burck, Jacob, 101
Burger, William T., 101n
Burliuk, David, 59, 103
Byzantine style, 54

Cabet, Étienne, 11, 14
Cage, John, 140-141, 141n
Calder, Alexander, 110-111
Campanella, Tommaso, 61
Cannon, James P., 63
Carpenter, Edward, 37
Carr, Edward H., 82n, 113n
Castro, Fidel, 141n, 144
Central Committee on Arts (U.S.S.R.), 84

153